Praise for *Liturgical Catechesis*

MW00477478

"Here is a gift to the Church as we e...   il'
in their prayer lives and 'remote' in th.... .... are being overwhelmed by the
values of our passing age. Liturgy can be our source of life in God if instruction is more
encounter, teaching more communion between learner and Christ, and catechesis more an
ignition of supernatural desire. All catechists, clergy, and theologians will benefit from this
book if they receive it for what it is: a cry to allow the *supernatural* to order the passing on of
the truths of our faith. Only then will knowledge give birth to devout worship."

Deacon James Keating, PHD
Director of Theological Formation
Institute for Priestly Formation
Creighton University, Omaha, NE

"Pope Francis teaches us that the Church must initiate everyone into the 'art of accompaniment.' James Pauley does just that, painting a road map for personal discipleship
through the liturgy. A much needed read to counter the drop in sacramental understanding and participation."

Curtis Martin
Founder and Chief Executive Officer
Fellowship of Catholic University Students

"In *Liturgical Catechesis in the 21st Century,* Dr. Pauley invites us and those we catechize to
a deeper encounter with Christ in the Church's liturgy. He listens with us to the voices of
faithful Catholics past and present, who offer new possibilities for helping Catholics of all
ages awaken to an encounter with the Divine in every liturgical celebration."

Lani Bogart
Director of Marriage and Family Life
Our Lady of Perpetual Help, Glendale, AZ

"'*Lex orandi lex credendi*' As we pray, so we believe. James Pauley offers ample food for
thought and prayer on the relationship between the liturgical and catechetical compo-
nents of the Great Commission. Dr. Pauley's book is insightful, practical, and useful for
enhancing how we teach the Faith."

Ken Ogorek
Director of Catechesis,
Archdiocese of Indianapolis
President (2015–2018), National Conference
for Catechetical Leadership

"In this inspiring book, James Pauley retrieves and updates the integrated catechetical
vision so much desired in the lead up to Vatican II. Like a true Christian scholar, he
brings forth things old and new—from the insights of Jungmann to the recent calls of
Benedict XVI and Francis for a mystagogical renewal. Pauley demonstrates that the
Liturgy is, and always has been, the key to effective catechesis. *Liturgical Catechesis in the
21st Century: A School of Discipleship* deserves to become a standard text for every religious
education program in the training institutes of the English speaking world and beyond."

Dr. Gerard O'Shea
Associate Professor of Religious Education
University of Notre Dame, Sydney, Australia

"Dr. James Pauley's work takes seriously the cultural challenges the Church faces in carrying out her mission today. Pauley answers the challenge via a liturgical catechesis that invites one into a deep and abiding communion with Jesus Christ—a much-needed message in an age starved for meaningful and lasting relationships. In youth ministry, he proposes catechesis that takes seriously the need for apprenticeship, which will serve any parish that takes youth discipleship seriously."

Brad Bursa
Director, Office of Youth Evangelization
and Discipleship
Archdiocese of Cincinnati

"Imagine a parish that is 'steeped in a culture of transformative liturgical encounter' with the risen Christ. James Pauley shows us how to be that parish, by exploring the early Christian process of liturgical catechesis as a process of apprenticeship in forming missionary disciples. He describes what is essential to liturgical catechesis, speaks about its challenges, and shares insights from concrete pastoral applications."

Ximena DeBroeck
Assistant Professor of Sacred Scripture,
St. Mary's Seminary & University, Baltimore

"With the skill of a historian and the heart of a catechist, James Pauley presents a compelling vision for a contemporary renewal of parish life, a renewal based on helping our people to better encounter God in the sacraments. This book will change the way we look at catechesis. *Liturgical Catechesis in the 21st Century: A School of Discipleship* is greatly needed by all catechists, youth ministers, RCIA directors, and liturgists—and the people who teach them. I highly recommend it. I hope it will be an instant classic."

Most Reverend James Wall
Bishop of Gallup, NM

"James Pauley's *Liturgical Catechesis in the 21st Century* is not only essential reading for any high school religion teacher, priest, deacon, seminarian, or catechist, but it is also an ideal resource for any person who desires a deeper understanding of how we encounter Christ and His Paschal Mystery within the celebration of the liturgy. Pauley is able to weave the insights of Cyprian Vagaggini, OSB, and Joseph A. Jungmann, SJ, into a dialogue with recent popes, saints, and the lived experience of catechists to develop a comprehensive and insightful work into liturgical catechesis. This work is an authentic response to the need for a new liturgical movement as it outlines the relationship between the liturgy, theology, catechesis, and evangelization."

Roland Millare, STL, STD (candidate)
Theology Department Chair
St. John XXIII College Preparatory,
Houston, TX

LITURGICAL CATECHESIS IN THE 21ST CENTURY

A SCHOOL OF DISCIPLESHIP

JAMES C. PAULEY

LITURGY TRAINING PUBLICATIONS

Nihil Obstat
Very Reverend Daniel J. Smilanic, JCD
Vicar for Canonical Services
Archdiocese of Chicago
February 13, 2017

Imprimatur
Very Reverend Ronald A. Hicks, DMIN
Vicar General
Archdiocese of Chicago
February 13, 2017

Figure 9.1, "Our Father Silhouette," on p. 148, figure 9.2, "Overall Thematic Progression Corresponding to the Liturgical Year," on p. 152; and figure 9.3, "Focus on the Sacrament of Reconciliation in the program for Seven-Year-Old Children," on p. 155 reprinted with permission of Sr. Hyacinthe Defos du Rau, OP, in the name of the Dominican Sisters of St. Joseph, Lymington, UK. All rights reserved.

Figure 10.1, "This Is Equal to . . . This," on p. 169; and figure 10.2, "Ari's Image of Baptism," on p. 173 © 2014 Catechesis of the Good Shepherd, USA. All rights reserved. Used with permission.

LITURICAL CATECHESIS IN THE 21ST CENTURY: A SCHOOL OF DISCIPLESHIP © 2017 Archdiocese of Chicago: Liturgy Training Publications, 3949 South Racine Avenue, Chicago, IL 60609; 800-933-1800; fax 800-933-7094; e-mail: orders@ltp.org; website: www.LTP.org. All rights reserved.

This book was edited by Kevin Thornton. Michael A. Dodd was the production editor, Anna Manhart was the designer, and Kari Nichols was the production artist.

Cover: Garcia painting courtesy the Redemptorist Renewal Center

22 21 20 19 18   2 3 4 5 6

Printed in the United States of America.

Library of Congress Control Number: 2017935912

ISBN 978-1-61671-360-7

LCC

To my wife, Kate.
Your self-sacrificing love is
a vivid reminder to me of how God wills
the good of the other for the other's sake.

To my daughters,
Grace, Mairen, and Monica.
You are each a tremendous light.
God takes great delight in you.

To my parents,
John and Kathleen.
Thank you for our beautiful family
and for bringing us to the sacraments.

CONTENTS

Chapter 7: The Trajectory of Liturgical Catechesis: From the Visible to the Invisible 108

Chapter 8: Liturgical Catechesis as a School of Discipleship: Apprenticing Skills for Sacramental Living 120

Part III: Emerging Practices: What It All Means for Parish Liturgical Catechesis 141

Chapter 9: Come Follow Me: A New Model for Children's Catechesis 145
❧ Sr. Hyacinthe Defos du Rau, OP

Chapter 10: The Liturgical Encounter and the Child: Insights from the Catechesis of the Good Shepherd   165
◈ **Mary Mirrione**

Chapter 11: The Liturgy's Vital Role in Discipleship Ministry with Teenagers   180
◈ **Jim Beckman**

FOREWORD

The *Catechism of the Catholic Church* tells us that the liturgy is "the privileged place for catechizing the People of God" (CCC, 1074). This is not principally because the homily offers a venue for catechetical instruction, though this is certainly not precluded, but because, as St. John Paul II said, "it is in the sacraments, especially in the Eucharist, that Christ Jesus works in fullness for the transformation of men" (CT, 23, cited at CCC, 1074). The liturgy is intrinsically catechetical because Christ is the principal agent at work in the liturgy. His formation of those joined to him in celebration of the sacraments configures them to his love. Their sensibilities are formed by the symbolic actions and words that constitute the rites and the pictures and statues that enrich them. It is a formation involving all five of the senses and the imaginations of young and old alike. The liturgy, as the primary locus and instrument of catechesis is therefore intrinsically ordered towards a more explicitly catechetical moment that would draw out its meaning and explain its significance without, on the other hand, reducing the liturgy to such explanations. This latter kind of catechesis the *Catechism* calls "liturgical catechesis" (CCC, 1075).

James Pauley has written a superb, much needed book on just this subject. It draws together the best thought on the topic from the whole of twentieth-century theology and in particular from the Liturgical Movement which grew up in the early part of the century and played such a pivotal role at Vatican II. It draws into the conversation, in a constitutive way, the documents of Vatican II and other magisterial documentation such as Blessed Paul VI's *Evangelii Nuntiandi*, Saint John Paul II's *Catechesi Tradendae*, the *Catechism*, the *General Directory for Catechesis*, Pope Francis' *Evangelii Gaudium*, etc. The reader can feel confident that Pauley's book presents a synthesis of classic liturgical theology and its reception in magisterial teaching that is authoritative and creative. Not only that, but there are four chapters (out of thirteen total) written by expert practitioners of liturgical catechesis so that the reader receives both theory and recommendations for practice. The book ends with a splendid brief conclusion on the liturgy as a lifelong school of discipleship and on liturgical catechesis as a lifelong mystagogy. The liturgy offers us an "experience of transformative communion with God," an encounter with God "in his incarnate presence" who thereby "becomes more and more incarnate in us." But this transformation "becomes most fruitful over the years when it is enveloped in effective approaches to liturgical catechesis," and as a result of the whole process we become better and better able to bear the incarnate presence of God "into the world" (pp. 218–220).

These accomplishments notwithstanding, in my view the most important contribution of Pauley's book is the way in which it invites us to move beyond what has seemingly become a sterile (and false) dichotomy between "cultural Catholicism" and an "evangelical" emphasis on intense subjective religious experience, especially the experience of a "personal relationship" with Jesus. Where such a dichotomy is prosecuted, the liturgy more often than not will find itself on the side of merely "cultural Catholicism," while personal prayer, or extraliturgical prayer meetings would be the locus of an experience of a "personal relationship" with Jesus. Pauley's book exposes this false dichotomy definitively. While it is true that experience of the liturgy without the liturgical catechesis towards which it is intrinsically ordered can remain on a superficial level, exposure to well thought out liturgical catechesis based on the correct theology of the sacraments and of the Church can deepen one's experience of liturgy so that one can find the most intimate and even mystical "personal relationship" with the Incarnate Lord arising out of the liturgy and, precisely as liturgical, pervading the whole of life.

This is only logical because, as Pauley brings out well, the liturgy is ultimately centered around communion with Christ truly present in the Eucharist, and proper liturgical catechesis reminds us that "it is for [communion with] this most intimate Presence—real contact with Infinite Life and Perfect Love—that every human being yearns" (p. 22). The job of liturgical catechesis is to help people to understand the experience of communion with "this most intimate Presence" and how to nurture such intimate communion so that it is sustained in a "personal relationship" afterwards and as a lifelong process. Nor does this result in privatizing the liturgical experience so that we are left only with "me and Jesus" as a spirituality. Pauley shows how the more truly intimate this communion becomes, the more it is also a communion with others and an outreach to the world. We become, as Pope Francis has most recently put it, missionary disciples whose job is to leaven the world with the good news of the love of God revealed in Christ. Thus we become agents of evangelization in a world sorely in need of good news, and in a society that is rapidly losing the depth dimension that religion is supposed to provide, and which the practice of the Catholic faith can provide at its deepest level. James Pauley's book thus continues the legacy of theological and pastoral reflection on the topic of evangelization in the modern world which runs from *Gaudium et Spes* through *Evangelii Nuntiandi* all the way to Pope Francis' *Evangelii Gaudium* in the present. I am pleased to be able to recommend it to the widest possible audience.

John Cavadini, PHD
McGrath-Cavadini Director
McGrath Institute for Church Life
Professor of Theology,
    University of Notre Dame

PREFACE

I love my job. I have the great privilege of working with university students who desire to spend themselves in loving service of God and his people in the New Evangelization. I also am blessed to spend many days each year encouraging catechists and catechetical leaders in various dioceses in their vital work of evangelization and catechesis. There are many signs of hope today, initiatives being carried out by kind and passionate people who desire to see that "new springtime" St. John Paul II anticipated as the fruit of the Holy Spirit's movement in our day.

In recent years, in my conversations with these dedicated people, I have heard much concern expressed regarding the current downward trends in sacramental practice.

Our three most recent popes have shared thoughtful insights on how to address this issue, reflective of their reading of the times. We all join them in understanding that the answers have to go deeper than merely revising our sacramental policies or reminding parents of their *obligation* to attend Mass on Sundays and ensure that their children are well catechized. St. John Paul II, Pope Benedict XVI, and Pope Francis have each looked to the roots of these challenges—calling for new efforts to first evangelize our own parishioners, plan liturgical celebrations that are beautiful and nourishing of people's faith, increase opportunities for mystagogical catechesis, and rediscover our shared responsibility to proclaim unabashedly the mystery of Christ crucified. These are ways forward that have the potential to ignite a great contemporary renewal.

Inspired by their gentle insistence upon what is most essential for today's Catholic faith and life, I offer this book as a step in engaging an important issue that impacts sacramental practice: the need for a revitalized liturgical catechesis.

Many Catholics today live with an impoverished understanding of the power of the sacraments for how we live. The best way we can help our brothers and sisters out of this poverty is to help them see, above all else, how God uses the sacraments to give himself to us, to heal and elevate us into a new life suffused with his divine grace. The whole liturgical life brings us into the greatest possible encounter with God—and such a meeting does not leave us unchanged. If we consciously give ourselves to the eternal exchange of love which the liturgy makes present to us, we will find in abundance what each of us most deeply desires. And, finding this "pearl of great price," we will want to give it away to those we meet.

This text focuses on what we Catholics call the *liturgy*. This term does not mean merely the Mass, though this is the act most central to it. When we use this word in the following chapters, we use it in its broadest sense. The liturgy refers to the Church's whole public prayer of worship and sanctification, experienced in the Mass, each of the other sacraments, and the entire array of ritual celebrations found in the Liturgy of the Hours, the Rite of Christian Initiation of Adults, and the *Book of Blessings*.

This book is a work of *catechetics*. While readers rightly understand *catechesis* to be that task of communicating the content of the faith in a way that deepens understanding and brings about a change of heart, the two terms are not interchangeable. *Catechetics* is the scientific study of the artful work of *catechesis*, much like a course in economics provides an examination of the various dynamics influencing the working of particular economies. Catechetics studies the multiple factors impacting the mission of catechesis, including its history, sources, content, methodology, participants, evangelistic context, and its cultural, philosophical, and ideological influences. This book, therefore, critically reflects upon the work of liturgical catechesis. It suggests new approaches to preparing today's Catholics to give their full selves to God in the liturgy.

There is much discussion in the Church today concerning how to best help Catholics and all people become missionary disciples of our Lord. In the following chapters, we will explore the sacred action most essential to forming genuine disciples: the transformative encounter with God in the liturgy. We will also focus on the catechesis which envelops it and helps us into full, conscious, active, and *fruitful* participation in the sacred mysteries. It is my deepest conviction that the more catechesis and the liturgy are harmonized with one another in how they are conducted today, the more transformative they both will be, to the great good of the Church and the world.

There are a number of people to whom I wish to express my deep gratitude.

Professor Barbara Morgan first opened up for me the Church's vision for transformative catechesis. I owe so much of my own understanding and passion for catechetics to my extraordinary friend and mentor. In so many ways, she has inspired me toward holiness in my day-to-day life as a parent, catechist, and university professor.

During my doctoral studies, I had the pleasure of working under the direction of a truly great liturgical scholar, Fr. Douglas Martis. Fr. Martis' course on the liturgical movement inspired me with the original ideals of the leaders of the movement and set me on the trajectory of writing this book. His support for me throughout the dissertation writing process, and particularly in preparation for my defense, will not be forgotten.

I was uniquely fortunate to work with Kevin Thornton as this book's editor. Kevin's encouragement, expert editorial critique, and good humor helped me over numerous hurdles and greatly increased the quality of this text. Every step of the way, it was an absolute joy to work with him. I am also grateful to Nancy Allen, Fr. Randy Stice, and Dr. Petroc Willey for their insightful assessments of various chapters in the book.

I thank, too, my colleagues on the theology faculty at Franciscan University for their tremendous support, particularly those dear friends who specialize in catechetics. I also thank my students for their patience with me as I wrote this book and for their tremendous witness of joyful discipleship which inspires me every day. I love my work because of the amazing people I get to serve.

Most importantly, I want to express my debt of gratitude to my wife, Kate. Not only has she taken on the weight of so many additional responsibilities while I spent many nights and Saturdays writing, she also offered her help as a first reader, vastly improving these chapters with her ability to help me to the essentials. Neither of us had any idea of her editorial talents when I began this project. Her wisdom and good judgment are the reasons why I am no longer laboring over this manuscript in my basement. Thank you, Kate!

ABOUT THE AUTHOR

Dr. James Pauley is professor of theology and catechetics at Franciscan University of Steubenville. In 2014, Dr. Pauley was appointed editor of *The Catechetical Review*, the university's journal dedicated to catechesis and the new evangelization. He received his doctorate in sacred theology from the Liturgical Institute at the University of St. Mary of the Lake and is a frequent speaker in dioceses and parishes across the United States.

Dr. Pauley began working as a parish catechetical leader in 1989 in Phoenix and has served professionally in parish, diocesan, and university catechetical formation for twenty-eight years. A native of Arizona, James is married to Kate, and they are blessed with three beautiful daughters.

ABBREVIATIONS

AG   *Ad Gentes*. In *Vatican Council II: The Conciliar and Post Conciliar Documents*. Edited by Austin Flannery. Northport, NY: Costello Publishing Company, 1996.

CCC   *Catechism of the Catholic Church*. 2nd ed. Washington, DC: Libreria Editrice Vaticana–United States Catholic Conference, 2000.

CT   Pope John Paul II. *Catechesi Tradendae*. Boston: Pauline Books and Media, 1979.

EG   Pope Francis. *Evangelii Gaudium*. Vatican Translation. Boston: Pauline Books and Media, 2013.

EN   Pope Paul VI. *Evangelii Nuntiandi*. Boston: Pauline Books and Media, 1976.

GCD   *General Catechetical Directory*. Washington, DC: United States Catholic Conference, 1971.

GDC   *General Directory for Catechesis*. Washington, DC: United States Conference of Catholic Bishops, 1997.

NDC   *National Directory for Catechesis*. Washington, DC: USCCB Publishing, 2005.

RCIA *Rite of Christian Initiation of Adults: Study Edition*. Chicago: Liturgy Training Publications, 1988.

RM   Pope John Paul II. *Redemptoris Missio*. Vatican Translation. Boston: Pauline Books and Media, 1991.

SC   "Sacrosanctum Concilium." In *Vatican Council II: The Conciliar and Post Conciliar Documents*. Edited by Austin Flannery. Northport, NY: Costello Publishing Company, 1996.

SCa   Pope Benedict XVI. *Sacramentum Caritatis*. Boston: Pauline Books and Media, 2007.

PART I

The Relationship of Liturgy and Catechesis and Why It Matters

In the early decades of the twentieth century, by many cultural markers, Catholicism was flourishing in the United States. Churches were regularly full on Sundays. The Catholic school system was expanding. Children frequently were raised in intact families, received the sacraments, memorized their Baltimore Catechisms, prayed their devotions, and grew up presuming the Church's teaching authority. Movies such as *The Song of Bernadette* (1943) and *The Bells of St. Mary's* (1945) received widespread popular acclaim, to the point of being nominated for Best Picture in their respective years for Academy Awards. By most accounts, Catholicism was thriving and was making a strong impression upon the broader American populace.

Yet during this exact period there arose on the international scene dedicated Catholic men and women who were uneasy as they observed this seemingly robust Catholic milieu animating many countries. They applauded the exterior indications of a thriving Church, but as they looked a little deeper they found systemic causes for concern. Much of their apprehension had to do with the *quality* of the catechesis of the day. While many children knew by heart an admirable breadth of doctrinal content, catechesis was failing to propose the glad tidings of the salvation offered us in Christ and the need for a free and conscious response. This under-emphasis of what is most essential to Christianity was affecting both liturgical practice and how the Christian life was being lived in the world. Was this thriving Catholic culture signaling that the faith had been deeply embraced? Did it indicate that many were heeding what the Second Vatican Council of the early 1960s would call the "universal call to holiness"? Did Catholics of the time possess a sufficient inner dynamism and rootedness in their faith so that adverse geopolitical events—or radical social upheavals— would refine and strengthen them, yet not overcome them?

The Lord himself had counseled his disciples that they must establish themselves in their Christian life as a house that is built on solid rock rather than one built on shifting sand. For the house built on rock, "the rain fell, the floods came, and the winds blew and buffeted the house. But it did not collapse; it had been set solidly on rock" (Mt 7:25). Some during this time juxtaposed twentieth-century Catholic life to that of the early Christians and became convinced that something essential was missing from how the sacraments were celebrated and how the faith was received in catechesis. They became more and more concerned that the marvelous edifices of a prospering Catholicism were not built as securely as they seemed.

In these years, the world was engulfed in two world wars. Many would be concerned soon after World War II over the possibility of a third and perhaps final conflict as the Soviet Union and the United States and their allies descended into the Cold War. In the United States, the various cultural revolutions of the late 1960s began an era of unique confusion and upheaval, frequently resulting in a collective grasping for a misguided version of personal freedom and autonomy from outside authority. These experiences deeply challenged the Catholic belief of many within the Church, as well as the faith of many outside of it.

In those *first* decades of the 1900s, though, perhaps in preparation for what was to come, we can see how the Holy Spirit was moving the Church towards profound renewal. Many pastoral leaders were inspired to reorient the Church to more closely parallel the Church of the early Christians—in its zeal, purity of focus, Trinitarian-Christocentricity, vibrant catechesis and sacramental expressiveness, and the fervor of its members. Relying upon early Christian sources, as so many twentieth-century Catholic intellectuals and pastoral thinkers did, they were able to see what was critically needed: a revitalized catechesis and sacramental life. This need, as we will examine in the next chapter, has become even more acute.

In these first four chapters, we will construct a vision for catechesis and the liturgy that is inspired by the tremendous ideals of the Second Vatican Council, the postconciliar magisterial vision, and the best insights of the pioneers of twentieth-century ecclesial renewal. Exploring how we can more fruitfully envision the liturgy and catechesis today, in the light of the immense wisdom of our forebears, will establish important foundations for the practical proposals described in the rest of this book.

CHAPTER 1

The Catholic Impulse in Adversity: An Introduction

We live in days of great consequence.

C. S. Lewis put it quite well, in words expressed by college professor Dr. Dimble in *That Hideous Strength*, the climactic book of Lewis' fantasy space trilogy. Dimble and his wife were members of a small partnership, working to repel a catastrophic threat to humanity. In their struggle against forces of great evil—concentrated, interestingly, upon a small, stuffy, business-as-usual liberal arts college in the heart of twentieth-century England—Dimble makes this observation to his associates:

Have you ever noticed . . . that the universe, and every little bit of the universe, is always hardening and narrowing and coming to a point? . . . If you dip into any college, or school, or parish, or family—anything you like—at a given point in its history, you always find that there was a time before that point when there was more elbow room and contrasts weren't quite so sharp; and that there's going to be a time after that point when there is even less room for indecision and choices are even more momentous. Good is always getting better and bad is always getting worse: the possibilities of even apparent neutrality are always diminishing. The whole thing is sorting itself out all the time.[1]

It is as if the contours of good and evil, over the progression of time, are continually narrowing into sharper contrast, into greater dissonance, with one another.

As we move deeper into this third millennium, perhaps Lewis' insight expresses well our experience as Christians in the contemporary world.

---

1. C. S. Lewis, *That Hideous Strength: A Modern Fairy-Tale for Grown-Ups* (New York: Scribner, 1996), 280–81. First published in 1945 by The Bodley Head, London.

We know that the drama for the world's salvation has unfolded as a great and prolonged struggle. To understand the origins of this conflict, we need look no further than the early pages of the Book of Genesis in its description of the strife resulting from the original choice against God. "Then the Lord God said to the snake . . . I will put enmity between you and the woman, and between your offspring and hers; they will strike at your head, while you strike at their heel" (Gen 3:14–15). In the twentieth century, St. John Paul II memorably described a deepening clash between the culture of life and the culture of death. He wrote, "This situation, with its lights and shadows, ought to make us all fully aware that we are facing an enormous and dramatic clash between good and evil, death and life, the 'culture of death' and the 'culture of life.' We find ourselves not only 'faced with' but necessarily 'in the midst of' this conflict."[2] While this decisive conflict has been germinating from the moment of the original temptation, if we are to adopt Lewis' idea, the struggle itself is becoming more perceptible as it intensifies.

Choosing to authentically live the Christian life—today as in any time period—is never for the faint of heart. While an unthinking, seemingly unconscious, Catholicism has been inherited by many in recent decades, true indifference and neutrality in this dramatic confrontation is quickly becoming unrealistic. The struggle is unmistakable. Radical ideologies explode into violence and terrorism around the world—often against innocents. Our Christian brothers and sisters in the Middle East, among other minorities, are frequently targeted for genocidal atrocities. Shootings multiply within our own country, leaving us grappling with loss and wondering at the kind of evil that leads to such hateful acts. Western cultures continue their steep decline in how we collectively view the human person, pushing the envelope both anthropologically and morally and bringing us into uncharted waters.

Such disturbing patterns in our contemporary world lead to the question: On the level of the person, will an unconvinced Christian faith last? St. John Paul II warned in 1988 of the significant danger facing the laity of a tendency to separate faith from life.[3] Earlier voices had cautioned of the likely fallout from so many being outwardly attached to the Church

---

2. See Pope John Paul II, *Evangelium Vitae* (Boston: Pauline Books and Media, 1995), 28.

3. John Paul II, *Christifideles Laici* (Boston: Pauline Books and Media, 1989), 2.

but not interiorly converted, unchanged in how they think and live. Twenty-four years earlier, in fact, the great Austrian liturgical-catechetical scholar Joseph A. Jungmann, SJ, observed that "a pure habitual Christianity, a pure Christianity living by tradition and conservation cannot last much longer or it must sink into insignificance, into a paganism which ekes out its life on the mere crumbs of a past life."[4] Both the pontiff-saint and the Jesuit scholar were prophetic as they looked to the future. Many today are sacramentalized but divided in what they believe and ambivalent to the light of Divine Revelation. Others continue to identify as Catholics on account of family history or cultural tradition alone. Unfortunately, without an inner conviction for God and the Church, many Catholics today are being easily overwhelmed by an aggressive secularism.

How will the Church be affected by the propensity of so many to live an uncertain Christian life? Joseph Ratzinger's sober prediction may indeed become the eventual reality. As a young forty-three-year-old theologian, back in 1970, he wrote:

> [The Church] will become small and will have to start afresh more or less from the beginning. She will no longer be able to inhabit many of the edifices she built in prosperity. As the number of her adherents diminishes, she will lose many of her social privileges. In contrast to an earlier age, she will be seen much more as a voluntary society, entered only by free decision. As a small society, she will make much bigger demands on the initiative of her individual members. It will be hard-going for the Church, for the process of crystallization and clarification will cost her much valuable energy.[5]

---

4. Joseph Jungmann, *Pastoral Liturgy* (New York: Herder and Herder, 1962), 332.

5. Joseph Ratzinger, *Faith and the Future* (San Francisco: Ignatius Press, 2009), 116–17. This English translation is based on the German original: *Glaube und Zukunft* (Munchen: Kosel-Verlag, 1970). This reduction of the number of Christians, though, will not be the end of the narrative. Ratzinger foresaw the emergence of a more vibrant and dynamic Church, evangelizing the world with the vitality of the early Christians. He continued: "But when the trial of this sifting is past, a great power will flow from a more spiritualized and simplified Church. Men in a totally planned world will find themselves unspeakably lonely. If they have completely lost sight of God, they will feel the whole horror of their poverty. Then they will discover the little flock of believers as something wholly new. They will discover it as a hope that is meant for them, an answer for which they have always been searching in secret. And so it seems certain to me that the Church is facing very hard times. The real crisis has scarcely begun. We will have to count on terrific upheavals. But I am equally certain about what will remain at the end: not the Church of the political cult, which is dead already with Gobel, but the Church of faith. She may well no longer be the dominant social power to the extent that she was until recently; but she will enjoy a fresh blossoming and be seen as man's home, where he will find life and hope beyond death" (118).

If such a projection proves accurate, the Church of the future will closely resemble the early Church of the apostolic era in both its size and in the scope of its mission.

The Problem of Attrition

The markers of such a downsizing are clearly observable today. Readers of this book know well the acute problem that is bubbling to the surface in most Catholic parishes. The number of American adults who were raised Catholic and still consider themselves to be Catholic is on a severe downturn, a trajectory that must be urgently and substantively addressed. At the press conference announcing his appointment as auxiliary bishop of Los Angeles, Bishop Robert Barron chose to highlight this specific issue. He observed, "The most significant challenge facing the Catholic Church today is the attrition of our own people."[6]

At this precise time when the world is in such desperate need of Christ, the Church herself is facing a growing internal crisis of diminishing interest and practice. Of the nearly one-third of American adults who say they were raised Catholic, 41 percent no longer consider themselves to be so. More than six people leave the Catholic Church today for every one new convert. And among millennials, fully 50 percent who were raised in the Church no longer self-identify as Catholics.[7]

Other studies reveal a dwindling vitality in Catholic sacramental practice. As of 2015, approximately 24 percent of American Catholics attend Mass on a weekly basis.[8] While Sunday Mass attendance has dropped precipitously over the past several decades, it is not the only form of sacramental participation on the decline. Catholic marriage rates have waned, with nearly 65 percent fewer weddings being celebrated in the Church in 2014 than in 1970.[9] Such numbers are staggering in their implications for the future of Catholic life in the United States.

---

6. Jim McDermott, "Three New Bishops for the Archdiocese of Los Angeles," *Dispatches* (blog), *America*, July 21, 2015, http://www.americamagazine.org/content/dispatches/three-new-bishops -archdiocese-los-angeles.

7. Pew Research Center, "America's Changing Religious Landscape," May 12, 2015, http://www. pewforum.org/2015/05/12/americas-changing-religious-landscape.

8. Center for Applied Research in the Apostolate at Georgetown University, "Frequently Requested Church Statistics," accessed October 10, 2016, http://cara.georgetown.edu/frequently -requested-church-statistics/.

9. Ibid. In 1970, there were 426,309 Catholic marriages in the United States, whereas in 2015, there were 148,134.

In the midst of this negatively trending ecclesial landscape, the call for the Church to regain its evangelistic identity reverberates. We remember that Christ commanded members of the nascent Church in Matthew 28 to not merely preserve their faith in the midst of adversity, but to go out into the world with courage to make disciples. The first-century world responded frequently enough by demanding of them the supreme testimony of martyrdom. Many of our brothers and sisters around the world offer the same witness today, a cause for deep concern. Yet, no matter the hardship, those who know divine love understand that they must give it away, for "the love of Christ impels us" (2 Cor 5:14) to fearlessly propose the Gospel.

Catholic evangelist Fr. Tom Forrest, CSsR describes why Christians today must embrace their urgent responsibility to evangelize: "We perform a vast number of good deeds, but one is supreme: proclaiming Jesus Christ as the only Savior of the world. Those who do not know Christ have no guaranteed way of getting to heaven." Mirroring the zeal for evangelization that has driven the magisterial vision since St. John XXIII, Fr. Forrest declares, "Too few Catholics realize that evangelization is the only adequate and convincing proof of their Christ-like love for both God and neighbor."[10]

Wisdom from Our "Cloud of Witnesses"

Evangelistic determination can be difficult to sustain today. The current against which we swim is strong. We can turn for inspiration and wisdom to the "great cloud of witnesses" (Heb 12:1), men and women who, through the centuries, overcame obstacles large and small by humbly turning to Christ.

As Peter became overwhelmed by the natural consequences of stepping out of the boat, seeing as he did the rising depths between his feet, he had to choose. Peter's instinct in such a dire circumstance—certainly under the influence of Christ's nearness—was to cry out, "Lord, save me!" In that terrible moment, with his need before him, Peter abandoned himself into the power of the Savior.

The great saints teach us what this graced instinct looks like in circumstances where they experienced difficulty. For instance, when

---

10. Tom Forrest, CSsR, "Why Should Catholics Evangelize" in *John Paul II and the New Evangelization*, ed. Ralph Martin and Peter Williamson (Ann Arbor, MI: Servant Books, 2006), 31, 34.

entrusted with the responsibility of teaching younger Carmelite sisters (a task for which she felt deeply inadequate), St. Thérèse shows us both her awareness of her own weakness and also her glorious childlike trust in Christ the Teacher. She writes:

> I saw immediately the task was beyond my strength. I threw myself into the arms of God as a little child and, hiding my face in his hair, I said: "Lord, I am too little to nourish your children; if you wish to give through me what is suitable for each, fill my little hand and without leaving your arms or turning my head, I shall give your treasures to [them]."[11]

Thérèse demonstrates what it is to teach as one abides in the Vine who is Christ, utterly dependent upon the sustaining hand of God.

While the challenges facing the Church and all Christians today are vast, we can take courage in the example of Peter and of the Little Flower, reaching as they did for Christ. Theirs is the impulse of the true disciple— always a turning to Christ. Such a movement is never without effect. Nearly four centuries later, the great Augustine must have smiled when he remarked, "lo, what Peter was in the Lord!"[12]

This determination to entrust ourselves entirely to Christ must be our Catholic impulse when facing today's challenges—both within the Church and in the world. We can see an important expression of this instinct present in the work of many Catholic liturgical leaders in the early to mid-twentieth century. During those calamitous years encompassing the first and second world wars, a growing number of priests, religious and members of the laity labored to vivify Catholic liturgical practice, even as they suffered grievously along with their countrymen. It is perhaps jarring to think of Catholics investing themselves into the question of how to better engage the faithful in liturgical prayer during those terrible years when the world was on fire. This movement to renew the Catholic liturgy, however, was a collective turn to God in our utter poverty, a need intensely experienced under the scourge of these wars.

Here is one pointed example. During the German occupation of France, in 1943, Paris' Centre de Pastorale Liturgique was founded and

---

11. *Story of a Soul: The Autobiography of St. Thérèse of Lisieux*, trans. John Clarke, OCD, 3rd ed. (Washington, DC: ICS Publications, 1996), 238. For a helpful reflection on this impulse of the 33rd doctor of the Church, see Teresa Hawes, "Trusting Thanks to our Weakness: The Spirituality of the Catechist," *The Catechetical Review* 2, no. 2 (April 2016): 32–33.

12. Augustine, Sermon 26, LXXVI Ben.

dedicated to the work of liturgical renewal. In 1944, at a congress of this liturgical institute, Dominican cofounder Fr. A.M. Roguet articulated the institute's missionary orientation beginning with these words: "We have not come together for a scholarly work of restoration. We are not a congress of archeologists, nor of esthetes, nor of fragile eccentrics of the past, amateur dabblers in things of rare beauty. What moves us, what inflames us, is a missionary zeal."[13] This speech was given during the same year as the D-Day Normandy invasions. During these two years, France was a war zone.

While Fr. Roguet makes clear that the institute's purpose was not one of academic pursuit far removed from the real needs of the world, still many might wonder at the timing of this missionary zeal for the liturgy. Does the establishment of a liturgical institute in the capital of wartime France seem a bit odd? Was such a conference an indication of liturgical theologians and pastoral thinkers being out of touch with the realities surrounding them?

On the contrary, these pioneers of the liturgical movement were convicted by their experience during both world wars. The Catholic faithful, they believed, must understand their vital potential within the Mystical Body of Christ and unite themselves to the liturgy, the prayer of the Church, to significantly impact the darkened state of the fallen world. The liturgy is, after all, the source of the supernatural life of the Christian, which is God's very transforming power. The liturgy plunges us into the Paschal Mystery, puts us into contact with Divine Love, perfect and total Self-Donation. Intentional, knowing immersion into the life and love of the Blessed Trinity brings about mighty effects. All things in the world and in ourselves can be made new.

This confidence in the transformative liturgical encounter is the exact conviction that must animate us today, just as the impulse of the saints to turn to Christ in adversity must also be ours. This book presumes that the Church is right when she teaches that the liturgical encounter with God is the source of transforming grace in the life of the Christian and in the life of the Church. Members of the Mystical Body of Christ, then, are propelled through love to work towards the sanctification of the temporal order, towards establishing a civilization of life, love,

---

13. *Etudes de Pastorale Liturgique* (Lex Orandi I), Paris 1944, 8–9, cited in Cyprian Vagaggini, OSB, *Theological Dimensions of the Liturgy*, trans. Leonard J. Doyle (Collegeville, MN: Liturgical Press, 1976).

and profound respect for persons. It will be from liturgy's divine encounter that individual Christians will be transformed and be given the capacity for a heroic outreach with the Good News of Christ—a development upon which the potential of the New Evangelization rests.

The Scope of This Book: Revitalizing Our Catechetical Vision

This book is intended as another point of engagement for those who wish to consider how to best advance the work of the new evangelization in families, parishes, and schools.

Others have addressed the reality of diminishing sacramental practice from the broader context of the overall life of the parish. This book examines and confronts this challenge from the perspective of our catechetical approaches and structures and their impact upon sacramental living. A fresh look is needed at how we envisage the relationship between sacramental practice and catechesis. If we can get this crucial relationship right, both conceptually and in practice, we have the potential to reinvigorate the sacramental practice of many within our parishes today. Much depends, however, on our vision and priorities concerning the essential work of catechesis.

The proposals offered in the following chapters hinge on three important convictions.

1. We must clearly understand what the liturgy is, what catechesis is, and the interdependent relationship they share in the Church's evangelistic mission. We will work within the invaluable framework provided by the Second Vatican Council and the postconciliar catechetical documents. The scholarship of two important twentieth-century theologians, the Italian liturgical theologian Cyprian Vagaggini, OSB, and the Austrian Jesuit Joseph A. Jungmann will additionally be highlighted for their ingenuity and forward thinking in uniting the previously disparate fields of sacramental theology and what we now call catechetics. These towering figures—both important contributors to the council— were among the first to substantively address the interdependence of the liturgy and catechesis in the Church's mission of bringing the Gospel to the world.

2. After coming to understand the liturgy and catechesis in their relationship to one another, we will explore a second vital conviction. Sacraments are opportunities for a transformative encounter with God. Helping Catholics we serve to embrace this truth will make accessible to them the ever-present source of living water, the cause of deepest joy, and the impetus for understanding our missionary responsibility in the world. Because God generously gives himself—his very life and love—to those who seek him in the encounter of the liturgy, extraordinary fruits are possible for each of us.

3. Above all else, catechesis presents us an opportunity to cultivate a deep desire for God in the liturgical encounter. Through well-conceived catechesis, we can be drawn to seek Divine Love where it may best be found. Catechists can strive to prepare those they teach to find God in the liturgy, to actively invest themselves in it, and to identify and receive his grace. The encounter, then, becomes a source of divine assistance, joy, and freedom. Such an experience—particularly when it deepens over the course of time—changes everything about how we view reality and invest ourselves in life.

What does such a catechesis look like? What are its contours, its priorities, and its potential outcomes? What is required of parents, pastors, and catechists to bring about such a transformative catechesis? This forms the trajectory of the second part of this book. The principles and pastoral applications integrated into this part are intended to be conceptually and practically helpful to the catechist.

Part 3 of the book features contributions by four catechetical leaders who have significant experience in leading others to a dynamic living of the sacramental life. These chapters will offer concrete applications of the principles advanced in this book and will share practical wisdom, insights, and innovative strategies for effective liturgical catechesis.

As we examine the potential of catechesis to prepare us to experience the wellspring of worship in all its power and beauty we focus on something essential to the movement of disciple making. For it will be from the very grace of God transforming ordinary Christians into missionary disciples that the twenty-first-century Church will be revitalized to evangelize the world.

CHAPTER 2

An Evangelizing Catechesis: Today's Great Need

"Now when they heard this, they were cut to the heart, and they asked Peter and the other apostles, 'what are we to do?'" (Acts 2:37).

What are we to do? These are the charged words of those who heard the very first apostolic catechesis, when Peter stood up with the Eleven and gave an exhortation so deeply gripping that these early Christians-to-be moved to instantaneous response. They immediately sought Baptism, joining themselves to the Mystical Body of him whom they had come to know through the teaching of the Church's first catechists.

In today's Church, where do such life-altering convictions surface and take root? Many encounter the One who is the Way, the Truth, and the Life in the context of the Mass, the Sacrament of Reconciliation, or in silent prayer before the Blessed Sacrament. They might also come to know him in a different way on a retreat, at a youth conference, during a Cursillo, in a bible study, or at a prayer group. Some recognize Christ "in his most distressing disguise"[1] as they stand before a person in need, perhaps being opened at the same time to their own humanity and deep need for the presence of others. Reflecting, though, on this compelling *catechetical* account from the life of Peter the apostle, those of us who teach the faith today could ask ourselves: Can Christ also be encountered through the experience of catechesis? Can those we teach be moved to a personal responsiveness through the teaching of Christian doctrine?

Many today would instead be inclined to say that if a person is seeking a transformative encounter with God, this is most realistically found in experiences outside of catechesis. Catechesis, they might argue, is the

---

1. This phrase is attributed to St. Teresa of Calcutta.

educational phase of Christian formation—where we read, study, and discuss—but rarely *a place of life-changing encounter* in itself.

This chapter proposes a very different view not only of the potential of catechesis, but of what it must become.

Before moving into the central issues of this book—and its culmination in a new vision for fruitful liturgical catechesis—we must find our footing. The foundations established in this chapter are essential as we explore the sacramental mysteries in their potential impact on catechesis.

Catechesis today—even amidst great challenges[2]—remains a pivotal opportunity to impact how young people and adults alike see God, the Church, and their mission in the world. As we consider ways to rehabilitate and strengthen catechesis, it is time to "roll up our sleeves," think big, honestly evaluate the effectiveness of our approaches, and seek hopeful and promising ways forward.

The Church needs catechetical revitalization. Our programs and methods must better prepare Catholics to draw from a deep reservoir as thinking disciples of Christ, ready to navigate their way—by faith and reason—through a complex and incongruous world.

Before he was named auxiliary bishop, Fr. Robert Barron said as much in his 2014 keynote address at the Los Angeles Religious Education Congress. In this address, he implored attendees, "Don't dumb down the message." Reflecting on the exodus of so many of his contemporaries from the Church in the past several decades, Fr. Barron said:

> There were a lot of people in my generation who just opted out of Catholicism. How come? They grew up and life hit them in the face. They saw the complexity of things and a childish, superficial Catholicism was no answer to the deep problems of life.

Fr. Barron went on to ask why teenagers in our catechetical programs and Catholic schools can't read Aquinas, Augustine, Newman, Chesterton, and Dante. If they are required in literature courses to grasp the intricacies of a writer such as Shakespeare—and if some are aiming

---

2. One challenge is this: as the numbers of those receiving sacraments has decreased over the past five decades, the numbers of those receiving catechetical formation are also substantially lower. For instance, the number of students in Catholic elementary schools has dropped from 4.431 million in 1965 to 1.358 million in 2015. The number of primary school-age children in parish religious education has also dropped from 4.175 million in 1970 to 2.631 million in 2015. See Center for Applied Research in the Apostolate at Georgetown University, "Frequently Requested Church Statistics," accessed October 14, 2016: http://cara.georgetown.edu/frequently-requested-church-statistics/.

for careers in the sciences, technology, business, and as lawyers and doctors—they will only take Catholicism seriously as adults if they have some contact with its resplendent intellectual treasury.[3] Where will such access be provided if not in our schools, parishes, and families?

Of course Aquinas, Augustine, and Newman did not describe a speculative Christianity, but wrote insightfully about a Christianity that is lived. Today's Catholics must be given access to the Tradition in a way that the call to communion with God resonates, so we may have the opportunity to come to know God personally. Catechesis should offer the opportunity to learn from Christ *as Teacher* and also from Christ *our Life*, who brings us into loving communion with the Father in the Holy Spirit. Such a communion changes everything about how we will see the world.

There is no question that today's needed recalibration of catechesis depends on creative solutions to many issues that are outside the scope of this book. New strategies are required to centralize adult evangelization and faith formation in parish life, to win parents over and empower them to embrace their responsibilities as primary catechists of their children, and to prioritize a rich spiritual formation for catechists. While needs such as these affect the proposals of this book, we will focus now on the imperative that underpins each of these, that our catechesis become an *evangelizing catechesis*. To this end, this chapter establishes a baseline understanding of the most significant magisterial catechetical development of the past fifty years: the prophetic relocation of catechesis within the mission of evangelization. Correctly understanding catechesis in its relationship to evangelization provides the fertile soil from which will spring today's catechetical renewal.

Evangelization and Catechesis: Postconciliar Developments

Over the past fifty years, the Church has gradually focused her expression of how evangelization and catechesis operate in the mission of bringing the Gospel to the world. This increasing clarity will, by God's grace, lead to

---

3. To watch this outstanding address to religious educators, see "REC 2014 | Keynote | Rev. Robert Barron," YouTube video, 53:31, posted by "RECongress," March 19, 2014, https://www.youtube.com/watch?v=fRzDBro3FiE.

increased evangelistic fruitfulness in the years to come. Three historical markers are particularly useful in seeing these advances.

First, in the 1971 *General Catechetical Directory*, evangelization and catechesis—along with the liturgy and theology—were classified as the four forms of the ministry of the Word. Each form was understood to be distinct yet related in the mission of communicating the Gospel. Evangelization, defined somewhat narrowly as "missionary preaching . . . [which] has as its purpose the arousing of the beginnings of faith so that men will adhere to the Word of God" (GCD, 17), was understood to be a first proclamation of the Good News directed to those in need of initial faith. Strictly speaking, this paradigm presumed that evangelization normally should precede catechesis. Yet, the authors of the directory were certainly grounded in reality, recognizing that "often, however, [catechesis] is directed to [people] who, though they belong to the Church, have in fact never given a true personal adherence to the message of revelation" (GCD, 18). In such cases, evangelization ought to accompany catechesis.

The great conviction with this model was that if an initial decision for Jesus is the fruit of the missionary preaching of evangelization, this attachment could give rise to a new receptivity for what is given in catechesis. Of course, any catechist of any generation would wholeheartedly affirm the need for this preliminary giving of ourselves to the Lord, and would savor the possibility of teaching such a willing group of learners.

It is important to see, however, a negative association that could emerge from this paradigm for how we see the ministry of catechesis. If evangelization is conceived as the missionary preaching that ought to be preliminary to catechesis, it becomes quite possible in practice that catechesis be compartmentalized from evangelization as a merely cerebral endeavor. In this understanding, evangelization speaks to the heart and brings a person into relationship with Jesus, while catechesis has to do with the head and is concerned merely with the communication of doctrine and the promotion of knowledge. While catechesis would, within this paradigm, benefit from evangelization, it can also get along without it, meeting its obligations as students pass exams or finish exercises in their religion workbooks. The *General Catechetical Directory* did not propose such a bifurcated view of evangelization and catechesis, explicitly acknowledging that "the element of conversion is always present in the dynamism of faith, and for that reason any form of catechesis must also perform the role of evangelization" (GCD, 18). Nonetheless, a widespread tendency has continued in both schools and parishes to catechize in ways that do not consciously promote the conversion process that the directory describes. When the faith is taught in a merely academic-theoretical fashion, when catechesis is not permeated with the proposal of communion with Christ and the consequent call to holiness of life, catechesis becomes intellectualized and its results widely miss the mark.

Such an approach in the postconciliar years does not genuinely heal what was frequently flawed in the catechesis before the council. Pre–Vatican II models of instruction that fixated on doctrinal retention were marvelously effective at helping children remember doctrinal formulae, but there were also deficiencies that arose in limiting catechesis in too narrow a fashion. Opportunities to come to know God personally, to receive the faith within the framework of culture, and to move towards the integration of faith and life were often scarce in these models, creating new challenges for many later in life in their relationship with God and the Church. Knowing Catholic doctrine without coming to know the One from whom this precious content originates was not the intent of the Church yet was frequently the effect of catechesis.

Many Catholics today, if they have any familiarity with the term "evangelization," continue to view it as something akin to the "missionary preaching" of the 1971 directory. Therefore, for them, evangelization belongs to the expertise and responsibility of three groups: (1) the missionaries who knock on doors or preach Christ to villagers in developing countries, (2) the extroverted, super-enthused, admirably motivated, saintly "born-again" types, or (3) those who are professional Church employees, that is, the *trained experts* (priests, religious, or lay people with degrees in theology, divinity, religious education, or catechetics) who evangelize in fulfillment of their job responsibilities. With each of these marginalizations comes a greater distancing of ourselves from our God-given personal responsibility to "make disciples of all nations" (Mt 28:19). Consequently, many members of our parishes would contend that it is important for the Church to evangelize, but only when it imposes no personal demands.

A second milestone in the evolution of the evangelization-catechesis relationship may be discovered in Pope Paul VI's 1975 postsynodal apostolic exhortation *Evangelii Nuntiandi* (On Evangelization in the Modern World).

In this important document, Paul VI moved the Church to a new understanding of evangelization and its relation to catechesis. The epicenter of this significant development may be located in these words:

> Evangelizing is in fact the grace and vocation proper to the Church, her deepest identity. She exists in order to evangelize, that is to say, in order to preach and teach, to be the channel of the gift of grace, to reconcile sinners with God, and to perpetuate Christ's sacrifice in the Mass, which is the memorial of his death and glorious resurrection. (EN, 14)

There are two important observations we can make from this groundbreaking paragraph.

First, evangelization is conceived in broader terms and is resituated into the center of the Church's life, mission, and self-understanding. No longer merely one form of the ministry of the Word, evangelization is now described as the Church's "deepest identity." If the whole Church "exists in order to evangelize," every member of the baptized is affected by Christ's command to make disciples. We all become responsible, a position clearly reflective of the Second Vatican Council's "universal call to holiness."

A second observation is equally momentous. This mission to evangelize is carried out by the Church not only in a "missionary preaching" intended to call people to initial faith as the GCD specified. Other ways are also identified: through teaching, being a channel of grace, reconciling sinners, and perpetuating Christ's sacrifice in the Mass. Initial proclamation will always be vital to the work of evangelization, but the term "evangelization" is to be indicative of far more, extending even to catechetical and sacramental initiatives. One important catechetical leader, in fact, summarizes the insight of Paul VI in this way:

> This view understands evangelization as a lifelong process of conversion in which the believer hears God's word over and over and responds to that word with an ever-deepening faith. Evangelization comprises all the Church's endeavors to proclaim the Gospel, so that faith may be awakened, develop and thrive. In this sense, evangelization motivates the overall mission of the Church and animates all of the Church's ministries.[4]

Both catechesis and the liturgy help accomplish evangelization. They are, when well executed, *evangelizing initiatives*.

---

4. John Pollard, "Catechesis: A Pastoral Priority," *The Living Light* 28, no. 3 (Spring 1992): 202.

A third and final marker of this paradigm shift between evangelization and catechesis came in 1997 with the revision of the original directory. The newer *General Directory for Catechesis* assumes and deepens the insights of Paul VI. Evangelization is defined again quite broadly as "the carrying forth of the Good News to every sector of the human race so that by its strength it may enter into the hearts of men and renew the human race" (GDC, 46). Additionally, the GDC specifies that the work of evangelization is accomplished by way of five distinctive elements or "means." The GDC explains, "proclamation, witness, teaching (or catechesis), love of neighbor, the sacraments: all of these aspects are the means by which the one Gospel is transmitted and they constitute the essential elements of evangelization itself" (GDC, 46). While Paul VI extended the concept of evangelization to sacraments and catechesis, the 1997 directory adds three more initiatives to our understanding of evangelization, thus dramatically expanding its radius. Through each of these modes, the Good News of Christ's life, Death, and Resurrection can be "carried forth" and when taken to heart can have a transforming impact on life and culture.

The distinction between the 1971 and 1997 directories in how they view catechesis is worth noting. In the 1997 GDC, catechesis is envisioned as an "essential moment" in the evangelization process[5] that must therefore be intrinsically evangelistic in its own right. Good catechesis penetrates the heart with the Good News and provokes conversion. It does so by helping us take in the Good News more deeply, not only for the sake of the "renewal of [the] mind" (Rom 12:2), but with the intent of the whole person being transformed. Thus, in the mind of the Church, the faith is to be presented today by way of an *evangelizing* catechesis.

In a 2010 telephone interview, Archbishop Alfred Hughes, the retired ordinary of New Orleans who had served as chairman of the editorial oversight board for the creation of the 2005 *United States National Directory for Catechesis*, identified the relocation of catechesis into the process of evangelization as one of the most significant differences from the earlier directory. The archbishop described catechesis as:

> an extended moment that involves the systematic unfolding of the content of evangelization. Emphasis is placed in the catechetical effort on leading people to acknowledge God, accept Christ as the Son of God, consciously

---

5. See GDC, 49, 59, 67.

accept the Holy Spirit, allowing them to be not only informed but to be transformed by the living encounter with Jesus Christ.[6]

As we see here, while evangelization and catechesis are intimately related, they are not indistinguishable. Catechesis brings faith to Christian maturity through a "systematic unfolding of the content of evangelization." St. John Paul II describes catechesis as the practice of "maturing initial faith and educating the true disciple of Christ by means of a deeper, more systematic knowledge of the person and the message of our Lord Jesus Christ" (CT, 19). Good catechesis, then, deepens our union with Christ by maturing our understanding of both the content of his teaching and the mysteries of his personhood. This results in a transformed and deeply rooted faith, one that is "living, explicit, and fruitful" (GDC, 82).

For St. John Paul II, catechesis develops "understanding of the mystery of Christ in the light of God's Word" and this understanding is meant to *change* each of us "by the working of grace into a new creature." The catechized person sets "himself to follow Christ and learns more and more within the Church to think like him, to judge like him, to act in conformity with his commandments, and to hope as he invites us to" (CT, 20). Catechesis, then, bears fruit in the full flowering of a life lived in genuine conformity to the way of Christ. This is how St. John Paul II understood the Christian maturity that is the goal of catechesis.

In addition to defining the parameters of evangelization, the GDC describes six tasks unique to catechesis, each of which is integral to this movement towards Christian maturity: "knowledge of the faith, liturgical education, moral formation, teaching to pray, education for community life and missionary initiation."[7] These six tasks correspond well to our need to *integrate* faith and life, extending the power of the Gospel into the various dimensions of our experience of Christian life. The directory warns against the neglect of any of these tasks, for, "maturity of Christian life requires that it be cultivated in all its dimensions. When one is omitted, Christian faith does not attain full development" (GDC, 87).

---

6. Archbishop Alfred Hughes, telephone interview by author, April 23, 2010.

7. GDC, 85–86. The first four tasks are inspired by the four pillars which structure the *Catechism of the Catholic Church*. The final two tasks bespeak a genuine and mature response of faith which leads a person into full participation in the life of the community and in the missionary dynamism of true evangelization (understood, of course, in the wider sense as the GDC understands "evangelization"—see art. 46ff.).

Through ongoing catechesis, maturing in our Catholic faith and life becomes a lifelong vocation and adventure. It cannot end at Confirmation or at high school graduation or with entry into adulthood. We can always go further and deeper and understand and experience more concerning the love, faithfulness, and mystery of God. Consequently, the Church sees the catechesis of all her *adults* as the "central task in the catechetical enterprise."[8]

Catechetical practice over the past century has been dominated by the swinging pendulum: on the one hand, understanding catechesis to be a systematic and comprehensive content-based endeavor and on the other hand seeing it as a creative and inculturated engagement of the many facets of human experience. One emphasized to the detriment of the other devastates the potential for young people (and older ones too!) to confidently, intelligently, and joyfully live the Catholic life today. When catechesis is contextualized within the evangelization process this division is healed. Authentic catechesis is always irretrievably both rich in content and ordered towards the transformation of our experience. Through our ever more intentional embrace of the teaching of Christ, the experience of life becomes more and more permeated by his saving presence.

The Proposal of Communion, the Invitation to Friendship

To be catechized, then, is to be offered the proposal of life in Christ. A close reading of the Gospels reveals Jesus himself repeatedly extending this exact invitation. To the rich young man he said, "If you wish to be perfect, go, sell what you have and give to [the] poor, and you will have treasure in heaven. Then come, follow me" (Mt 19:21). To the woman at the well, he said, "Whoever drinks the water I shall give will never thirst" (Jn 4:14). To Martha and Mary, mourning the devastating loss of their beloved brother, Lazarus, he said, "I am the resurrection and the life;

---

8. International Council for Catechesis, *Adult Catechesis in the Christian Community* (Washington, DC: United States Catholic Conference, 1990), 25. This document continues, saying that genuine Christian community is impossible without systematic catechesis for all members of the community. See also Pope John Paul II, CT, 43, where he wrote that adult catechesis is the "principle form of catechesis," and GDC, 275, refers to adult catechesis as the "axis" around which revolves catechesis for all other age groups. A further indication of the Church's emphasis on the centrality of adult evangelization and catechesis may be seen in the 2006 national catechism of the United States, which is not written for children as earlier catechisms were but is directed to adults. See USCCB, Ad hoc Committee to Oversee the Use of the Catechism, *United States Catholic Catechism for Adults* (Washington, DC: USCCB Publishing, 2006).

whoever believes in me, even if he dies, will live. . . . Do you believe this?" (Jn 11:25). To Zacchaeus the tax collector he said, "Today I must stay at your house" (Lk 19:5). To Matthew, he simply said, "Follow me" (Mt 9:9). Even his giving "the impression that he was going on farther" (Lk 24:28) was an invitation for the disciples on the road to Emmaus to appeal to him to stay with them. It is for this communion with God in Christ that we were made. Through it, we will find deepest joy and our sure purpose.

The term *communion* indicates one of those Catholic theological concepts that has become so familiar that the truth expressed by it has perhaps lost its hold upon our collective imagination. Blessed Marie-Eugene of the Child Jesus, OCD, the Carmelite founder of the secular institute of Notre Dame de Vie in France, describes the experience of communion with God with these almost alarming words:

> This contact is penetrating, and when we penetrate God, when the contact is established, there is a real exchange. God is an ocean, a fire, a living fountain. Each time we make contact with God we touch the ocean that He is, the flame that He is, and consequently we draw from him the divine substance. We receive an increase in that participation in divine life which is the grace within us.[9]

It is for this most intimate Presence—real contact with Infinite Life and Perfect Love—that every human being yearns. By grace, those joined to Christ are brought by him into deepest intimacy with the Blessed Trinity.

St. John Paul II moved right to the heart of things when he wrote, "The definitive aim of catechesis is to put people not only in touch but in communion, in intimacy with Jesus Christ: only he can lead us to the love of the Father in the Spirit and make us share in the life of the Holy Trinity" (CT, 5). The proposal of intimate communion with the Lord Jesus must become today the enveloping focus of every catechetical act. The *Catechism of the Catholic Church* beautifully emphasizes that no matter what is being taught, "the love of the Lord must always be made accessible, so that anyone can see that all the works of perfect Christian virtue spring from love and have no other objective than to arrive at love."[10] Such an invitation, rooted into the heart of our teaching, will help catechesis to become interesting, engaging, deeply relevant, and accurately perceived to be the

---

9. Marie-Eugene of the Child Jesus, OCD, *Where the Spirit Breathes: Prayer and Action* (New York: Alba House, 1998), 67.

10. CCC, 25. It is notable that this statement was original to the *Roman Catechism*, Preface, 10.

beginning of the greatest of enterprises. This proposal must be extended every time the catechist teaches, and no matter what the catechist teaches.

The Proposal and the Catechist

If the invitation to the communion of love is offered throughout our teaching, then every facet of the catechetical act becomes something extraordinary, transfigured by the grace and glory of the divine proposal being extended.

It is the catechist who bears this summons to communion with God. What can we understand, then, of the dignity of the catechist's work?

The Church uses astonishing language in describing the mission of the catechist, referring to the catechist as a "mediator" who "facilitates communication between the people and the Mystery of God" (GDC, 156). Reaching out from our own intimate friendship with God, catechists teach others, helping them perceive the call to life in Christ. This understanding of the catechist's mediatorial presence is provocative and worthy of any catechist's deeper reflection.

One catechetical writer, Msgr. Francis Kelly, understands the catechist to be the one who "helps create the conditions for the possibility of a deepening of God's Word in the hearts of those being served."[11] It is noteworthy that, in this understanding, the catechist does not deepen God's Word in the hearts of those being formed, for it is not within the power of any catechist to do so. The only way this happens is when a person freely chooses to take God's Word to heart, and such an act is always a free cooperation with the inspiration of the Holy Spirit, who is present and deeply invested in this work. All that the catechist can do is create the conditions for the possibility of this encounter.

A second application of this idea of the catechist's mediation may be found in the writings of the great catechist of children, Sofia Cavalletti. Believing that the primary encounter of catechesis takes place between God and the child, Cavalletti suggests that the catechist take steps to ensure he or she does not impede this meeting. Her ideas on this deserve to be quoted at length:

> The [catechist] should remind himself that he is the "unworthy servant" of the Gospel. . . . The catechist proclaims a Word that is not one's own and

---

11. Francis D. Kelly, *The Mystery We Proclaim: Second Edition: Catechesis for the Third Millennium* (Huntington, IN: Our Sunday Visitor, 1999), 138.

assists the child's potentialities, which in no way belong to oneself. The adult cannot help but recognize how often the results surpass the promises of one's work. The adult is so often made aware of the disproportion between what one has given and what the children manifest to possess and to live. At times our hands touch the presence of an active force that is not ours, and it is precisely because it is not our own that it fills us with wonder and deep joy. . . . The catechist's task is to create specific conditions so that this relationship may be established, but to withdraw as soon as that contact occurs. We should take the greatest care not to intervene between God and the child with our encumbering person, with our insistent words. The adult's mediation is a service that is offered to the Word of God and to the child, and it has all the limitations of a service. The catechist who does not know when to stop, who does not know how to keep silent, is one who is not conscious of one's limits and, after all, is lacking in faith, because, on the practical level at least, one is not convinced that it is God and His creative Word that are active in the religious event. The help the adult can give the child is only preliminary and peripheral, and one that halts—that must halt—on the threshold of the "place" where God speaks with His creature.[12]

These are the words of a true believer that when Christ said, "For where two or three are gathered together in my name, there am I in the midst of them," he meant it.

Regardless of how this mediation is envisioned, the catechist must above all be attuned to God and his inspirations within the catechetical setting. The Holy Spirit, after all, is moving in the heart of the catechist and in the hearts of those being catechized, calling all into intimate friendship with God. The catechist's primary responsibility, then, is to promote and cultivate the possibility for encounter with God in times of prayer, in moments of fraternity, and as God's Word is being studied. It is a challenging and beautiful responsibility.

The catechist's call to mission originates in God and is a "vocation." Though we may become catechists by way of seemingly natural events—such as a desperate plea from the pastor—God uses even these circumstances to call. The most mundane or messy of catechist recruitment processes has a hidden dimension, and if a person is called to become a catechist, it can be the vehicle for receiving a divine summons. Of course,

---

12. Sofia Cavalletti, *The Religious Potential of the Child* (Chicago: Catechesis of the Good Shepherd Publications, 1992), 52.

a dignified and prayerful approach to helping people discern this call is important for many reasons.

Because catechesis is a vocation, it is an authentic pathway to holiness. The message borne by the catechist—if pondered and taken to heart throughout the process of giving it away to others—cannot but have an effect. St. John Paul II said of this process, "faith is strengthened when it is given to others" (RM, 2). The Holy Spirit who is the "principal agent of evangelization" (RM, 21) wants to grow and stretch every catechist and draw us gradually into a life of profound sanctity. Embracing this vocation and cooperating with the grace of God in it will develop in us specifically catechetical virtues—such as a radical giving of ourselves to God as we prepare our catechesis, becoming more and more personally responsive to the Truth of Christ and of the Church, investing ourselves generously into those we teach, and willing their good, sometimes unto great sacrifice. In fact, the Church understands that this vocation of catechesis will "cause the catechist to grow in respect and in love for . . . those being catechized" (GDC, 239). With a stirring beauty, the GDC then quotes Pope Paul VI: "What is this love? It is the love, not so much of a teacher as of a father, or rather of a mother. It is the Lord's wish that every preacher of the Gospel, every builder up of the Church, should have this love."[13]

Of course, by bringing a child into the world, mothers and fathers are entrusted with the sacred responsibility to serve as catechists to our own children. We are our children's primary educators, their most influential catechists. Every parent has a catechetical vocation—at least for our own children. Embracing this responsibility of being primary catechists for our children—and pouring ourselves into this greatest work—will draw parents more deeply and richly into the mystery of Christ's self-sacrificial love.

Whether a parent, schoolteacher, or parish catechist, the catechetical vocation must also be sustained over the course of the years. Perhaps the essential scripture for every catechist's reflection may be found in John 15:4–5. At the most solemn hour, possibly even during that grave march from the upper room to the garden of Gethsemane, the Lord gives this teaching:

---

13. GDC, 239, quoting Paul VI, EN, 79.

Remain in me, as I remain in you. Just as a branch cannot bear fruit on its own unless it remains on the vine, so neither can you unless you remain in me. I am the vine, you are the branches. Whoever remains in me and I in him will bear much fruit, because without me you can do nothing.

The fruitfulness of the catechist—whether pastor, parent, or first grade teacher in the parish school—is always directly related to the depth of his communion with Christ.

The Proposal and our Catechetical Methods

The extraordinary content of our teaching has another impact on the catechetical process. *How* the catechist teaches must always serve the content of the Mystery, in all its power and beauty, that has been entrusted to the Church.

Our understanding of the relationship of content to method within catechesis becomes therefore quite important. Every other educational discipline bears witness to the necessary deference given to *what* is being taught. Whether we are teaching algebra, geography, history, or how to change the oil in a car, *what it is* that we teach determines *how we are going to teach it*. Each educational endeavor is geared towards the attainment of a specific scope of knowledge. If that outcome is not reached, then our chosen methods must be evaluated, refined, or even replaced.

Upholding the content-method relationship is never more vital than when God's revelation and the call to discipleship is the "knowledge" being communicated. The content of this message is of such immeasurable value that it cannot be subjected to just any teaching methodology. One of the twentieth century's best catechists once wrote, "as we do not present to others jewelry and ordinary food in the same kind of wrapping, neither do we transmit religion and geometry to students by the same teaching method. Religious teaching demands a method in keeping with its nature."[14] Staying with this analogy, we know that jewelry is presented in a jewelry store with strategic forethought—with lighting and methods of display that accentuate the color and sparkle of the jewelry. Likewise, we must constantly be evaluating our catechetical methods to continually renew and refine how the invitation to communion with Christ is being

---

14. Johannes Hofinger, SJ, *The Good News and Its Proclamation* (Notre Dame, IN: University of Notre Dame Press, 1968), 87. The first edition of this text was published in 1957 by the same press under the title *The Art of Teaching Christian Doctrine: The Good News and its Proclamation*.

presented. St. John Paul II is unequivocal on this point: "A technique is of value in catechesis only to the extent that it serves the faith that is to be transmitted and learned; otherwise, it is of no value" (CT, 58).

When might our catechetical methods be less helpful to the content of catechesis? The unfortunate age-old method of reading too much straight from the textbook might serve as an apt example of a method that reliably results in boredom. Frequently these generous and heroic volunteer catechists who stray very little from the text may do so because they are not yet sufficiently confident as teachers or because they are concerned about leaving out a particular point in the book; they are in need of continued formation and mentoring in their teaching methods by more seasoned catechists. On the other hand, a method might be so high-energy or free-flowing that the activities or lack of structure overshadow whatever content is given. In instances such as these, many will leave the catechetical setting bereft of the deeper understanding of the faith which they so need. Such a catechesis can, unfortunately, have very little lasting effect.

In her wisdom, the Church directs our gaze toward what she terms, "the Pedagogy of God," so that we might be inspired by God himself in communicating what has been divinely revealed and entrusted to us.[15] Exploring the scriptures from the perspective of the divine pedagogy is to see God's approach in sharing himself with human beings. Such a study is invaluable today for learning how to offer the invitation to divine love.

The Proposal and Those We Catechize

St. John Paul II wisely described catechetical methodology as being in a relationship of service to the content of the faith and the conversion of those being catechized.[16] Therefore, the catechist embraces the *content* that is to be conveyed and at the same time the *needs of the person*. Only this double embrace makes it possible for catechetical participants to be attracted to the Divine Teacher and choose to enter into the process of discipleship and conversion.

For catechists, the learning process (how our learners best respond) must be the preoccupation of our planning and prayer—and not just the

---

15. See especially GDC, 139–43; NDC, 89–95; Petroc Willey, "The Pedagogy of God Part 1," *The Sower* 30, no. 2 (April 2009): 7–9; and Petroc Willey, "The Pedagogy of God Part 2," *The Sower* 30, no. 3 (July 2009): 17–18.

16. John Paul II, *Catechesi Tradendae*, 52. The subheading preceding this section states as much: "Method at the Service of Revelation and Conversion."

teaching process (what we say and do). Teaching and learning are the two sides of the coin of catechesis, with one being a means (teaching) and the other the end (learning).

As we have seen to this point, both the person of the catechist and the methods employed must be attuned to the divine content of catechesis—but what of the people we catechize? What do we hope for them as they receive the content of Divine Revelation, this proposal of intimate communion with Christ? There are several conclusions we might draw for how we approach catechetical participants with the mystery of Christ.

First, the content of the faith must always be inculturated. The Church's conviction for inculturation is rooted in the fact of the incarnation, which is the "original inculturation of the Word of God" (GDC, 109). Because God took upon himself the imperfect human condition out of love for us, we learn from him the importance of accommodating the content of faith to the receptive capacities of those whom we teach. Much depends here upon the diversity of cultures, ages, and intellectual abilities of those being taught. The faith is not, therefore, to be merely conceptual in its presentation but conveyed in such a way that there is the possibility for it to be heard, understood, taken to heart, and integrated into life by the unique individuals and groups entrusted to our care. Jesus himself makes it clear that the one who sows is to be aware not only of the life within the seed, but also the conditions of the soil into which the seed is received.[17]

In his great encyclical focused on evangelization, St. John Paul II maintains that the saving Gospel must be offered in its full potency and in such a way that it might be well received. He writes, "This proclamation is to be made within the context of the lives of the individuals and peoples who receive it" (RM, 44). A doctrinal teaching which is somehow disembodied from the context of life and culture will remain purely theoretical, will not engage the full person, and will be unlikely to become leaven within a person's life. In these cases, there is the possibility that catechesis devolves into just another academic subject, to be grasped and studied for the sake of passing an exam, but lacking the more personal engagement which is germane to this work. He continues, "[The proclamation] is to be made with an attitude of love and esteem toward those who hear it, in language which is practical and adapted to the situation" (RM, 44). Life

---

17. GDC, 15, referencing Mk 4:1–9 and Lk 8:4–15.

context and language, of course, are heavily influenced by culture. The catechist, consequently, becomes more effective as she grows in knowledge and appreciation of how to propose the faith to people living within ever-evolving cultural contexts.

Since communion with Christ is the primary intended fruit of catechesis, our second consideration has to do with our awareness of where our learners are in the process of conversion. How and what we communicate of the content of catechesis depends greatly upon where an individual person stands in relation to God. This concept is not new as the GDC has already articulated five stages of evangelization.[18]

A particularly helpful approach may be found in the "thresholds of conversion" articulated by Sherry Weddell in her book *Forming Intentional Disciples*. Weddell argues that those attempting to reach others with the Gospel must, through friendship, discover at what "threshold" another person is in his or her "lived relationship with God."[19] Weddell's five thresholds are: trust, curiosity, openness, seeking, and intentional discipleship. A good deal hinges upon a person's actual location on this spectrum—and catechists need to genuinely know the individual persons being catechized if it is hoped that catechesis will be fruitful.

A natural objection will arise from experienced catechists: how is it possible to know my students and to tailor my catechetical approaches to them as individuals, when I am teaching a group of eight or twelve or twenty at a time? An important consequence results from this more personal approach. A catechesis tailored more individually is best envisioned as a process of apprenticeship.[20] Catechetical models and structures must

---

18. GDC, 47, describes five stages of evangelization: "Christian witness, dialogue and presence in charity, the proclamation of the Gospel and the call to conversion, the catechumenate and Christian initiation, and the formation of the Christian communities through and by means of the sacraments and their ministers." One important insight in these stages is the need expressed for "the proclamation of the Gospel and call to conversion" to be preceded by "dialog and presence in charity" for only when another person is respected, loved and treated with kindness might there be an authentic opening to the Truth of which we are all so in need.

19. Sherry Weddell, *Forming Intentional Disciples*, 128. How the person subjectively sees himself in his lived relationship with God must be distinguished, Weddell argues, from his sacramental position or catechetical level. As we all know, it is frequently the case today that a person is catechized and sacramentalized but lacks a consciousness of being in relationship to God as a disciple of Christ.

20. This term was used by the Council Fathers when they wrote of the RCIA process: "The catechumenate is not a mere expounding of doctrines and precepts, but a training period in the whole Christian life, and an apprenticeship duty drawn out, during which disciples are joined to Christ their teacher" (*Ad Gentes*, 14).

be pioneered today that promote the possibility of mentoring others in small groups or as individuals in the richness of the Christian life. First and foremost, parents can be better equipped to serve their children in their irreplaceable role as mentors in the life of authentic discipleship. The catechist serves in a supportive and complementary role, a very distant second place to the influence exercised by parents.

By employing the terminology of apprenticeship, mentoring, and discipleship we see that catechesis today extends beyond mere doctrinal explication. The catechist is instrumental in forming particular abilities and skills that become habits serving a person over the course of life. Catechists can know the joy of helping others learn how to pray, study scripture, enter into authentic liturgical participation, find and serve Christ in those who are in need, and effectively share the faith with others. In most cases, these skills must become habits by the time a young person is graduated from high school if these abilities are to be depended upon in adulthood. Adult catechesis, too, is instrumental in assisting adults in the development of the habits and skills needed for living the Christian life. These abilities, whenever learned, are the crowning fruits of a well-conceived catechesis.

Catechesis for Missionary Disciples

Catechesis proposes the Christian life and at the same time creates the conditions to embrace that life and conform ourselves to the way of Christ. The GDC describes the fruit of catechesis in this way: "The Christian faith is conversion to Jesus Christ. It is a full adherence to his person and the decision to walk in his footsteps. Faith is a personal encounter with Jesus Christ, making of oneself a disciple of him. This demands a permanent commitment to think like him, to judge like him and to live as he lived" (GDC, 53).

The final step in the learning process will be putting our own words to what we have learned. We likely know this in our own personal experience as catechists, as we have come into a more assured possession of the faith through the experience of communicating it to others. The final phase of catechesis—once the desire has arisen in our hearts to become true disciples of Jesus—is developing confidence in sharing the faith with others. Every one of our students has the vocation, by virtue of sacramental

Baptism, to missionary discipleship. In *Evangelii Gaudium*, Pope Francis describes this concept well:

> In virtue of their baptism, all the members of the People of God have become missionary disciples (cf. Mt 28:19). All the baptized, whatever their position in the Church or their level of instruction in the faith, are agents of evangelization, and it would be insufficient to envisage a plan of evangelization to be carried out by professionals while the rest of the faithful would simply be passive recipients. The new evangelization calls for personal involvement on the part of each of the baptized. (EG, 120)

In the end, learners who choose to genuinely live the Christian life must be prepared to embrace the richness and the challenge of living Christ's priestly, prophetic, and kingly mission, a responsibility that becomes our own by virtue of our membership in the Mystical Body of Christ.

While the new evangelization depends upon a revitalization of catechesis, it is important for catechists to know that we do not stand alone. The work of evangelization is the task of the whole Mystical Body of Christ. It is the work of God among us and includes all those in communion with God—to include the angels and the communion of saints. As we journey through life, the grace of God reaches those we catechize by many avenues, always for the sake of drawing us all to deeper conversion and missionary awareness. We can count on the love of God who is relentless in searching us out and inviting us into Life. There are, to take up the language of the GDC, numerous means by which we are all continually evangelized.

Among these, catechesis and the sacraments in their complementarity and interdependence are of particular importance to the issues addressed in this book. The next chapters will explore the immense potential to be found in reuniting the liturgy and catechesis for the sake of the new evangelization.

CHAPTER 3

Two Movements and a Council: Rediscovering a Fundamental Connection

When the Risen Christ entrusted his apostles with the mission of disciplemaking, he indicated two indispensable actions. They were to baptize "them in the name of the Father and of the Son and of the Holy Spirit," and they were to teach "them to observe all that I have commanded you" (Mt 28:19–20). With this mandate, the Lord made it clear there was to be (as we now understand) both a sacramental and a catechetical dimension to the work of making disciples.

Following any great teacher requires a slow process of coming into possession of his or her teachings. For those who are drawn to Christ, *knowing* the truth of his teaching becomes an immeasurable need. It is the way we gain access to the mind and will of the One who is the Word of the Father and Savior of the world. The disciple draws ever nearer to Christ through a sustained reflection upon his Word, much like the Lord's mother so frequently and lovingly pondered his mysteries in her own heart. The command of Jesus *to teach*, then, is integral to the apostolic mission of inviting others into the Christian life.

Not only does Jesus desire that we come to know his teaching, he also wishes us to *draw close to him*, to share in his Divine Life. Through the waters of baptism, the one seeking Christ finds him in marvelous fashion. Baptism objectively puts us into a profound communion with the One we follow and this intimate union is deepened through a life of sacramental participation. This union is so profound and real that Paul exclaims, "Yet I live, no longer I, but Christ lives in me" (Gal 2:20). The disciple is able to know and live like Christ because it is the Lord Himself, dwelling within the disciple, who empowers him to do so.

In the language of the Great Commission, then, we see how important both the sacramental and catechetical encounters are to coming to know and enter into union with Christ.

The 2005 US *National Directory for Catechesis* describes the liturgy and catechesis as being "intimately connected" (NDC, 110). If our pastoral vision today comes to reflect this deep harmony, then both catechesis and the liturgical life will be what Christ intended from the very beginning: his principal means of transforming people into authentic missionary disciples who are in close union with Him.

Before we can explore the complexities of today's pastoral situation, we must truly be convinced of *the need* for liturgy and catechesis to be conducted in a concerted way. We will turn now to the persuasive insights of those who quite recently made this rediscovery: the early-twentieth-century pioneers of the liturgical and catechetical renewal movements. In this matter of the interdependence of liturgy and catechesis, they are excellent guides.

To study the ideas of the great pastoral thinkers who led the way to the Second Vatican Council—as well as the teachings of the Council itself—is no dry, dispassionate endeavor. We have much to gain by putting ourselves in touch with movements that prepared the ground for a Council whose pastoral initiatives are fruits of God's inspiration. Many of those conciliar insights faded into obscurity in the years following Vatican II and were never brought to fruition. Giving them the chance to challenge us anew is important to recovering the inspired wisdom of the Second Vatican Council, which continues to hold great promise for today's evangelistic initiatives.

The Liturgical Movement: Beginnings

On the feast of St. Cecilia, November 22, 1903, Pope St. Pius X published *Tra Le Sollecitudini (On the Restoration of Sacred Music)*. This motu proprio was intended to more widely promote sacred music in the Church's liturgies at the turn of the twentieth century. In the introduction, using words that were, at first, widely overlooked and seemingly inconsequential, the pope expressed his "most ardent desire," which was "to see the true Christian spirit flourish again in every way among all the faithful."

This spirit, the pope believed, could be acquired only "from its first and indispensable source, namely, active participation in the most sacred mysteries and in the public and solemn prayer of the Church."[1] Pius X's linking of the "flourishing of the true Christian spirit" with its "indispensable source" in the liturgy was to become the tour de force of the coming liturgical movement.

The origins of this movement to renew the Church's liturgical life may be traced to a Belgian monk who was inspired by this ideal of Pius X. After entering the Benedictine Monastery of Mont César in Leuven, Belgium, in 1906, Lambert Beauduin, OSB, (1873–1960) discovered the liturgy to be not only the vivifying influence for his life as a Benedictine monk, he also believed the liturgy to be the true source of life for the whole Church. Sonya Quitslund relates how influential the Scriptures, liturgical texts, the writings of the Church fathers, and numerous conciliar statements were for Beauduin in coming to these conclusions.[2] Leo XIII's 1891 encyclical *Rerum Novarum* also inspired Beauduin, helping him to correlate his earlier experience as a labor chaplain with his love for the Church's liturgy. His experience of the beauty and power of liturgical prayer as a Benedictine was likewise deeply formative. Through these influences, Beauduin became convinced that the liturgy is essential to the Christian's relationship with God and has the power even to transform society.[3] He became intensely motivated to spread more widely the burgeoning liturgical vitality being lived in many European monasteries.[4]

An important opportunity arose for Beauduin in 1909, when he was invited to present a paper on the liturgy at the National Congress of

---

1. Pope Pius X, *Tra le Sollecitudini*, in Pamela Jackson, *An Abundance of Graces: Reflections on "Sacrosanctum Concilium"* (Chicago: Hillenbrand Books, 2004), 220.

2. Sonya A. Quitslund, *Beauduin: A Prophet Vindicated* (New York: Newman Press, 1973), 10–16. She also credits Blessed Columba Marmion, OSB, the prior of Mont César when Beauduin entered, as a significant influence on Beauduin's understanding of the liturgy and its importance to the spiritual life of the Christian. Marmion, beatified during the Great Jubilee Year of 2000, was the author of *Christ the Life of the Soul* and *Christ in His Mysteries*, early examples of a spirituality for the liturgy.

3. Keith Pecklers, SJ, "Liturgical Movement I: Catholic," in Berard Marthaler, ed., *New Catholic Encyclopedia*, 2nd ed. (Detroit: Thomson Gale, 2003), 8:672.

4. This renewal in monastic liturgy may be traced even further back to Prosper Guéranger's emphasis on the Roman rite in his 1833 refounding of the monastery at Solesmes in France.

Catholic Action at Malines, Belgium.[5] Unfortunately, the presentation of his paper, entitled *La vraie prière de l'Eglise* (*The True Prayer of the Church*), was relegated to an obscure position within the congress itself, which perhaps reveals how the liturgy was viewed at this time. After unsuccessful attempts to have the presentation included in the doctrinal and then the moral sections of the congress, his paper was finally also excluded from the section on piety. In the end, it was decided that the paper would be presented in the division titled "Literary, Artistic, and Scientific works," under the newly created category "Liturgy and Religious Music."[6] While the theme and content of Beauduin's paper failed to cultivate the attention he hoped it would before its delivery, his conclusions were incorporated into the formal resolutions of the congress.[7] In later years, many saw the delivery of this paper as the humble beginning of the twentieth century's far-reaching movement to renew the liturgical life of the Church.

In 1964, Joseph Jungmann, SJ, described the contribution of Beauduin's Malines speech with these words:

> It was [Beauduin] who put forth the ideas which others seized upon and which finally aroused widespread enthusiasm. What he said—the viewpoint which he had long cherished—amounted to this: We are making tremendous efforts to gather together into our parish centres little groups of faithful souls, so as to win them to a truly Christian life and to lead them to a corporate Communion; and yet, in every village, we have already got a centre for the entire Christian people—the church, which is . . . full of sacred mysteries and sources of grace, where Sunday after Sunday all the people assemble to renew themselves in spirit, where there is the priest whose vocation it is to instruct, to bless and to offer sacrifice, where the patron saints are at hand, where feasts and fasts, festivities and funerals are held, where the

---

5. Quitslund relates the interesting story of how this invitation was extended from Cardinal Désiré-Joseph Mercier to the abbot of Maredsous, Abbot Hildebrand de Hemptinne, to choose a monk with liturgical expertise to present a paper at the congress. The abbot suggested E. E. Vandeur, who wrote *La Sainte Messe, Notes Sur la Liturgie* and later became prior of Mont César. After hearing of this decision, Beauduin's students "expressed their dismay, for Vandeur could not begin to compare with Beauduin's impressive and vivid style of delivery. Finally, persuaded by their enthusiasm, Abbot de Hemptinne asked Abbot de Kerchove (of Mont César) for permission to assign the task to Beauduin" (23).

6. Quitslund, *Beauduin: A Prophet Vindicated*, 23.

7. Alcuin Reid, OSB, *The Organic Development of the Liturgy: The Principles of Liturgical Reform and Their Relation to the Twentieth Century Liturgical Movement Prior to the Second Vatican Council* (Farnborough: Saint Michael's Abbey Press, 2004), 20, 24. See also 69 for a list of these formal resolutions.

community finds its centre, and a marvelously rich liturgy is already available for these purposes. Why do we go on making little or no use of all this while exhausting ourselves with labours in other directions?[8]

Beauduin persuasively argued in this speech to recenter the entirety of a parish's pastoral work in the celebration of the liturgy. Pius X's insistence that the liturgy is the "first and indispensable source" of a flourishing Christianity resounded throughout Beauduin's address. The speech was well received, but what happened afterwards was breathtaking.

Almost immediately following the Malines Congress, the influence of Beauduin's ideas surged. In 1910, his monastic community founded *Questions Liturgiques*, a publication edited by Beauduin that offered a desperately needed liturgical formation for parish clergy.[9] Also in 1910, Mont César began the first of the annual liturgical study weeks, bringing together many who were interested in investigating more deeply the true nature of the liturgy. In 1914, Beauduin published *La Piété de L'Eglise* (*Liturgy the Life of the Church*). This book was enormously influential, identifying the liturgy as not merely one among many prayer forms, but the *central prayer* of the Church. In this book, Beauduin described the primary idea of the liturgical movement to be inviting the Christian faithful to "all live the same spiritual life, to have them all nourished by the official worship of holy mother Church."[10] Beauduin's book was a stirring call to action, an appeal to Catholic leaders to awaken the faithful to their enormous potential in Christ. It is helpful to hear again Beauduin's literary voice, to gain some sense of the urgency of his plea:

All [the] truths which find expression in every liturgical act, are asleep in [people's] souls; the faithful have lost consciousness of them. Let us change the routine and monotonous assistance at acts of worship into an active and intelligent participation; let us teach the faithful to pray and confess these truths in a body: and the liturgy thus practiced will insensibly arouse a slumbering faith and give new efficacy, both in prayer and action, to the latent energies of the baptized souls.[11]

---

8. Joseph A. Jungmann, SJ, *Liturgical Renewal in Retrospect and Prospect*, trans. Clifford Howell, SJ (London: Burns and Oates, 1965), 16–17.

9. This journal is available in English today under the title *Studies in Liturgy*.

10. Lambert Beauduin, OSB, *Liturgy the Life of the Church*, 3rd ed., trans. Virgil Michel, OSB (Farnborough: St. Michael's Abbey Press, 2002), 52.

11. Beauduin, OSB, *Liturgy the Life of the Church*, 21.

Through the efforts of Beauduin and his collaborators, the liturgical movement began to influence Christians in many other European countries, extending eventually to the United States and beyond.

The optimism and progress of the liturgical renewal came to an abrupt standstill in the harsh reality of the First World War. The high social ideals of the movement, that the world could be refashioned through the "active and intelligent participation" of the faithful in the liturgy, were put to a severe test. In the end, the experience of the war only further crystallized the motivation to help Christians, beginning with the soldiers fighting in the trenches, to find real sustenance in the Church's liturgical life.

After World War I and into the years preceding the Second World War, the pioneers of the liturgical movement continued to discuss and publish their ideas and the movement expanded in its influence. In 1918, annual liturgical study weeks began again in Belgium. The proceedings from these weeks were published in a growing number of periodicals dedicated to the germinating ideals of the liturgical renewal.[12]

World War II, of course, inflicted terrible violence and suffering upon millions of people. Confronted with great evil, the ideals of the liturgical movement sometimes emerged in acts of extraordinary faith and courage. Fr. Timothy Vaverek, parish priest in the diocese of Austin, Texas, relates this experience of a former parishioner who came of age in Germany during the war:

> "Anna" grew up in Bavaria and joined the German Catholic youth movement as a teenager in the 1930s. At that time, this movement had as its chaplain Fr. Romano Guardini, one of the leaders of the liturgical movement. Those responsible for this youth movement saw the trajectory in which their country was moving and used the movement as a way to prepare young people for the coming hostility.

> The Catholic youth movement was an important vehicle for introducing liturgical renewal into Germany. Young people experienced the beauty and power of a fuller participation in the liturgy and were encouraged to go back

---

12. These periodicals included the previously mentioned *Questions Liturgiques*, *Ecclesia Orans* (begun at Maria Laach in 1918), *Bollettino Liturgico* (launched in Italy in 1923), and *Orate Fratres* (published by St. John's Abbey in Collegeville, Minnesota, beginning in 1926). Additionally, some of the most influential books of the liturgical movement were published during these years as well—books such as Romano Guardini's *Vom Geist der Liturgie* (*The Spirit of the Liturgy*, 1918) and Odo Casel's *Das Christliche Kultmysterium* (*The Mystery of Christian Worship*, 1932).

to their parishes and do what they had experienced. These young people understood deeply the connections between the liturgy and life in Christ.

On March 10, 1937, Pius XI issued his encyclical *Mit Brennender Sorge* ("With Burning Anxiety") and it was read from the pulpits of Catholic churches throughout Germany on Palm Sunday. In his encyclical, the pope warned, "whoever exalts race, or the people, or the State, or a particular form of State or the depositories of power . . . above their standard value and divinizes them to an idolatrous level, distorts and perverts an order of the world planned and created by God; he is far from the true faith in God and from the concept of life which that faith upholds" (8). The Catholic youth movement, which had, to that point, served as a permissible alternative to the Hitler Youth movement, was consequently suppressed by the Nazis.

After its suppression, members of the youth movement would wear pins to secretly identify themselves to each other. In the summers, they would go in small groups—so as to avoid attracting attention—into rural areas to be formed in their Christian life. Much of the catechesis offered was liturgical in its focus, helping the young people to see the transformative power of their encounter with God in the liturgy.

On one occasion, in the summer of 1939 or 1940, 15-year-old Anna returned from one of these illegal gatherings in the Bavarian mountains. She received a phone call from a close friend alerting her to the fact that the Gestapo was on its way to her home to interrogate her about her participation. For two hours she was questioned by three members of the Gestapo. She denied knowing anything about the gathering and gave them no information. As they left her home, the officer turned around, came back through the door, looked her in the eye, and said, "Now, listen, fräulein. You have not fooled us. We know you were there. We're only leaving because I too have a fifteen-year-old daughter. Do not go back there and do not make me come back here again."

In the Winter of 1945, during the Nazi collapse, Anna received a telegram ordering her to report for service. She told her mother, "Prepare yourself! I will not serve this regime. They can hang me!" She was never contacted again, as the Nazi hold on power was rapidly coming undone. In later years, she lamented, "I was so close to going home! No one came looking for me. I had to live another sixty years!"

Those last words may come as a shock. Anna grew up as a woman who loved life and treasured the next seventy years during which she married, raised a family, and served the Church as a catechist, spiritual director, and formator of Third Order Carmelites. The familial and liturgical catechesis she received as a young person helped her to live with an abiding awareness that this life is a pilgrimage and her true home is not in this world. Her desire for God and for heaven have remained strong. Now nearing ninety and suffering a degree of dementia, her journey is reaching its goal. At times mistaken about time and place, she speaks with joy and gladness of all the Lord has done and she still longs for his coming.[13]

Acts of everyday bravery such as these stemmed from a catechetical formation that put maximum emphasis on the connection between liturgy and life.

After the war, in 1947, Pope Pius XII published his encyclical *Mediator Dei*. This encyclical formally embraced many of the priorities of the liturgical movement.[14] According to one important contributor to the movement, this encyclical "looked like a charter granted to the liturgical movement."[15] And with the legitimization of *Mediator Dei*, the postwar liturgical movement began to flourish, establishing the framework for the eventual liturgical reforms of the Second Vatican Council.

Catechetical Motivations of Liturgical Renewal

In its essence, the liturgical movement sought to reawaken Catholics and all Christians to their need for the living font of the Church's life, the sacred liturgy, so that the Church and the world might be transformed. Annibale Bugnini, an important voice in the liturgical reforms of the

---

13. Fr. Timothy Vaverek, telephone interview by author, January 11, 2016.

14. See especially, Pius XII, *Mediator Dei*, 4–5: "You are of course familiar with the fact, Venerable Brethren, that a remarkably widespread revival of scholarly interest in the sacred liturgy took place towards the end of the last century and has continued through the early years of this one. The movement owed its rise to commendable private initiative and more particularly to the zealous and persistent labor of several monasteries within the distinguished Order of Saint Benedict. Thus there developed in this field among many European nations, and in lands beyond the seas as well, a rivalry as welcome as it was productive of results. Indeed, the salutary fruits of this rivalry among the scholars were plain for all to see, both in the sphere of the sacred sciences, where the liturgical rites of the Western and Eastern Church were made the object of extensive research and profound study, and in the spiritual life of considerable numbers of individual Christians.

"The majestic ceremonies of the sacrifice of the altar became better known, understood and appreciated. With more widespread and more frequent reception of the sacraments, with the beauty of the liturgical prayers more fully savored, the worship of the Eucharist came to be regarded for what it really is: the fountain-head of genuine Christian devotion. Bolder relief was given likewise to the fact that all the faithful make up a single and very compact body with Christ for its Head, and that the Christian community is in duty bound to participate in the liturgical rites according to their station."

15. Bernard Botte, *From Silence to Participation: An Insider's View of Liturgical Renewal*, trans. John Sullivan, OCD (Washington, DC: The Pastoral Press, 1988), 78.

twentieth century, wrote, "The liturgical movement was an effort to reunite rites and content, for its aim was to restore as fully as possible the expressiveness and sanctifying power of the liturgy and to bring the faithful back to full participation and understanding."[16] These words reveal two important threads that may be discerned in the work of the movement: the attempt to "restore as fully as possible the expressiveness and sanctifying power of the liturgy" (a reform of rites) and that of deepening the "participation and understanding" of the faithful (an elevation in the liturgical capacities of Christians). This second motivation is primarily a catechetical concern and was a mainstay of the movement.

Expressions of this catechetical objective may be found everywhere in the writings of the liturgical pioneers. An anonymous liturgical publication (but generally believed to be written by Virgil Michel, the founder of the liturgical movement in the United States) expressed the hopes of the movement in these words:

> What is really being striven for is a change in the spiritual orientation of the faithful, which, it is hoped, will result in a much needed strong, virile Catholicity. The liturgical movement, therefore, as the words indicate, is a movement—a movement towards the liturgy. It means the sum of all the efforts being made in our day to bring the faithful back to an active participation in the liturgical acts and prayers of the Church.[17]

Another writer in the 1950s observed that "the end of the liturgical movement is education toward the worship of God."[18] Strategies and resources were needed to help all the baptized—including the clergy—strengthen their liturgical understanding.[19]

When it came to catechesis in those years, many became convinced that the liturgy needed to be integral to every aspect of the faith as it was

---

16. Annibale Bugnini, *The Reform of the Liturgy: 1948–1975*, trans. Matthew J. O'Connell (Collegeville, MN: Liturgical Press, 1990), 6.

17. "The Liturgical Movement: Its General Purpose and Its Influence on Priestly Piety," in *The Liturgical Movement*, Popular Christian Library series 4, no. 3 (Collegeville, MN: Liturgical Press, 1930), 8.

18. F. Arnold, "Liturgy in the School," *The Catholic Educator* 24 (1953–54): 169, quoted in Keith F. Pecklers, *The Unread Vision: The Liturgical Movement in the United States of America: 1926–1955* (Collegeville, MN: Liturgical Press, 1998), 151.

19. Chapter 4 of Pecklers' *The Unread Vision* provides a helpful history of the printing and production of liturgical aids and resources to help the faithful understand how to pray and participate in various liturgical celebrations. The author additionally explores the development of liturgical education in schools, various local initiatives for adult liturgical education, and a history of the development of academic liturgical programs at Catholic colleges and universities.

taught. An excellent example of this idea may be seen in Virgil Michel's introduction to the *Christ-Life* religion textbook series:

> The religion course should have a solid liturgical basis. More than that, the liturgy must be the very fibre of its being. The liturgy is not merely a phase of religious instruction; it is the life of Christ in His Church; it is the glorious triumphant Christ teaching and sanctifying His members who are of good will. It is through the sacred liturgy that Christ instructs and transforms souls into Himself. The work of the teacher in religion, then, is to bring children to a conscious participation in the sacred liturgy, wherein Christ Himself teaches and sanctifies them.[20]

For Michel, the liturgy was not to be studied as merely one subject among many, but must be integrated throughout catechesis. He wanted Catholics to see the liturgy as essential to living the Christian life, gaining, above all, the capacity to be taught and sanctified by Christ through encountering him in liturgical prayer. Michel insisted that the catechist provide consistent contact with liturgical texts that would prepare people well to encounter Christ in the liturgy:

> How can we teach the whole Christ without bringing as much as possible of the liturgy into our actual classroom instruction, and without bringing into these truths as they are taught all the wealth of inspiration and meaning that the liturgy gives to them in its very formulas and texts? The liturgy and the liturgy alone is the truth of Christ prayed by the continuing Christ, and prayed as an inspiration for the faithful living of this same truth at all times.[21]

Michel believed, in fact, that the catechesis of his time was gravely deficient in how frequently it separated doctrine from the Church's living liturgy. This estrangement weakened people's ability to live the Catholic life to their full potential. He lamented how catechesis did not give our youngest what they most needed, the ability to draw close to God in the liturgical wellspring of grace. He wrote that the catechesis of his time "had separated both our teaching efforts and the learning efforts of the children as far as possible from the sources of divine grace in the liturgy, which alone could produce the divine effects we were really

---

20. "Fundamental Character and Purpose of the Christ-Life Series" (unpublished manuscript), St. John's Abbey Archives: Z–29 quoted in Pecklers, *The Unread Vision*, 173–74.

21. Virgil Michel, "Timely Tracts: Liturgical Religious Education," *Orate Fratres* 11, no. 6 (1937): 268.

aiming at."[22] Living a supernatural life in Christ is just not possible apart from the source of that life.

Therefore for Michel and many in the liturgical movement, a catechetical formation that accentuates the place of the liturgy in the Christian life was critical to the success of the renewal they envisioned. This renewal would only be possible with a raising of the liturgical intelligence and desire of every Christian.

As influential as it was, the liturgical renewal was not the only movement that was attempting to influence the liturgical understanding of the faithful at this time. Another group of thinkers during these same decades was likewise becoming convinced that catechesis needed new vigor. They knew that catechetical renewal would have an immense impact on the people's experience of the liturgy.

The Catechetical Renewal and Joseph A. Jungmann, SJ

As we consider the catechetical renewal movement, it is particularly fascinating to remember the work of the Austrian liturgical theologian Joseph A. Jungmann, SJ (1889–1975), whose study of the history of the liturgy led him to see the need for catechetical renewal.

As professor of pastoral theology at the University of Innsbruck, Jungmann taught courses in both catechetics and liturgical theology, contributing to both disciplines over the course of his life. He published a number of important works recovering and critically examining the history of the liturgy, the most influential of which was his study of the historical development of the Mass, entitled *Missarum Sollemnia*.[23] Benedictine scholar Bernard Botte respectfully wrote of Jungmann, "On the international scene the greatest worker of my generation is without any doubt the Austrian Jesuit Joseph Jungmann." Botte describes Jungmann's study of the Roman Rite as "a summa of everything that can be said about the history of the

---

22. Michel, "Timely Tracts: Liturgical Religious Education," 268. He went on in this article to emphasize the significant impact of this grave deficiency in catechesis: " . . . how the prince of this world must have laughed up his satanic sleeve at the spectacle of the redoubled human efforts trying to achieve Christ but ignoring to a maximum degree the only possible source of success in this attempt."

23. In English, *The Mass of the Roman Rite: Its Origins and Development*, trans. Francis A. Brunner, CSsR (London: Burns and Oates, 1959). This is a translation of the German revised edition from 1949.

Mass."[24] Another scholar describes *Missarum Sollemnia* as "the jewel of the academic liturgical movement."[25] Jungmann's scholarship catapulted him to a prominent position within the movement. He was eventually chosen to be a member of the preparatory commission on the liturgy that drafted Vatican II's *Constitution on the Sacred Liturgy*. He also served as a *peritus* (expert) for the Council and after its conclusion, was invited to be a consulter of the Concilium, the commission entrusted with the implementation of the liturgical constitution. While Jungmann's influence on academic liturgical thought in the twentieth century is well established, his catechetical writings were equally momentous for catechetical practice.

The twentieth-century renewal of catechesis did not, however, begin with Jungmann. In his overview of the catechetical renewal's early history, Jungmann referred to the Englishman, Canon Francis Drinkwater, who singled out 1910 as the year the renewal began. This is the year Pope Pius X published *Quam Singulari*, which decreed that the first reception of Holy Communion be moved earlier in childhood, to the age of reason ("about the seventh year, more or less"). Drinkwater wrote that this decision "forced us all back on the psychological realities of childhood" and claimed that the "origin of the reform [can be found in] the child, his needs and capacity."[26] Focusing in this way on the learning capacities of the child stirred a deep dissatisfaction with the formulaic, memorization-dominated methods of the time.[27]

The eruption of war in 1914 brought catechetical renewal to a four-year impasse. The catastrophe of the First World War and its accompanying test of Catholic faith and life brought into stark realism the deficiencies of the catechesis of the time. Jungmann explained the new motivation that World War I produced for the catechetical renewal, describing the experience of Francis Drinkwater:

---

24. Botte, *From Silence to Participation*, 54.

25. Virgil C. Funk, "The Liturgical Movement," in Peter E. Fink, SJ, ed., *New Dictionary of Sacramental Worship*, 2nd ed. (Collegeville, MN: Liturgical Press, 1991), 696.

26. F. H. Drinkwater, *Educational Essays* (London, 1951), 95–96, as cited in Joseph Jungmann, *Handing on the Faith: A Manual of Catechetics*, trans. A. N. Fuerst (New York: Herder and Herder, 1959), 56.

27. These methods were frequently modeled on the "format, language and assumptions of the theological manuals that were used to train seminarians." The methodology of these theological manuals "treated questions as distinct from each other, sought intelligibility by virtue of those distinctions, and pursued a precision of expression based on a specific Neo-Scholastic vocabulary and worldview." See Michael Horan, CFC, "Kerygmatic Catechesis: An Analysis of the Writings of Jungmann and Hofinger as Reflected in Post-Conciliar Catechetical Documents" (PHD diss., The Catholic University of America, 1989), 20, 19.

The war of 1914 . . . gave Father Drinkwater, who became a chaplain in the army, an opportunity to observe at first hand the effects of the traditional system when put to the supreme test. He found that what the soldiers had learned of the abstract formulas had been forgotten for the most part, but that the practical things like the sacraments were still familiar even to those who had lapsed. This influenced the next stage [of the renewal]. Religion is not only something to learn but something to be lived, and every effort must be made to insert religious instruction into life, into the life of the Church (hence the liturgy), into the life of the family, and so far as possible it must be a preparation for life in the world.[28]

Drinkwater's experience of what remained familiar and fruitful to the soldiers in combat was not an isolated observation. Many began more intensely considering how to improve catechesis as a result of the experience of the war. And so, the catechetical renewal picked up again after the war with new vitality and perspective.

Eighteen years later, in 1936, Jungmann published his seminal catechetical work, *Die frohbotschaft und unsere glaubensverkundigung* (*The Good News and Our Proclamation of the Faith*). The publication of this book was a pivotal event, inaugurating a new phase in the efforts to enhance catechesis.[29] It would be difficult to overstate the historic importance of this work, as it moved the catechetical renewal beyond methodological concerns into a new discussion of how the content of the faith was formulated and presented.

Johannes Hofinger, SJ,[30] describes this book's important thematic contribution to the catechetical renewal: "What we must really strive for is not so much a better method as a better understanding and a more

---

28. Jungmann, *Handing on the Faith*, 56–57.

29. Hereafter, *The Good News*. Jungmann, *Die frohbotschaft und unsere glaubensverkundigung* (Regensburg: Verlag Friedrich Pustet, 1936). This text was not published in English until 1962 when it was published along with four essays by prominent catechetical scholars focused on the different parameters of the impact of this much celebrated text. It may be found in Johannes Hofinger, SJ, ed., *The Good News: Yesterday and Today*, trans. and ed. William A. Huesman, SJ (New York: William H. Sadlier, 1962).

30. Johannes Hofinger, SJ, (1905–1984) was Jungmann's most influential student and closest collaborator in the kerygmatic renewal of catechetics. Hofinger was a prolific author, developing in pastorally concrete form many of Jungmann's theoretical ideas regarding the kerygmatic renewal. His most important book was *The Art of Teaching Christian Doctrine*, in which he set forth a kerygmatic formulation of the content of the faith. At the age of 66, he began studying Spanish in order to bring the kerygmatic message to Latin America. During the final years of his life, Hofinger moved to the United States and accepted a position as the associate director of the Office of Religious Education for the Archdiocese of New Orleans, Louisiana.

relevant presentation of the very core and substance of the Christian message."[31] For Jungmann, the doctrinal distinctions integrated within catechetical texts were important. However, the underpinning framework within which these truths are situated, what he referred to as the *kerygma*,[32] had been largely underemphasized or altogether left out. To not grasp the central announcement of Christianity is not merely educationally problematic, but it undercuts Christians in their need to know Christ and root their lives in him. Jungmann was concerned for what was missing in the Catholic cultural experience for so many, separated as they were from this living knowledge of the kerygma. He put the problem this way:

> All that is genuinely Christian, *the truly supernatural*—the merciful plan of God revealed in the humanity of Christ, calling for man's inmost participation—all this has been largely lost from sight. Christianity such as this is not the Good News proclaimed by Christ.[33]

Jungmann believed that the gaze of Catholicism had lost its supernatural mooring in what God has done and is doing in us for the sake of the world. He therefore sounded the alarm that the content of twentieth-century catechesis little resembled the Gospel originally proposed by Christ and the apostles. It is not difficult to imagine how such an assertion was received by some as a provocation, "ruffling the feathers" of many during this time. While *The Good News* initiated a new phase in the catechetical movement—called the kerygmatic renewal—there was such a strong

---

31. Johannes Hofinger, sj, "The Place of the Good News in Modern Catechetics," in ed. Johannes Hofinger, trans. William A. Heusman, sj, *The Good News: Yesterday and Today* (New York: William H. Sadlier, 1962), 173.

32. This word, *kerygma*, is a Greek term used frequently in the New Testament (e.g., Lk 4: 18–19, Rom 10:14, and Mt 3:1). It indicates the activity of "preaching" or "proclaiming." The content of this preaching is, for Jungmann, the "Good News," those aspects of the New Testament which are meant to be announced and proclaimed. Jungmann describes the content of the Good News in this way: "The Mystical Christ sets forth most clearly the luminous center from which the whole of faith grows together unto clear unity, since it is from the radiance of Christ that God's merciful plan, as well as its concrete realization, is rendered immediately intelligible. Christ is the pivotal point of all God's ways—those by which His mercy descends to His creation and those by which the creature mounts back to its Source. All dogmatic treatises converge about Christ. His person and work form the true core of the Christian message of salvation. In this sense, Christ may rightly be called the center of all doctrine . . . " (Jungmann, *The Good News*, 9–10). Present in this text is the idea of the "Mystical Christ" (he will in other places substitute St. Paul's term "Mystery of Christ"), which is the content of the kerygma, the Good News.
Louis Bouyer sums up the meaning of the kerygma as "the proclamation by the Church, as sent by Christ, of the salvation-event that finds its accomplishment in him" in Louis Bouyer, ed. *Dictionary of Theology*, trans. Charles Underhill Quinn (Tournai, Belgium: Desclee, 1965), 260.

33. Jungmann, *The Good News*, 4 (emphasis mine).

initial reaction against Jungmann's ideas that his book was removed from circulation by his Jesuit superiors just three weeks after its publication.[34] The text wasn't published in English until 1962. Eventually, however, Jungmann's ideas were widely embraced.

In 1950, Jungmann summed up the twentieth-century catechetical problem as he had described it in *The Good News*:

> Most people know all the sacraments; they know about the Person of Christ as well as about Our Lady, Peter and Paul, Adam and Eve, and a good many others. They know enough about the commandments of God and of the Church. But what is lacking among the faithful is a sense of unity, seeing it all as a whole, an understanding of the wonderful message of divine grace. All they retain of Christian doctrine is a string of dogmas and moral precepts, threats and promises, customs and rites, tasks and duties imposed. . . .[35]

For Jungmann, the kerygmatic renewal was concerned with restoring the *missing center* to the Church's catechetical proclamation, which, over the years, had been diminished. The primary elements of the Church's kerygmatic announcement needed fundamental emphasis once again: the divine love of the Blessed Trinity as the origin of all things, the fall from grace through the original alienating sin, the need for a Savior and the Good News of our redemption accomplished through the incarnate paschal love of the Word Become Flesh. These are truths that must be understood not merely as distinct doctrinal formulae but as indispensable saving truths that emerge from the biblical story of salvation history. These indispensable truths should be proclaimed once more in their unity, as Good News. Such a message, announced with great joy by the early Christians, needed to be restored to the center of catechesis and all of Catholic life.

Jungmann, again in 1950, used these words to summarize the goals of the kerygmatic movement:

> To restore the kerygma to its full power and clarity into one single message proclaiming with joy and love the beauty and promise of the kingdom of God is the task of the kerygmatic renewal. Its chief aim is to present the truths of Faith as an organic whole. The core is the Good News of our redemption in Christ. Its fruit should be our grateful and loving response to God's loving call.[36]

---

34. Anne Marie Mongoven, OP, *The Prophetic Spirit of Catechesis* (Mahwah, NJ: Paulist Press, 2000), 47.
35. Jungmann, "Theology and Kerugmatic Teaching," *Lumen Vitae 5* (1950): 258.
36. Jungmann, "Theology and Kerugmatic Teaching," 5.

The movement proposed the kerygma as the animating truth of every aspect of Christian doctrine. Jungmann expressed his motivation with these words: "Christian doctrine ought to be led back to its original, unified power, so that above all else it is the kerygma itself that is heard."[37]

An analogy may be helpful. Jungmann's conviction can be understood by envisioning two images: the links in a chain and the spokes of a wheel.[38] In conceptualizing catechesis according to the first image, one doctrinal truth is linked to another, which is further connected into a whole chain of interlocking points of doctrine. If this is how the content of Revelation is learned, not only is it difficult to see how the first link is related to the fiftieth, but it is also nearly impossible to identify any sense of hierarchy in these truths. The kerygma risks being seen as just another link in the chain, as one teaching among many, which reduces what is most essential to just another teaching point. The inner cohesion of Christian faith and life in such a construct is difficult to intuit.

Jungmann preferred an approach to doctrine that resembled the connectivity of spokes to the hub of a wheel. With the supernatural reality of what God has done for us embraced as the central truth in catechesis, every other doctrinal point can then be seen in its relation to the "hub" of revealed truth. Such a way of formulating the content of the Christian message emphasizes above all else the supernatural mystery of Christ's redemptive act. Jungmann, of course, understood that the liturgy uniquely makes this redemptive act present to us. Catechesis, then, becomes an opportunity to understand one's whole life within the context of what is given us in the liturgy.

Seventy-seven years after Jungmann published *The Good News*, Pope Francis used the term "kerygmatic catechesis" for the first time in a magisterial document.[39] In *Evangelii Gaudium*, Pope Francis writes, "in catechesis too, we have rediscovered the fundamental role of the first announcement or kerygma, which needs to be the center of all evangelizing activity and all efforts at Church renewal." Using remarkably direct and personal language, Pope Francis articulates the kerygma with these words: "Jesus Christ loves you; he gave his life to save you; and now he

---

37. Joseph Jungmann, SJ, *Announcing the Word of God* (London: Burns and Oates, 1967), 59.

38. See Jungmann, "Theology and Kerugmatic Teaching," 261.

39. See Pope Francis, *Evangelii Gaudium*, Vatican Translation (Washington, DC: USCCB Publications, 2013), 163–65.

is living at your side every day to enlighten, strengthen and free you" (EG, 164). He then suggests that the kerygma be *ever* on the lips of the catechist and not merely presented at the beginning of the catechetical process. These paragraphs form the clearest of papal approbations for how important Jungmann's timeless work is today.

The motivations of the liturgical movement and kerygmatic renewal were remarkably similar. Both aimed to bring Catholics into greater contact with the Divine Mystery and to become convinced of the implications of this Mystery for all of life. Liturgical and catechetical leaders came to esteem each other's work and ideals, discovering many points of intersection. Hofinger observed that, "as in other countries, a growing interest in the liturgy in the U.S. was soon followed by a growing interest in kerygmatics."[40] He went on to explain that this closeness between the liturgy and catechesis "derives necessarily from their respective natures. Each is intrinsically related to the other and can achieve its own purpose only by working together with the other in a well-planned and organic manner."[41] Seeing the liturgy and catechesis in their interdependent relationship was a great good that emerged from both movements.

Sacrosanctum Concilium: A Foundational Vision

The promulgation of the *Constitution on the Sacred Liturgy* in 1963 is the apex moment of the liturgical movement in the twentieth century, effecting the reform of the Church's liturgical life advocated by so many of the liturgical pioneers. The Council Fathers maintained that the liturgical life of the time depended not just on the reform of rites but also on a more effective liturgical formation of the People of God—clergy, religious, and faithful alike. Thus, the impact of the catechetical renewal may also be seen throughout this document.

---

40. Hofinger, "The Place of the Good News in Modern Catechetics," 181. Hofinger continued, "It is not without significance that the University of Notre Dame, which gave such a great impetus to the liturgical revival in the United States through its Liturgy program, offered the first kerygmatic course in the summer of 1955. In 1957, again through the initiative of the Liturgy Program, the University of Notre Dame Press published *The Art of Teaching Christian Doctrine* [an important book written by Hofinger demonstrating a kerygmatic articulation of the Deposit of Faith]. This was the first manual in English for priests and catechists which gave a detailed account of the kerygmatic approach to Christian doctrine, together with a systematic exposition of the Christian message" (181). See also Hofinger, "Catechetics and Liturgy," *Worship* 29, no. 2 (January 1955): 89–90.

41. Hofinger, "Catechetics and Liturgy," 90.

To conclude our treatment of the history of these two renewal movements, we will briefly examine seven key moments within the constitution which help us better envision the complementarity of the liturgy and catechesis in the Church's mission.

A Conciliar Vision: What Is the Liturgy?

The first section of the constitution (paragraphs 5–13) is titled "the nature of the sacred liturgy and its importance in the Church's life." In these few paragraphs, we find a liturgical catechesis of particular brilliance—as it was initially drafted by some of the foremost pastoral-theological leaders of the liturgical movement.

The Council Fathers' liturgical vision in these paragraphs is compelling. The liturgy is described as a reconciling encounter with the Blessed Trinity, where the Paschal Mystery is made accessible to people of every place and time. Christ Jesus, our "One Mediator with God," makes himself uniquely present to us as his work is accomplished, that work of "redeeming mankind and giving perfect glory to God" (SC, 5). We learn that we who are present enter into a mystical participation in this great work by virtue of our membership in the Mystical Body of Christ, which offers to God the priestly sacrifice of Christ himself. And, "from this it follows that every liturgical celebration, because it is an action of Christ the priest and of his Body which is the Church, is a sacred action surpassing all others; no other action of the Church can equal its efficacy by the same title and to the same degree" (SC, 7).

So few Christians of this era had received an adequate liturgical education at any level—whether elementary school or seminary formation. Consequently, with these paragraphs the Council Fathers were intent on reversing the trend of poor liturgical formation in the early 1960s. They understood that a new understanding and love for the liturgy would begin with how well they captured its meaning. in these few crucially important pages.

This opening section assists us as we consider today's need for a robust liturgical catechesis. In these paragraphs, the Council Fathers made clear, above all else, that the liturgy is a divine encounter and an ecclesial action of the Mystical Body of Christ. We can have confidence that He may be met in every liturgical celebration—and such a confidence will be contagious for those whom we teach.

The Mission of the Apostles: Effecting What Is Proclaimed

Reflective of what we see in the Great Commission at the end of Matthew's gospel, 28: 19–20 ("Go, therefore, and make disciples of all nations, baptizing them in the name of the Father, and of the Son, and of the holy Spirit, teaching them to observe all that I have commanded you"), the Council Fathers emphasize that the Church's mission to the world is at once both sacramental and catechetical. First, we see that the apostles were sent out to preach and teach:

> Just as Christ was sent by the Father, so also He sent the apostles, filled with the Holy Spirit. This He did, that, by *preaching* the gospel to every creature, they might *proclaim* that the Son of God, by His death and resurrection, had freed us from the power of Satan and from death, and brought us into the kingdom of his Father. (SC, 6)

But the apostles did more than preach about the Paschal Mystery of Christ. Arriving at a confidence in the objective act of redemption is but the first step. Something more is necessary. The document continues:

> His purpose also was that they might *accomplish the work of salvation which they had proclaimed*, by means of sacrifice and sacraments, around which the entire liturgical life revolves. (SC, 6)

We see here that the Paschal Mystery is preached and then "accomplished" through the liturgy, which makes present the act that saves us all. The link between the liturgy and catechesis is clear.

The Need for Faith and Conversion

A meaningful and fruitful sacramental life, the constitution teaches, depends upon the predispositions of faith and conversion.[42] With the new way of seeing that accompanies the gift of faith and with a repentant heart,[43] a great passion arises for a transformative encounter with Christ

---

42. See SC, 9.

43. In Fr. Robert Barron's masterful theological treatment of Christian conversion, he explains well the change in sight that accompanies the encounter with Christ. Drawing upon the account of the healing of the man born blind in the gospel of John, Fr. Barron writes, "When the man washes his eyes in the pool of Siloam as Jesus had instructed him, his sight is restored. The crowds are amazed, but the Pharisees—consternated and skeptical—accuse him of being naive and the one who healed him of being a sinner. With disarming simplicity the visionary responds: 'All I know is I was blind, and now I see.' This is precisely what all Christians say when they have encountered the light of Christ. It was St. Augustine who saw in the making of the mud paste a metaphor for the incarnation: the divine power mixing with the earth, resulting in the formation of a healing balm. When this salve of God made flesh is rubbed onto our eyes blinded by sin we come again to see" (Robert Barron, *And Now I See: A Theology of Transformation* [New York: Crossroad, 1998], 1).

in his Paschal Mystery. If we do not recognize the liturgy as an encounter, it is not because God isn't present, but because our perception of him—and of ourselves—is obscured.

Faith and conversion also must be cultivated throughout life if our discipleship in Christ is to continually mature. Before approaching the liturgy, then, nonbelievers must come to believe, to "know the True God . . . and be converted from their ways." But those who believe are also continually and deeply challenged:

> To believers also the Church must ever preach faith and penance; she must prepare them for the sacraments, teach them to observe all that Christ has commanded and encourage them to engage in all the works of charity, piety and the apostolate, thus making it clear that Christ's faithful, though not of this world, are to be the lights of the world and are to glorify the Father before men. (SC, 9)

Without lifelong growth in faith and conversion, our experience of the liturgy risks devolving into a merely external ritual act. Such mechanical ceremony fails to evoke either an interior purposefulness during the act of worship or the missionary responsiveness that is its fruit.

Attuning Ourselves to God

While the liturgy is objectively "the summit toward which the activity of the Church is directed [and] it is also the fount from which all her power flows" (SC, 10), there is also a critical subjective dimension to the liturgical experience. What the celebration of the Paschal Mystery achieves—worship of God and our sanctification—is not automatically, effortlessly, thoughtlessly accomplished in participants. Something important is required on our part. We must invest ourselves in the liturgy, give ourselves to God through it, and receive the gift he makes of himself if we are to be impacted in this divine encounter.

> But in order that the liturgy may be able to produce its full effects it is necessary that the faithful come to it with proper dispositions, that their minds be attuned to their voices, and that they cooperate with heavenly grace lest they receive it in vain. . . . It is [the duty of pastors] to ensure that the faithful take part fully aware of what they are doing, actively engaged in the rite and enriched by it. (SC, 11)

If we approach the liturgy from a position of desire, well prepared to invest our total selves in the Church's prayer, then it becomes possible for the "full effects" of this most sacred prayer to be realized in us.

Full, Conscious, and Active Liturgical Participation

In article fourteen, the Council Fathers describe the central objective of the intended reform: "Holy Mother Church earnestly desires that all the faithful should be led to that full, conscious, and active participation in liturgical celebrations, which is demanded by the very nature of the liturgy."

We should avoid facilely correlating "active participation" with "external activity" as was done so frequently after the Council. Pamela Jackson, in fact, points out that authentic liturgical participation always includes both an interior and an exterior dimension.[44] In the first place, it is interior, with "worshippers uniting their whole beings to what God is doing in the liturgy, which they understand and want to be a part of."[45] Uniting ourselves to God in this way presumes two things: first, that we desire union with God and, second, that we have some sense of "what God is doing in the liturgy." Both of these dispositions can be the fruits of a well envisioned catechesis.

This interiority, however, in no way detracts from the exterior dimensions of sacramental participation:

> The point being made . . . is not that participating in external actions is unimportant. Such actions are very important—because they are vehicles through which one participates in the celebration of the Paschal Mystery as part of Christ's Body, the Church. While participating fully, consciously, and actively in the Church's liturgy today involves such actions, these actions in themselves do not constitute full, conscious and active participation.[46]

---

44. Pamela Jackson, *An Abundance of Graces: Reflections on Sacrosanctum Concilium* (Chicago: Hillenbrand Books, 2004), 15.

45. Jackson, *An Abundance of Graces*, 12.

46. Jackson, *An Abundance of Graces*, 15. Francis Cardinal Arinze makes the point that one of the most fundamental liturgical activities each member of the assembly must do is that of attentively listening during the liturgical celebration. Anticipating the objections of some liturgists to such a notion, Arinze wrote, "Listening is not a passive affair. It is an active openness to God's action in us. It makes us ready to receive the Word of God proclaimed in the liturgical assembly. It leads us to listen to the homily as it applies the sacred readings to the realities and challenges of life on earth today." See Francis Arinze, "Active Participation in the Sacred Liturgy," *Cardinal Reflections: Active Participation and the Liturgy* (Chicago: Hillenbrand Books, 2005), 24.

Jackson offers a helpful picture of genuine active participation as it relates to the Mass. Recalling the conciliar teaching of the fourfold presence of Christ in the liturgy, Jackson explains that active participation in the Eucharistic liturgy is attentive to the

> Risen Lord who is present in his minister, in the proclamation of the Word, in his sacramental Body and Blood and in his Body, the Church. It calls for participants to enter reverently into this re-presentation of the Paschal Mystery, where the Risen Christ as high priest is offering himself to the Father and joining them, his Body, to himself in this act where God is perfectly glorified and they are made holy and drawn into union with God and each other.[47]

Active participation in the Mass will always be first and foremost Christocentric, that is, a determined effort to search out communion with Jesus Christ, so uniquely present to us in the Mass.

The Liturgical Formation of the Clergy

The Council Fathers understood that elevating the quality of the liturgical participation of the faithful would only be realized if "pastors of souls, in the first place, themselves become fully imbued with the spirit and power of the liturgy and capable of giving instruction about it" (SC, 14). In the years immediately preceding the council, seminarians were frequently trained to validly and licitly preside at liturgies, following rubrical prescriptions, but attempts were rarely made to form them in the sacraments' deeper theological meaning. To improve this, SC required liturgical theology courses in seminaries and religious houses of formation, so that the liturgy would "be taught under its theological, historical, spiritual, pastoral and juridical aspects" (SC, 16). The Council Fathers believed that if priests and religious better understood liturgical theology, this would benefit tremendously the whole People of God.

The Catechetical Dimensions of the Liturgy

In a later section of the constitution, the Council Fathers focus on the liturgy's catechetical quality: "Although the sacred liturgy is above all things the worship of the divine Majesty, it likewise contains much instruction for the faithful. For in the liturgy God speaks to his people and Christ is still proclaiming his gospel. And the people reply to God both by song and

---

47. Jackson, *An Abundance of Graces*, 11.

prayer" (SC, 33). Taking care to avoid turning the liturgy into a mere cate-chetical instrument, the Council Fathers nonetheless acknowledge how God Himself is able to form his people through the divine-human dialog that is liturgical prayer. We can be formed through the liturgy's rich tap-estry of words, signs, symbols, and gestures:

> Moreover, the prayers addressed to God by the priest who presides over the assembly in the person of Christ are said in the name of the entire holy people and of all present. And the visible signs used by the liturgy to signify invisible divine things have been chosen by Christ or the Church. Thus not only when things are read "which were written for our instruction" (Rom 15:4), but also when the Church prays or sings or acts, the faith of those taking part is nourished and their minds are raised to God, so that they may offer Him their rational service and more abundantly receive His grace. (SC, 33)

Therefore, the prayers offered are spoken on behalf of the whole Church and reflect her faith. Liturgical signs have been chosen either by Christ or the Church and have some definite purpose and inner sacra-mental logic—and can consequently be reflected upon and probed for meaning.[48] If we are attuned to the unique way the liturgy teaches, we are more likely to come under an extraordinary formative influence.

In reading through these seven points from *Sacrosanctum Concilium*, the earlier convictions of the liturgical and catechetical movement leaders ring out, expressing a pastoral wisdom we continue to need today. We can see what the Council Fathers wished to accentuate for the whole Church: that the liturgy and catechesis are interdependent in their respective roles within the Church's pastoral mission and that, if this vision for them is realized, both will be strengthened to the great benefit of today's efforts to make disciples.

---

48. As SC, 59, states: "Because [the sacraments] are signs they also instruct. They not only presuppose faith, but by words and objects they also nourish, strengthen and express it. That is why they are called 'sacraments of faith.' They do, indeed, confer grace, but, in addition, the very act of celebrating them most effectively disposes the faithful to receive this grace to their profit, to worship God duly, and to practice charity. It is therefore of the greatest importance that the faithful should easily understand the sacramental signs, and should eagerly frequent those sacraments which were instituted to nourish the Christian life."

CHAPTER 4

The Kerygmatic Mystery: Its Impact upon Catechesis and the Liturgy

For many of us working within the Church, harmonizing the liturgy and catechesis in pastoral practice may have been moved to the "to do" list, but it has not yet become essential, ubiquitous, instinctual. It is almost second nature today for most catechists to begin in a place of prayer or apply the content of the faith to the lives of participants. Helping catechetical participants into a liturgical way of living needs to become equally integral to how we approach our work.

On what grounds are the liturgy and catechesis to be so closely united in our pastoral vision? Is there a foundation upon which effective approaches might be constructed? We ask these questions so we can advance to a conviction that will inspire liturgists into a catechetical sensibility and catechists into a liturgical way of seeing.

What Unites the Liturgy and Catechesis?

The NDC refers to the liturgy and catechesis as "intimately connected." This close relationship originates in what the bishops describe as "the faith of the Church." Four parallel tasks are then identified which reveal this association:

> [Catechesis and the liturgy] "proclaim the Gospel; they call its hearers to conversion to Christ; they initiate believers into the life of Christ and his Church; and they look for the coming of the kingdom in its fullness when 'God may be all in all' (1 Cor 15:28)." (NDC, 110)

It is helpful for us to see this way of approaching the question. The NDC begins by describing the origins of their connection in the Church's *fides quae*[1] before identifying their shared pastoral initiatives. In other words, locating the genesis of the liturgy and catechesis in the "faith of the Church" is to see the source and reason for their unity in practice.

The theological basis for this claim is found in the GDC, as it teaches that the same Word of God that is communicated in catechesis "is celebrated in the sacred liturgy, where it is constantly proclaimed, heard, interiorized and explained" (GDC, 95). The content of the faith, then, which is revealed by God, is made available through both initiatives, though in distinct ways. The liturgy celebrates what catechesis teaches.

What we mean here by the "faith of the Church" is worth remembering. The content of the Church's faith is steeped in and anchored to the glad tidings of what God has done for us in Christ Jesus: Deeply wounded by sin, fallen from our original harmony with God and one another into a desolate alienation, God's loving faithfulness to man and woman is seen in his plan to prepare for the One who would restore all that was lost in the original sin. "In the fullness of time," God sent forth his Son, who offered himself in the supreme sacrifice, accomplishing by his self-emptying obedience on the Cross the reconciliation of humanity to God. Every human being is invited into the intimate union with God that Christ has won for us. Each of us must freely respond. The Paschal Mystery—that is the Crucifixion, Death, Resurrection, and Ascension of Christ into heaven empowers us for divine self-donation, an eternal life for which each of us has been created.

For numerous reasons, many today have yet to *truly hear* this extraordinary mystery, to receive it in a way they can take to heart. We are living in a time when many Catholic leaders are rediscovering the importance of kerygmatic proclamation to every facet of the parish's mission. This is a movement of the Holy Spirit and a cause for hope. The proclamation of the kerygma is the work for which Christ commissioned his apostles. It is the gift and responsibility of the whole Church to share the beauty of the Gospel with every human person.

The content of this kerygmatic mystery is what harmonizes every aspect of the Church's doctrinal teaching. This proclamation also catalyzes

---

1. The *fides quae* is the "faith which" the Church believes and holds to be revealed, "the content of Revelation and of the Gospel message." The *fides qua* on the other hand is the "faith by which" belief is possible, "an adherence, which is given under the influence of grace, to God who reveals himself" (GDC, 92).

our understanding of what is offered us in the liturgy and what we ourselves can give to God in this encounter with the Blessed Trinity. Additionally, it is the content of the Gospel that helps us realize the need that the liturgy has for catechesis and that catechesis has for the liturgy. While the union with God we discover in catechesis is offered us through the liturgy, catechesis prepares us to see and desire this encounter.

The Liturgy and the Kerygmatic Mystery

As we explored earlier, Joseph A. Jungmann, SJ, dedicated himself, beginning in the 1930s, to the great project of restoring the proclamation of the Mystery of Christ to the center of catechesis. He also wanted Christians to understand how the liturgy expresses—and makes uniquely present—this same mystery. In his 1936 book, *The Good News and Our Proclamation of the Faith*, Jungmann explains that the liturgy "as the divine worship of an assembled community, is oriented to *the expression* of what is communal and objective. . . ."[2] Jungmann details how it is a "religious reality" expressed through ritual prayer; it is "God and his work in the weak images of human words."[3] *God and his work*: this reality will only become clear for us as we come to better understand the story of salvation history, culminating in the redeeming action of Christ in his Paschal Mystery.

He offers us this example:

> [T]he prayer of the liturgy reflects Christ as our way to God. In the pre-Carolingian liturgy there was no preface (as is still the case) and no oration which was not directed to God *per Dominum nostrum Jesum Christum [through our Lord Jesus Christ]*. Even today formulas of this sort set the characteristic tone of our liturgical prayer. . . . Thus the exultation of redemption rings out from liturgical prayer and awakens in all who enter into this prayer the joyous consciousness that we are children of God, as well as the consciousness of the importance of holding fast to this one Leader through whom we have access to the Father.[4]

---

2. Joseph Jungmann, "The Good News," in William A. Heusman, SJ, trans. and ed., and Johannes Hofinger, SJ, general ed., *The Good News: Yesterday and Today* (New York: William H. Sadlier, 1962), 114 (emphasis mine).

3. Ibid.

4. Ibid., 115.

Even such a simple phrase as "through our Lord, Jesus Christ" puts us into contact with the kerygma, which is what the liturgy expresses with such clarity of language.

In another place, Jungmann stresses how important it is to have "the essential core [of the Mass] before our eyes to see what it is."[5] He sets this "essential core" before his readers by providing a rich scriptural summary of how the redemption of humanity was accomplished through the Paschal Mystery:

> In this mystery our Lord sealed with His blood His testimony to truth (Jn 18:37), to the Kingdom of God which had come in His own person, and thus had "borne witness to the great claim" (1 Tm 6:13). With a heroic obedience that was steadfast even to the death of the Cross (Phil 2:8), He had in this mystery fulfilled the will of His Father against whom the first Adam had set himself with defiant disobedience. With free resolve our Lord had put himself into the hands of His enemies, silently, making no use of his wondrous might, and had offered up His life as "a ransom for many" (Mk 10:45). He had taken up the warfare against the invisible enemy who held mankind imprisoned in sin, and as one who is stronger still, He had been victorious (Lk 11:22): He had cast out the prince of this world (Jn 12:31). He took His place at the head of mankind, striding forward through suffering and death, thus entering into His glory (Lk 24:26). As high priest He has offered up in the Holy Spirit the perfect sacrifice: with His own blood He has entered the sanctuary and set a seal upon the new and eternal covenant (Heb 9:11ff.). He himself became the Paschal Lamb whose blood procured our ransom out of the land of bondage, whose slaughter inaugurated our joyous Easter feast (1 Cor 5:7ff.), the Lamb that was slain and yet lives, the Lamb for whose wedding feast the bride has clothed herself (Rev 5:6ff.; 19:7ff.).[6]

This description of the kerygmatic mystery is prefaced with these words: "this is what is continually being made present and actual—in the institution of the Last Supper."[7] As we can see, the story of salvation history is the very air we breathe in the liturgy. This kerygmatic context is integral to the experience of the liturgy and to perceiving its underlying cosmic drama. Jungmann believed that fruitful catechetical and liturgical

---

5. Joseph Jungmann, SJ, *The Mass of the Roman Rite: Its Origins and Development*, trans. Francis A. Brunner, CSsR (London: Burns and Oates, 1959), 176.

6. Ibid.

7. Ibid.

practice hinges on whether we are seeing, accepting, and responding to the kerygmatic proposal.

> A kind of faith such as is illuminated in the Roman liturgy as heir to Christian antiquity ought to be unfolded with equal and greater clarity, in the actual teaching of the faith. Sermon and catechesis, religious art and the organization of services ought to strive jointly to promote a consciousness of *the faith* upon which the liturgical and sacramental life may be based, and from which a joyful Christian faith can arise. This will be possible only when out of the many accretions of the centuries the one single message, the kerygma of the early Church, is once again allowed to emerge. To accomplish this, Christ must be restored to the center of the faith. The restoration of the kerygma to its full power and clarity is, therefore, a principal task of modern pastoral work.[8]

We can note here Jungmann's assertion that a consciousness of the *fides quae* leads to a joyful living of the Christian life. This joy, he believed, results only when that faith is specifically understood in its kerygmatic quality—that is, when the Mystery of Christ's redeeming love forms how we see all of Christian faith and life.

Consequently, for Jungmann, we discover the full potency of both liturgical prayer and the doctrinal content of catechesis when we are changed by the illuminating radiance of the kerygma. This conviction can help us appreciate the full significance of the NDC's later statement that the liturgy and catechesis "originate in the faith of the Church." As we will see, the kerygma provides us a theological basis capable of sustaining the pastoral reunification of the liturgy and catechesis amid all of our contemporary challenges.

Historical Observations: Kerygma, Liturgy, and Catechesis

As a leading twentieth-century historian, Jungmann's instinct was to root the reforms of the liturgical and catechetical renewal movements in the historical precedents of early Christianity. By doing so, he preserved both movements from accusations of being illegitimate innovations out of sync with earlier traditions. Johannes Hofinger addressed this aspect of Jungmann's contribution:

---

8. Joseph Jungmann, *Handing on the Faith* (New York: Crossroads/Herder & Herder, 1964), 397 (emphasis mine).

Catechetical renewal, as indicated in *The Good News*, is not a dangerous innovation but a most desirable restoration of the very best and oldest catechetical traditions of the Catholic Church, based on the example and directives of Our Lord Himself, and of His apostles. Jungmann thus cut the ground from under the objections sure to be raised by catechetical "traditionalism," showing, as he did, that the "traditional" approach was actually suffering a great loss as a result of its lack of contact with the best catechetical traditions of apostolic times.[9]

Jungmann's study of history also informed his most compelling critiques of the catechetical practice of his time.

Jungmann raised one such critique in his treatment of what he calls "conscious Christianity." In his book *Pastoral Liturgy*,[10] he suggests that the best way to measure the Christian vitality of the faithful in each era of history is by studying their "consciousness" of the essential core of the Gospel message. He explains it in this way:

Conscious Christianity exists when a person also knows why he is a Catholic Christian—not simply in the sense of a purely intellectual apologetic argument, but in the sense of having grasped the unique value of Christianity. Conscious Christianity is present then when a person does not merely possess the treasure in the field in fact, but also knows that he possesses it and would be prepared to give his whole inheritance to win it or to keep it.[11]

While Jungmann agreed the medieval era was the golden age of the integration of Catholic faith within European culture, he also described this period as a time of widespread unconscious Christianity. These centuries, for Jungmann, featured an interesting confluence of a weakened practice of formal catechesis with a flourishing Catholic culture. Acknowledging

---

9. Johannes Hofinger, "The Place of the Good News in Modern Catechetics," in *The Good News*, 177.

10. Joseph Jungmann, *Pastoral Liturgy*, trans. Challoner Publications (Liturgy) Ltd. (New York: Herder and Herder, 1962), 325–34. This English translation is based on the German original: *Liturgisches Erbe und Pastorale Gegenwart* (Innsbruck: Tyrolia–Verlag, 1960).

11. Jungmann, *Pastoral Liturgy*, 330. In describing the content of which a Christian must be conscious, Jungmann offers a particularly eloquent description of the central Christian mystery. He wrote, "It must be made abundantly clear that in Christianity God has given us very much more than we could have claimed; that in Christ He has restored in a still more marvelous manner that human nature which originally He created most wonderfully; that in the God-man has shone out brightly the dignity to which God has called us, for we are to share in His Sonship of God and so in His closeness to God and in His divine glory . . . that there is no other way by which we can find God than this highway which Christ has opened up for us; that for this reason, the kingdom of God is a treasure hidden in a field for which a man would have to give up everything—it is the pearl of great price, to buy which, a man would have to sell all his possessions. Whoever has grasped this and made it the plumb-line of his life possesses a conscious Christianity" (ibid., 331–32).

the existence of cathedral, monastic, and parish schools for only the minority of children, Jungmann describes how the majority of children and adults were most frequently catechized: after the homily, when the Creed, the Lord's Prayer, or—in the late Middle Ages—the Hail Mary would be recited and gradually explained. Such a narrowly explanatory approach, separated from the rich *narratio* of salvation history, was far removed from the kerygmatic vision of the early centuries of Christianity. It was therefore insufficient even to these times, permeated as they were with such a vibrant Catholic culture. Jungmann writes:

> We would . . . be quite wrong if we were to attribute the flourishing Catholic life found in all lands of Christendom at the height of the Middle Ages to the state of catechetical instruction then prevailing. For the most part, the latter consisted in a certain amount of memorizing of doctrinal formulas with emphasis on questions of morality, as is evidenced by the manuals of preparation for confession which were the forerunners of the catechism. What the children assimilated of Catholic doctrine and Christian morality they owed, in the main, not to the schools nor to indoctrination by the priests of the Church, but to the home and to the environment in which they grew up. Their training came from their surroundings, their milieu, their way of life or whatever one wishes to call it. It came from the formative influence of a world imbued with a Christian spirit in every least detail. . . . A child born into such a world as this had only to keep his eyes open, and he saw all around him representations of the next world. He learned about religion and its precepts and practices just as one learns one's mother tongue, spontaneously and without formal instruction, simply from contact with his environment.[12]

Jungmann concludes, then, that the Catholic culture of the Middle Ages, influential as it was in the lives of its citizens, was not as robust as it appeared on the surface. The cultural milieu so prevalent in the medieval period proved, in fact, to be a meager preparation for the coming storm to be unleashed in the early-sixteenth century. He writes:

> This era contented itself too easily with religious usage and paid too little attention to the religious formation of the mind, knowledge and the understanding. Thus the people of the Middle Ages remained mentally immature. Only in such a way can we adequately explain the speedy collapse of religious

---

12. Jungmann, "Religious Education in Late Medieval Times," in *Shaping the Christian Message: Essays in Religious Education*, ed. Gerard S. Sloyan (New York: Macmillan, 1959), 39–58.

thought which the Reformation caused in so many spheres and in such a widespread fashion."[13]

This unconscious Christianity of so many during the European Middle Ages was not at all ideal and proved, in the end, enormously problematic. Yet, Jungmann speculated that, in itself, unconscious Christianity did not pose an *immediate* risk to the Christian life of the faithful, provided the robust Catholic family and cultural environment endured no serious challenges. He wrote:

> Such a state of Christian awareness is only tolerable, it is true, when men are living without serious disturbance in the full security of simple conditions where not only the family but also the whole community is imbued with Christian tradition and where all the requirements of the business of salvation are guaranteed by Christian customs and a fixed usage.[14]

With the protestation of Luther's Ninety-Five Theses, the stability of the Medieval Catholic synthesis of faith and culture was deeply shaken and its vulnerabilities revealed. The consequences of the massively inadequate approach to catechesis during this time soon became apparent.

It is quite important to see that Jungmann did not write on these matters from a position of scholarly detachment. He was deeply concerned for the sustainability of the faith and life of the Christians of his own age. Twentieth-century members of the Church, he believed, were also receiving an ineffectual catechesis, yet they were benefitting less and less from the supports of a vibrant Catholic societal or familial culture as the medievals did. He explained:

> If now, in an age when there is a resurgence of heathendom, we do not once more foster a conscious Christianity as we have described it . . . then Christians will not remain Christian for long.[15]

Of course, five decades after Jungmann penned these prophetic words, the erosion of the Christian foundations of both family and culture is significantly more advanced. Jungmann's prescient solution, a return to a

---

13. Ibid., 19.

14. Jungmann, *Pastoral Liturgy*, 327.

15. Ibid., 332. He also suggested that sacramental grace is obstructed in the unconscious Christian by using a leading image of the liturgical movement: the image of the vine and the branches. "Most of the people affected [by unconscious Christianity today] still remain outwardly attached to the Church; they remain on the fringe of the Christian community, but the sap of the sacramental life reaches them no longer" (ibid., 329).

catechetical and liturgical experience permeated by a dynamic understanding of the saving Mystery of Christ, has become much more urgent today.

From Jungmann's catechetical histories,[16] we can arrive at this helpful axiom: throughout history, the more that Catholics have grasped the significance of the kerygmatic proclamation to their life, the more closely united the liturgy and catechesis have been in pastoral practice. It is as if kerygmatic consciousness gives rise to an instinctual conviction that what is experienced in the liturgy must be prepared for and understood, and what we learn in catechesis must be encountered.

For Jungmann, the era of most pristine attunement to the kerygmatic mystery was the era of "Christian antiquity," from the Pentecost event through the end of the fifth century. Beginning with his examination of the body of preaching attributed to St. Paul, Jungmann wrote, "the immediate impression we get from his letters and the accounts about him in Acts is that of a wholly Christ-centered preaching. Christ appears everywhere. . . ."[17] Jungmann then describes how this focus remained prevalent throughout Christian antiquity as evidenced by both Patristic sermons and early Christian art.[18]

Throughout this period, the fact of the redemption won by Christ and offered to all was *essential* to preaching—and at the same time, the liturgy and catechesis enjoyed an organic integration. The first pages of Jungmann's *Handing on the Faith* paint a picture of the liturgy and

---

16. See especially chapters 3–7 in *The Good News*; chapter 1 ("The History of Catechesis") and appendix 2 ("The Kerygma in the History of the Pastoral Activity of the Church") in *Handing on the Faith*; "The Pastoral Idea in the History of the Liturgy," *Worship* 30, no. 10 (November 1956): 608–22; and the first chapter in part 3 of *Pastoral Liturgy*, entitled "Christianity—Conscious or Unconscious?"

17. Jungmann, *The Good News*, 17. Jungmann's brief overview of Pauline teaching concentrates on the Christological emphasis in his treatment of ecclesiology (referencing Eph 1:23; 2:5; 4:12ff. and Col 2:5ff.), Baptism (Rom 6:3ff.), the life of grace (Rom 8:14; 8:9–17, Eph 4:15ff. and Gal 4:19) and soteriology (Rom 5:12–21, Gal 3:24, 1 Cor 15:24–28, Phil 2:5ff.; 12:12ff.; 1:13; 6:15; 8:11; 10:21).

18. Jungmann, *Handing on the Faith*, 388. In *The Good News*, Jungmann offers the examples of the formulation of the Apostles' Creed and the Christocentricity of St. Gregory the Great's Ezekiel Homilies (20–26). In *Handing on the Faith*, when discussing the subject matter of the instructions for those in the catechumenate, Jungmann refers to Origen's use of the Books of Esther, Judith, Tobias, and the Sapiential books to demonstrate proper Christian conduct. Jungmann refers as well to Augustine's instructions for offering the content of the Christian doctrine of salvation as well as the *narratio* of salvation history from the fall to Parousia in *De Catechizandis Rudibus*. Additionally, Jungmann points to the nineteen prebaptismal catecheses of Cyril of Jerusalem as sources of the content of the catechesis taking place in the early catechumenate on the topics of sin, Baptism, and faith (the first five) and the Creed (the final fourteen). Finally, he makes brief mention of the mystagogical catecheses of Cyril, Ambrose (*De Sacramentis* and *De Mysteriis*), and Theodore of Mopsuestia as important examples of Patristic mystagogical teaching (3–7).

catechesis operating in a beautifully interdependent fashion in the life of the early Church. At the end of the second century, as Jungmann describes, catechesis was becoming increasingly prevalent and focused toward liturgical celebration. During these nascent years of the catechumenate, catechesis was carried out in communal settings and new Christians participated in liturgical rites leading to full sacramental initiation at the Easter vigil. Jungmann describes a process rich in theological meaning and ritual celebration. "Catechesis was closely bound up with the liturgy: Easter as the time for baptism, assistance at the Mass of the catechumens, special celebrations in the course of religious training."[19] The liturgy exercised a formative influence not only on the individual but also on the community. Jungmann continued:

> An active participation in the liturgy was on the whole the most desirable way in which the individual Christian and the Christian community were able to acquire the necessary religious knowledge. The liturgy, the forms of which were clearly recognized and the language of which was understood, was in a certain sense the continuation of catechesis and a substitute for those who had already been baptized as infants.[20]

Jesuit theologian Fr. Walter Burghardt comes to a similarly positive conclusion about catechesis and the liturgy in this period of history. In his overview of catechetical history, Burghardt describes the liturgical-catechetical relationship evidenced in the era of the Patristic catechumenate:

> The pre-baptismal instructions . . . were orientated towards incorporation into the worshiping Body of Christ; and the post-baptismal instructions had this liturgical life as the springboard of all that was said. Religious instruction leads to liturgy, and religious instruction stems from liturgy– this is basic to early Christianity.[21]

The Fathers of the Church enveloped the sacraments of initiation in a robust catechesis, with the Easter sacraments clearly situated as the apex of early Christian life. Early Christian catechesis, then, was profoundly influenced by the liturgical encounter.

It is also true that, from these early centuries, those who developed the rich sacramental language of word and sign employed in liturgical

---

19. Jungmann, *Handing on the Faith*, 2.

20. Ibid., 10–11.

21. Walter J. Burghardt, SJ, "Catechetics in the Early Church: Program and Psychology," *The Living Light* 1, no. 3 (Fall 1964): 106.

prayer understood the formative potential of worship. In the second section of his article "The Pastoral Idea in the History of the Liturgy," Jungmann describes the Church's early and perennial concern that liturgical prayer be composed in such a way that it would not only "bring the faithful together, so that they might stand before God as the Church, as the people of God," but also cultivate in the faithful a "conscious Christian faith." Instead of merely administering the sacramental actions "which were entrusted to her by her Founder," the early Church has, in her liturgical rites, "striven also to *give expression to her faith* by prayer—in all simplicity before God, but likewise before her own faithful." Jungmann offers this example: in the prayers written for the early rites of Baptism, "she has . . . not been satisfied with merely pouring water over the head of the baptismal candidate: already in the third century she blesses the water with solemn prayer, and led the catechumen by one ritual step after another to the sacrament of rebirth."[22] The Church's efforts to construct liturgical rites that express the theological meaning of liturgical actions are the basis for the well-known Latin axiom *lex orandi, lex credendi.* Indeed, how we pray (*orare*) in the liturgy has from earliest times expressed what we believe (*credere*). The corporate prayer of the Mystical Body forms faith because it reflects the Church's inspired view of reality.

For Jungmann, the first Christian centuries were the golden age of kerygmatic consciousness and also of liturgical-catechetical interdependence. He believed that much could be learned by reflecting on this experience of the young Christian Church and drawing wisdom from it for our present-day challenges.

A Limitation in Jungmann's Historical Approach

Jungmann studied early Church life to bring new energy to the catechetical practice of his time. His contributions to twentieth-century renewal are well established, but the conclusions of his historical study do require one subtle qualification. While effusive concerning the strengths of early Christian catechesis, Jungmann brushes aside any kerygmatic qualities in the catechesis between the decline of the catechumenate and the time of his work in the early twentieth century. This is quite a stretch of history!

---

22. Jungmann, "The Pastoral Idea in the History of the Liturgy," 613, emphasis mine. Additionally, Jungmann offers helpful examples concerning Holy Orders and the Eucharist.

In retrospect, there are certainly exceptions. We need only consider the renewal effected by the great preachers of the thirteenth-century mendicant orders or the contributions made to catechesis during the Counter-Reformation period. Jungmann is critical of the lack of kerygmatic emphasis he perceived in the various catechisms published in the wake of the Council of Trent. However, we find in that era's *Roman Catechism* this earnest appeal for catechists to connect doctrine with the love of God:

> Hence it is the duty of all who do this pastoral teaching to form and motivate the faithful to a love of God's infinite goodness towards us. Thus those who are taught will burn with a sort of divine ardor and will be powerfully attracted to the supreme and all-perfect good. Adhering to God in this way is our true and solid happiness. . . . This is that more excellent way which St. Paul points out (see 1 Cor 12:31), when he refers all his teaching and instruction to the love which never ends (see 1 Cor 13:8). Whatever the pastor proposes in this teaching, whether it be the exercise of faith or hope or some moral virtue, should be presented in the light of the love of God, so as to show clearly that all the works of perfect Christian virtue can have no other origin or purpose than divine love (see 1 Cor 16:14).[23]

Recognizing exceptions to Jungmann's characterization of a significant swath of Church history is helpful to balancing his criticism of various eras of organized catechesis. While his sweeping historical critique tends slightly towards overgeneralization on this issue, there were clearly weaknesses from the kerygmatic perspective during much of Church history. This said, Jungmann's assessment of the kerygmatic deficiencies of the catechesis of his time remains the great unassailable insight of the twentieth-century catechetical renewal.

Today's many initiatives attempting to recenter homilies, catechesis, and Catholic education on the kerygmatic mystery are not only an extension of the work of Jungmann and his collaborators. They are a work of the Holy Spirit. Such work logically tends towards the realization of important fruit: as we come to appreciate the centrality of the kerygma in catechesis, a yearning will arise to encounter the mystery in the liturgy. And, as we truly encounter God in the liturgy, a consequent desire will

---

23. *The Roman Catechism*, trans. Robert I. Bradley, SJ, and Eugene Kevane (Boston: St. Paul Editions, 1985), 8. Readers might recognize that a different translation of an excerpt of this statement finds a prominent position in the *Catechism of the Catholic Church* (25).

surface to more deeply study and understand the content of his saving actions, undertaken for the sake of every human being.

The Kerygma and Parish Life: Challenges

Many Catholics today, accustomed to approaching God collectively at Sunday Mass, are not yet comfortable with the language of personal relationship with God. This presents us all a significant opportunity to grow. The Christian proclamation must be personally received in such a way that it resonates deeply and challenges us to turn radically to Christ so that we might live in the energy of his transforming love. In this sense, being sacramentalized may not yet mean we have been evangelized. Sacramental membership in the Mystical Body of Christ becomes more fruitful as we grow more conscious of this new relationship with God in Christ.

Many of us might feel uneasy not only with the concept of seeking Jesus in a personal way, but even more so in speaking with others about our relationship with him. Sherry Weddell writes, "I have been part of many conversations about the Catholic discomfort at using the naked name of Jesus. We talk endlessly about the Church but so seldom about Christ as a person with whom we are in a relationship."[24] If we have any doubts about how germane the personal relationship with Jesus is to Catholicism, we need look no further than the first apostolic catechesis in Acts 2. Peter, in the power of the Holy Spirit just received at Pentecost, stands up and delivers as potent an invitation to relationship with Christ as has ever been given.

Practically speaking, parishes will see great fruit today as we make the proposal of life in Christ central to every facet of our mission. One friend of mine, who serves as Director of Evangelization and Discipleship in a Michigan parish, told me how her work revolves almost exclusively around planning opportunities for parishioners to *consciously* encounter Jesus. She certainly agrees that the sacraments are the most excellent way this can happen, but many parishioners need to be awakened and respond through a personal, intentional encounter with the Lord before they can appreciate what is possible in the sacraments. And so she plans retreats,

---

24. Sherry Weddell, *Forming Intentional Disciples* (Huntington, IN: Our Sunday Visitor, 2012), 141–42.

pilgrimages, initial evangelization courses, seminars—and the list continues to evolve.

The kerygmatic mystery and invitation to relationship with God can be reproposed through homilies, as the focal point of parish retreats, as the unifying element in catechesis across the generations. The more we become comfortable with naming "the Name" and exploring what God has done and continues to do in us, the more parish life will be permeated with an atmosphere of discipleship. Pope Francis helps us to see that the kerygmatic proclamation never gets old since it is at the heart of Christianity:

> This first proclamation is called "first" not because it exists at the beginning and can then be forgotten or replaced by other more important things. It is first in a qualitative sense because it is the *principal* proclamation, the one which we must hear again and again in different ways, the one which we must announce one way or another throughout the process of catechesis, at every level and moment. (EG, 164)

When a parish makes the kerygma central to its vision, parishioners will eventually become more confident in seeing Catholicism as a life of knowing and following the Lord Jesus, who in the Holy Spirit, brings us into communion with the Father. They will also come to be more at ease speaking with others about their own personal encounters with the Lord and speaking too, in their own words, a proclamation of what Christ has done. Greater familiarity with the kerygmatic mystery will help Catholics to place all of life within the context of the saving mystery of Christ. Vibrant faith helps us to see the many upheavals experienced in the world and in our own lives through the lens of God's plan for the world. While we live in a time of deepening darkness, we are enabled by God's grace to choose to live the virtue of hope, knowing with certainty that God is the Lord of history. As Pope Benedict XVI writes, "a distinguishing mark of Christians . . . is not that they know the details of what awaits them, but they know in general terms that their life will not end in emptiness." The Christian understands that, "I am definitively loved, and whatever happens to me—I am awaited by this Love."[25] The life of discipleship is the way of the *evangelii gaudium*, where we come to know the deep and lasting joy that comes from the Gospel of Christ.

---

25. Benedict XVI, *Spe Salvis* (San Francisco: Ignatius Press, 2007), 2–3.

In addition to helping those whom we serve to take the Gospel message to heart, there are other ways liturgists and catechists can put into practice the liturgical-catechetical interdependence described in this chapter.

Catechists and catechetical leaders can uniquely contribute to the new evangelization through orienting their teaching to the liturgy, which is the summit and font of the catechetical mission. Every catechist wants to bring others into contact with God and his Word. We know that the liturgy is the most efficacious place where this encounter with God unfolds. The catechist, then, has many opportunities to stir up a desire in those being taught for the wellspring of worship and the sacramental presence of Christ. Part three of this book will explore more practically how this may be done.

Liturgists have marvelous opportunities to direct every element of the liturgical celebration—to include music, homily, environment, and hospitality—towards the encounter with God. The more that our people experience liturgical prayer as a place of transformative encounter with God, the more those being catechized can verify through their own experience what they are learning about the liturgy.

In the end, those who have made the decision to live the faith consciously—particularly those who are parents, pastors, teachers, and parish leaders—must put our *desire for union with Christ* at the forefront of how we approach the liturgy and catechesis. By observing this desire and how we act on it, others will see that being a Christian means entrusting ourselves completely to our communion with the Blessed Trinity, cooperating with the God who is Love as he brings us deeply into his mystery.

CHAPTER 5

Liturgical Catechesis: An Apprenticeship

As we have seen in earlier chapters, pastoral thinkers and leaders enthusiastically promoted the remarriage of catechesis and the liturgy before the Second Vatican Council. It was only in the Council's *Constitution on the Sacred Liturgy*, though, that the concept and the term "liturgical catechesis" was first employed in magisterial teaching. In one place, the document refers to "instruction that is more explicitly liturgical . . ." (SC, 35) and in another the actual term *catechesis liturgica* is used (in the original Latin) in its treatment of the season of Lent (SC, 109).[1] In 1963, the meaning and parameters of liturgical catechesis were in their earliest stages of development, so the references here can come across as somewhat obscure. It was left to subsequent magisterial teaching and also to catechetical thinkers to define this new term in the Church's pastoral vocabulary. Let's take a few moments here to be clear on what we mean when we use the expression "liturgical catechesis."

What Is "Liturgical" Catechesis?

Broadly speaking, most catechesis is *fundamental*, offering a basic formation in all the themes of the treasury of Revelation entrusted to the Church by Christ. It is also possible, in many instances, to distinguish various catechetical *forms*, each focusing on a particular facet of the Christian message for a more narrowly defined purpose. While our primary concern in this book is for the liturgical form of catechesis, there are others that could be identified. For instance, a growing number of Catholics today engage in scripture studies, which are examples of biblical

---

1. Veronica Rosier, OP, *Liturgical Catechesis of Sunday Celebrations in the Absence of a Priest* (Leuven: Uitgeverij Peeters, 2002), 24.

catechesis. In Catholic schools, individual courses might be taught on Catholic social teaching, prayer and spirituality, and the moral life (to name a few)—and each of these courses could be considered a distinct catechetical form. There are two ways we might discern a specific form of catechesis: by identifying its sources[2] and objectives.

Sources

Every form of catechesis has as its primary source the Word of God, expressed in both Sacred Scripture and Sacred Tradition and definitively interpreted by the Magisterium. Catechesis can also be enriched by various secondary sources. The *National Directory for Catechesis*, in fact, identifies four examples of secondary sources:

1. the celebration of the liturgy,

2. theology,

3. the life of the Church, especially in the lives of the saints and in the Christian witness of the faithful, and finally,

4. moral values (NDC, 54).

Each of these source categories can enhance and expand our understanding of the Word of God, which always occupies the pivotal position within catechesis. In most cases, a particular form of catechesis corresponds to the specific secondary source relied upon by the catechist. Consequently, a *liturgical form* of catechesis will draw primarily from the context of God's Word, but additionally from the language and rites of the liturgy.

Objectives

Considering our "intermediate objectives" in a given catechesis is a second way to see how catechesis may be specialized. While such objectives are indeed important—just consider a catechists' hopes for increasing biblical literacy or developing a virtue such as chastity—every form of catechesis ultimately aims at the principal aspiration motivating every catechetical act: assisting a person into a more intimate communion with Christ. "Only he can lead us to the love of the Father in the Spirit and make us share in the life of the Holy Trinity" (CT, 5). A *liturgical form* of catechesis, then, prepares participants for communion with God in

---

2. A discussion of sources of catechesis may be found in NDC, 53–54.

Christ, specifically by leading them into an increased sacramental understanding and a greater desire and capacity for full, conscious, and active participation in the liturgy.

Sacramental Preparation and Mystagogy

One further point about *liturgical catechesis* is helpful here. When exploring what liturgical catechesis is, we can see that it is conducted in two primary modes:

1. as a preparatory process for the first reception of sacraments (as we might see in marriage preparation, the catechumenal process, first communion programs) and also

2. as a mystagogical formation that helps us understand our sacramental experience.

The bishops of the United States put it this way: "Catechesis both precedes the liturgy and springs from it" (NDC, 110).

Sacramental preparation—also called sacramental catechesis or initiatory catechesis—is described by the NDC as a preparation for "full, conscious and active participation in the liturgy by helping [participants] understand its nature, rites and symbols" (NDC, 110). Those approaching a sacrament for the first time have a clear need to understand the human and theological meaning inherent in this extraordinary encounter with God, a meeting that gives rise to the possibility of real transformation and new life in Christ.[3] They also need to understand this encounter as it takes place within the atmosphere of ritual, through the mediation of signs and symbols. These ritual elements of the liturgy, quite foreign to many people today from a cultural perspective, can become a stumbling block to sacramental practice. Drawing from the rich content of the rite itself, then, is an important way of helping people enter into the unique language employed by the liturgy.

---

3. The introduction to the *Rite of Baptism for Children* captures this need when it insists that parents take part in the rite "with understanding." See "Introduction," in Congregation for Divine Worship, *Rite of Baptism for Children* (1969), no. 5 §1, quoted in *Catholic Rites Today: Abridged Texts for Students*, ed. Allan Bouley, OSB (Collegeville, MN: Liturgical Press, 1992), 139. The English word *understanding* is a translation of the Latin *consciam*. This Latin term is also used in SC, 12, when the necessary quality of participation in the liturgy is described as "plenam illam, *consciam* atque actuosam liturgicarum celebrationum participationem ducantur." In the context of no. 12, *consciam* is frequently translated into the English word *conscious*. Perhaps this word has richer connotations, particularly in light of Jungmann's treatment of the idea of "conscious Christianity," as described in the last chapter.

The second form of liturgical catechesis is mystagogical catechesis. This catechesis *springs from* the liturgical celebration itself, bringing us more deeply into its underlying mystery. Strictly speaking, mystagogy is the formative period that begins within the Christian initiation process, following the Easter reception of sacraments. At the Easter Vigil, the new Christian becomes a "neophyte." This new Christian finds himself or herself in need of a catechesis that teaches from the experience of sacramental grace begun at the Vigil. The neophyte formation—encouraged by the Church as at least a yearlong process—is the starting point for mystagogical catechesis.[4] More broadly, though, because the Christian mysteries are infinite in their depth, bringing us into communion with God who is "the inexpressible, the incomprehensible, the invisible, the ungraspable,"[5] mystagogical catechesis never ends. The *National Directory* explains,

> Mystagogy represents the Christian's lifelong education and formation in the faith. . . . Conversion to Christ is a lifelong process that should be accompanied at every stage by a vital catechesis that leads Christians on their journey towards holiness. (NDC, 117)

When the expression "liturgical catechesis" is used today, many even in professional catechetical positions will draw a blank with this term, not quite sure what is meant. In this book, we use the term to indicate any catechetical endeavor that has the meaning of the Mass, another sacramental celebration, or any other liturgical encounter with God as its content. While significant emphasis is placed on sacramental preparation in most parishes, and rightly so, neophytes (and all of us in the mystagogical period of life!) need to be *accompanied* into the new life of grace now available through our participation in the sacraments. Mystagogical catechesis is the logical implication of understanding the liturgy as the divine encounter that it is. If it truly is the "summit" and "font" of the whole Christian life, then our understanding of it must continue to deepen if we are to grow into mature Christian discipleship.

In order to understand what liturgical catechesis must become to meet our contemporary need, we turn now to an important trending

---

4. Offering the realistic possibility of a neophyte year is a great challenge for many parishes today and as a result a well-functioning neophyte process can be difficult to find. An excellent article was published in 2016 detailing one parish's approach to forming neophytes: Elizabeth Siegel, "Beyond RCIA: Accompanying the 'Newly Planted,'" *The Catechetical Review* 2, no. 3 (July 2016): 32–34.

5. *Liturgy of St. John Chrysostom*, Anaphora as cited in CCC, 42.

discussion among pastoral leaders. Many today are proposing a more individualized approach to evangelization and catechesis for the sake of helping these initiatives become more impactful. After briefly reflecting on three recent expressions of this ideal, we will see how the paradigm of accompaniment is vital to our vision for fruitful liturgical catechesis.

Today's Movement towards a More Personal Approach

In recent years and in various quarters, a growing sense of the inadequacies of a generic approach to evangelization and catechesis has begun to pick up steam. A number of pastoral thinkers and strategists have come to a challenging conclusion: presenting a prepackaged catechetical content to people without considerable personal guidance is not working as it may have for previous generations. Jim Beckman, a well-known national youth ministry leader, describes his realization of this problem:

> I was at the Saturday evening session of a teen retreat that we had spent months planning. This was the typical "powerhouse" moment of the weekend, and I expected teens to experience similar breakthroughs as I'd seen in previous years. But as I watched the young people around me, I could tell that something was not connecting. . . . That Saturday night I watched as volunteer team members poured themselves out in skits, personal testimonies, and a passionate talk by one of the other youth ministers. But the crowd of teenagers seemed distant, as if they were watching something on TV, had grown tired of it, and were ready to change the channel. . . .

> I have talked with many youth ministers—one after another—who feel that the ministry they're doing is waning in effectiveness. They struggle to connect with teens, the teens seem to respond differently than they expect, and their ministry seems to lack "staying power" in the teens' lives, meaning beyond high school but often even just through the students' senior year. Many teens were unplugging from the ministry well before their junior or senior year.[6]

Beckman suggests an alternative youth ministry model that is small group based, led by adults who have experience knowing and living the Christian life and who are able to guide young people in a more personal way towards an informed and vibrant life in Christ. What is needed, in

---

6. Jim Beckman, "Rethinking Youth Ministry" in Sherry Weddell, ed., *Becoming a Parish of Intentional Disciples* (Huntington, IN: Our Sunday Visitor, 2015), 117–18.

Beckman's view, is the raising up of parents and catechists who are able to more personally invest in a smaller group of young people, intensifying their impact. The Fellowship of Catholic University Students (FOCUS) and the Canadian campus ministry program, Catholic Christian Outreach (CCO) are two Catholic approaches to campus ministry that adopt similar views. Both are experiencing growth and success in the most difficult of cultural terrains: today's public university campuses. Whether catechetical leaders employ a large group or small group methodology, the need for personal mentoring in how to live a Christian life has never been greater.

Sherry Weddell, too, suggests a Catholic evangelization that begins with the needs and real faith position of the individual person. Her efforts at motivating Catholics to a greater love for those who do not know Christ—and her wisdom in basing personal evangelization on the particular "threshold of conversion" where a person may be found, are exceptionally valuable. The key ability recommended by Weddell is the desire to genuinely befriend another person, respecting him where he is and summoning the words and approach that might best *encourage* him towards the next threshold, and ultimately into an intentional relationship with Christ in the Church. Evangelization, for Weddell, happens best in an individual way and in the context of sustained personal presence and real friendship.[7]

And, finally, Pope Francis also frequently proposes what he terms, "personal accompaniment." Best described in his post-synodal apostolic exhortation *Evangelii Gaudium*, he suggests that we evangelizers must "remove our sandals before the sacred ground of the other." The Holy Father emphasizes relational evangelization, that moves at a "steady and reassuring [pace], reflecting our closeness and our compassionate gaze which also heals, liberates and encourages growth in the Christian life" (EG, 169). Evangelistic accompaniment, as described by Pope Francis, is a respectful dialog, leading ultimately to God.

Entering into genuine dialogue with another means entering a conversation where truly hearing the other is equally important to helping the other understand our own position. This kind of authentic exchange

---

7. See especially, Sherry Weddell, *Forming Intentional Disciples: The Path to Knowing and Following Jesus* (Huntington, IN: Our Sunday Visitor, 2012), chapters 5–8, which propose a series of "thresholds of conversion" and ways of respectfully approaching people who find themselves at each threshold.

requires us to listen and receive the concerns and convictions being voiced, so that we can arrive at real understanding. This can be done, *even if we are not in agreement with the other's position.* Such an approach to communication bespeaks a profound respect, kindness, and desire to truly understand as a first step. Certainly our Holy Father believes—showing us by his own example—that this must be the way forward in fruitfully proposing Christ today. If others are going to truly *hear* the truth of Christ, it is necessary that they must at the same time be *heard.* Such an approach represents a desire for genuine solidarity with the other, even when disagreement is present. Of course, an approach to dialogue within evangelization and catechesis that moves proclamation to the periphery is disingenuous. While Jesus most certainly entered into dialogue with the disciples on the road to Emmaus, that dialogue ("What are you discussing?") prepared them for proclamation ("Was it not necessary that the messiah should suffer these things?") (Lk 24:13–35).

Cardinal Timothy Dolan has described well the need for accompaniment *and* call to conversion in evangelization. He writes, "If we only accompany but do not convert, then we simply walk beside people farther into the night, away from the community of faith in Jerusalem. If we only question and listen, then we withhold from people the saving news of salvation." The Cardinal suggests we learn from the full Emmaus account, as he suggests our mission today is "to draw near, to accompany, to question, to listen, to rebuke the lack of faith, to teach the truth of the Gospel, to reveal Christ, to restore hope, to convert, to return to the Church."[8]

This idea of a more personal accompaniment in inviting others to live the Christian life is not a new concept. Vatican II's *Decree on the Church's Missionary Activity* uses the term *apprenticeship* to describe the newly restored Rite of Christian Initiation of Adults (RCIA) and the Council Fathers' intent for this process through which adults would join themselves to Christ's Mystical Body. "The catechumenate is not a mere expounding of doctrines and precepts, but a training period in the whole Christian life, and an apprenticeship duty drawn out, during which disciples are joined to Christ their teacher" (AG, 14). This ideal introduced by the Council was a move away from a purely doctrinal-explanatory

---

8. Cardinal Timothy Dolan, "Lord, To Whom Shall We Go?" *Catholic New York*, Oct. 26, 2015, http://cny.org/stories/Report-on-the-Synod,13240.

approach (often delivered by the parish priest who "offered instruction" to adults interested in becoming Catholic). Rather, the catechumenal model was understood to be an integral formation of the whole person, carried out by clergy and catechists who could teach *and* encourage catechumens into a living of Christianity. The process of becoming a Christian, in the minds of the Council Fathers, necessitated an environment of deeply personal engagement, which helped catechumens learn the content of Revelation, but in a dynamic and "livable" way.

For this reason, one of the most fascinating statements in the 1997 *General Directory for Catechesis* is found in the first part, where the document calls the baptismal catechumenate the model, the inspiration, for all catechetical activity (GDC, 90). Such an assertion means many things. One certain implication is that the emphasis on personal mentoring seen in the apprenticeship model is being recommended more broadly for the whole of the catechetical enterprise. This conviction within the GDC is shown in another part of the document, where catechesis in general—and not just the catechumenate—is described as initiating believers "in knowledge of faith and apprenticeship in the Christian life, thereby promoting a spiritual journey that brings about a progressive change . . . " (GDC, 56). Such a proposal is certainly well aligned with the ideas of Pope Francis, as well as Jim Beckman and Sherry Weddell. It also corresponds to the needs of those considering more deeply Catholic faith and life today.

What Is Apprenticeship?

My family recently had an extraordinary experience. To help celebrate our twin daughters' first Communions, a dear family friend, Celeine Minton, offered to visit us for four days and teach the twins (and our family) how to paint—or, more accurately, "write"—icons. Through Celeine's generosity, each of us entered into the experience of an abbreviated apprenticeship in iconography. Looking back on this time, the apprenticeship relationship she established with each of us was unique in three ways.

First, we placed ourselves *under Celeine's direction and expertise,* and she skillfully accommodated the scope of her teaching to our daughters' young ages and lack of experience.[9] When our daughters began the process, they were ready to create from their own individual ideas, when, in

---

9. There was, of course, an even more pronounced accommodation needed for their father.

iconography, the icon writer submits personal creativity to the authority of an earlier icon by keeping to a copied model. Rather than a process of self-expressiveness, icon writing is a prayerful process of observation and imitation. My wife and I would reassure them with a smile that, "Ms. Celeine is our teacher. We should see what she wants to show us first." Very quickly, they embraced this relationship with Celeine, who so well learned the capacities and potential of each of us gathered around the table.

Second, the purpose of our time was certainly about learning a new skill, but it was also about learning to properly see. In my case, my familiarly unimaginative instincts towards efficiency and production gradually gave way to a slowing down, an inner concentration. From this place of interior silence, contemplation became possible as the simple repetition of brush strokes stretched into the long hours.

Finally, the crux of this experience was without question the patient presence of our teacher. There was time in plenty for questions to arise and conversations to develop, and it was in the *spending* of time together that what was taught had a real chance to "sink in" and make an impression. This required a significant investment on the part of our dear friend. I'll never forget the last night, my wife and I calling it quits at around an hour before midnight. Celeine had a plane to catch early the next morning and we were all exhausted. The icon she had put so much time into, the one she planned to give my parents for their fiftieth wedding anniversary, looked like a masterpiece to me. She said, "I've just got a couple last things to do with this one" and we presumed that meant another twenty minutes. When I awoke at four in the morning to get a glass of water, I was shocked to see Celeine still sitting in front of this icon, sacrificially investing herself into it, brush stroke after patient brush stroke. Her time with us was no mere "instruction"; it was a loving gift of self that summoned so much of who she is as an artist and human being. Such a work enkindled real self-donation on her part, which brought a profound depth of sacredness to this time we spent with her.

What would it mean for catechists to apprentice those entrusted to them for formation in the faith? We can begin to imagine how such an approach would have the same three qualities described above.

First, the essential content of catechesis would of course be communicated, but those being catechized would be approached with a sensitivity to each person's respective movement towards the Lord and knowledge of his teaching. Only then could a respect begin to develop that would make it possible for those being catechized to (even without being explicitly articulated) put themselves under the direction—the apprenticeship—of a catechist. Perhaps those catechists doing the apprenticing could be entrusted with a smaller group, so that the dynamic of passive receptivity which plagues so many large group educational settings could gradually shift towards one of more accountability and personal engagement. Active engagement is a necessary ingredient to real change of heart and making a genuine commitment to follow the Lord and understand his teaching.

At the university level, particularly in our work with online programming, we hear much today about how to engage young adult and adult learners more actively, where they become motivated to take responsibility and initiative for what they are learning. Such approaches within catechesis teach the timeless truths of Christianity while promoting a responsiveness on the part of participants. Catechist-mentors allow time for a conversation to develop, where questions, concerns, objections could be expressed and addressed in a place where each person is respected because each is known. With such an approach, passive receptivity of doctrinal content can begin to give way to active learning.

How do we build in time for personal mentoring in our already busy catechetical sessions? It can be as simple as the approach taken by Sr. Mary Karolyn Nunes, FSGM, from Alton, Illinois, in her high school religion classroom. She is kind enough to share with us her experience:

> Having taught high school for seven years, I was blessed to experience the joy of accompanying students in their spiritual lives by making myself available to them and by not being afraid of asking them tough questions.
>
> Sometimes the mentor/student relationship comes naturally. This was true for the group of girls that regularly came to my classroom after school "just to chat," to show me the latest YouTube video, or to ask for prayers for particular situations in their lives. Over time, it became a chance for me to offer advice on prayer, relationships, overcoming vice, and vocational discernment.
>
> I discovered that the nets could be cast wider by asking a non-graded question at the end of a test, or giving students reflection questions for chapel time that would be discussed in one-on-one meetings. Those questions might include: How can I pray for you? What did you learn in this unit

that has the possibility of changing the way you live? How have you noticed God's gifts in the last week? Two or three times a semester (generally after grading a test or major assignment), I would pull my desk into the hallway, prop the door and sit in my "office" to meet with each student individually. During that time, I would show them their overall academic progress, go over the latest assessment and then discuss the answer to their non-graded question or latest reflection sheet. That gave me a window to encounter each student where he was, give advice if desired, and even pray together.

For me, mentoring my students has been a source of hope and reassurance in my role as a catechist. I have heard a student who claimed to be an atheist admit that there is a God and start to believe in love. I accompanied a student through the messy waters of her parents' divorce where she met Jesus as her friend and consolation. I encouraged a student through reconciling a broken friendship that was wreaking havoc on her daily life. I assisted a student in using principles of discernment to choose her college and proudly watched her step out in faith and see the hand of God in her decision. None of these experiences are because I am somehow a perfect catechist, but because I embraced the challenge of being more than just a teacher. I try to mirror the Lord's love for my students, whose restless hearts were looking for some-one to help them discover the fullness of life for which they were made.

One reason I respect the work of Sofia Cavalletti (the founder of the Catechesis of the Good Shepherd model of children's catechesis) is how she convincingly argues for the need that the child has to respond *within the catechetical space* to God's loving invitation. Sofia's answer to this need may be seen in how she allows time for silence, for meditation in a way suited to the child, and for individual mentoring conversations to take place between children and the catechists. Allowing such freedom and such opportunity for responsiveness is an important quality of any approach that seeks to apprentice those being formed.

Second, apprenticeship leads to a new way of seeing and a new way of living—these are its enduring fruits. Through catechesis, as we learn to see reality more clearly through our immersion in the truth, beauty, and goodness of all that has been revealed in Christ, this vision organically changes how we think, how we choose, and how we live. In mentoring others in this way, the catechist finds herself deeply challenged to be liv-ing this faith integration in her own life. Such a mentoring in holiness requires that the catechist not only teach the precious truths of Christ but also speak from experience about how the faith might best be lived.

Apprenticeship, therefore, leads not only to new convictions, but also to the development of a new set of abilities. Knowledge is not imparted in a way disassociated from the discipleship context. Such a catechetical approach teaches people not only to believe that the Bible expresses God's Word, but also to additionally find their way around it, inspired to become personally reliant upon it as an authoritative text. The apprentice does not merely learn to follow the catechist's lead in prayer, but also grows confident in the ability to pray *apart from the catechist*, employing the rich diversity of methods we receive from our rich spiritual tradition. The catechized person learns not just about the Mass, but also gains skills that can be employed when at Mass so that transformative participation becomes a real possibility. An apprenticeship vision for catechesis is precisely the approach needed if our people are to be equipped both with the vision and ability to live lives permeated by the Gospel.

Finally, there is no question that the apprenticeship model requires the involvement of catechists who are able to teach well and embody the living faith in how they live. It also presumes a certain generosity on the part of the catechist, who is called to offer a sustained—and sometimes heroic—presence to those being apprenticed. Herein lies perhaps the greatest challenge of apprenticeship: raising up adult catechists who can invest themselves in this way.

Apprenticeship and the Liturgy's Divine Encounter

When it comes to accomplishing all that is needed in liturgical catechesis, as the Council Fathers saw with the RCIA process, the apprenticeship model is the most amenable to our objectives. This is so because of the need that growing disciples have for learning the life of active sacramental participation. But even more importantly, those learning about the liturgy need to be apprenticed because of what the liturgy is: the place of divine encounter *par excellence*.

The liturgy affords us the chance to enter into a most intimate and personal exchange with God. Learning how to give ourselves and receive what is offered is best learned from human beings who themselves have been transformed through this exchange. We know on the theological level that something objectively real happens, that something of awesome proportion is offered us. The Council Fathers describe Baptism (for instance) as a plunging "into the Paschal Mystery of Christ: [we] die with him, are buried with him, and rise with him" (SC, 6). This is a reality of such magnitude, that ordinary and familiar educational approaches to content delivery are frequently inadequate.

As awe-inspiring as this mysterious immersion is, we as individual persons need to put ourselves consciously in front of such a life-giving truth—and learn to cooperate with all that is given us in Baptism—if this sacrament is to be transformative and fruitful. What is the Paschal Mystery? Why is it necessary that we be "plunged" into it? What about this dying, burial, and rising with Christ—what does it mean? What does such an encounter do to me and affect how I can live? Merely teaching about this sacred content, without an accompanying mentoring in how these truths can be personally (and communally) appropriated is sadly insufficient. Without this personal encouragement, there is a fundamental injustice that can begin to arise—a subtle transgression against the full reality of what we are teaching and an injustice too against those who so desperately need to understand and live new lives in Christ.

Approaching God in the liturgy and being able to live in the sanctifying atmosphere of divine worship requires a certain way of seeing and new abilities. These skills are best learned from those who already possess them. In the eighth chapter of this book, we will explore the most important of these abilities.

Implementing the Apprenticeship Model: Challenges

We should not, of course, underestimate how challenging a proposition it would be to move catechetical ministry in the direction of apprenticeship. Let's name a few of these challenges.

In a 2013 survey published by the University of Notre Dame's Institute for Church Life, the greatest weakness in catechetical ministry today, according to diocesan catechetical leaders, is the lack of trained and qualified personnel.[10] Many parish catechetical leaders, of course, struggle to find volunteer catechists for all the needed age groups. In a culture of ubiquitous busyness, it can additionally be quite difficult for those generous catechists who do step forward to set aside time to invest in their own formation. Ongoing study and encouragement is needed today for catechists perhaps more than ever before. Effectively teaching the faith today is an art that is in constant need of refining, and even more so when the catechetical model being employed is inspired by the ideals of personal mentoring.

The apprenticeship model presumes sufficient numbers of catechists who are, as Sherry Weddell describes, "intentional disciples." Disciple-catechists are those who have progressed in the conversion process and are committed followers of the Lord Jesus. Disciple-catechists have placed the Lord Jesus in the position of highest authority in their lives and they are personally being apprenticed—perhaps still by others whom they admire—but always most profoundly by Christ the King. They have given over authority to the One who has become the center of their lives and consequently are uniquely equipped to humbly lead others into this relationship. Of course, the disciple is not yet a canonizeable finished product, as clearly in the Gospels we read of so many shortcomings on the part of the Lord's own disciples. But today's disciples commit themselves to Christ, love his Mystical Body the Church, and move towards their life's great objective: the perfection of charity. Such people, at least at first, may be difficult to find. We can see how vital adult evangelization and catechesis is in the Church today!

There are certainly organizational challenges as well. Catechesis frequently takes place within the structure of larger groups, with just one or a few catechists teaching a relatively large group of people. How can our structures, and our use of time within them, be modified to allow the few to effectively mentor a larger group of participants?

These are questions that cannot be glossed over, but must be thoughtfully and creatively considered. The answers in most parishes will have to be found in beginning modestly, one catechist and catechetical

---

10. Brian Starks, Rita Tyson Walters, and Thomas P. Walters, *Joyfully Communicating the Living Mystery: A Profile of Diocesan Offices of Religious Education* (South Bend, IN: University of Notre Dame Institute for Church Life, 2013), 10. This report was accessed at icl.nd.edu/assets/130993/cspri_living_mystery_report.pdf on 8/9/2016.

group at a time, progressing slowly and with consistency towards a broader engagement of the apprenticeship model.

Finally, we can be encouraged that in many ways the apprenticeship model has numerous precursors in Catholic vision and practice. It remains a deep conviction within Catholic teaching that parents are the primary educators of their children. Parents are already, *ipso facto*, apprenticing their children in life. In most cases, there is no one more influential in a child's life.[11] Therefore, any investment the parish makes in building up a *catechetical* relationship between parents and children will yield the richest fruit, for the family is already the first place of apprenticeship. Family-based catechetical models build upon this already-existing apprenticing relationship and can effectively evangelize and catechize both parent and child.

Additionally, there are mentoring roles that are already defined within the context of liturgical catechesis, and these are excellent beginning points: not just the role of the catechist but also those of the sponsor and godparent. How do we help young people preparing for Confirmation, parents bringing a child for Baptism, and those journeying in the RCIA process to know how to choose a person who is capable of living up to this responsibility? How do we equip those chosen so that they can be impactful in their roles as mentors in the Christian life?

Many of us have taken advantage of the ancient practice of spiritual direction. Make no mistake about it: this is apprenticeship and spiritual accompaniment in a concentrated form. How could such a familiar model be expanded upon, in a way that would not overburden our beloved (and frequently overstretched) priests and religious? There is already one Midwestern American diocese that offers a substantive "spiritual mentorship" training program, which helps equip mostly lay people to provide spiritual accompaniment for aspiring disciples.

While there are inherent challenges in integrating apprenticeship within the catechetical setting, there are also many new initiatives today which have great potential. As has been the case with so many new

---

11. Christian Smith and Justin Bartkus gave a fascinating presentation at the University of Notre Dame Center for Liturgy's 2016 symposium. They previewed the results of Christian Smith's study on Catholic parenting and the faith convictions of today's adolescents and young adults. Their research, in my estimation, presents an encouraging argument for just how effective parents can be who embrace the ideal of apprenticing their children in the Christian life. See "Christian Smith & Justin Bartkus–'From Generation to Generation,'" YouTube video, 1:35:10, posted by "ICLnotredame," July 6, 2016, https://www.youtube.com/watch?v=v0FzwlM5iLM&feature=youtu.be.

movements in the Church over the millennia, much fruit has been borne by beginning humbly and simply. St. Teresa of Calcutta's luminous words ring true time and time again: "Do small things with great love." The practical implementation of apprenticeship within a Catholic parish would, in most cases, need to begin simply and humbly, taking "baby steps" forward as new disciples are made. It is not difficult to see how, with the passing of years, a parish could in this way become a true center for the New Evangelization.

One Parish's Experience

Let's end this chapter with a concrete example from a parish implementing some innovative approaches to apprenticeship. St. Thomas Aquinas parish in Ames, Iowa, has transitioned to a small group and one-on-one mentoring model for adult faith formation, and the pastor and staff have experience and wisdom to share. Fr. Jon Seda, pastor of this parish serving local Catholics and the students at Iowa State University, saw a need for his parish to take a new approach in how parishioners were being offered the Gospel.

> If you asked me what our parish needed more of, I would not say programs or events. What we need more of are disciple-saints. I think of my small home parish. We had no programs, no events, no lectures, no adult education, and no youth ministry. But we did have many quiet, simple, and behind the scenes saints. These relationships formed me in my youth.
>
> So our parish has shifted from a program paradigm to a relational one. People are transformed by relationships, with the Lord and each other. Our goal is to make disciples, and the best way I have seen to do this is to connect saints with wannabe saints.
>
> I believe people are transformed by stories, from Scripture but also about how God has worked in the lives of people you know. Many Catholic parishes have few opportunities for people to tell their faith story, or hear the faith stories of others. We are moving toward this relational model of ministry because of just how important relationships are to growing closer to God and strengthening our community within the Church.

The parish director of faith formation, Tyler Wheeler, offers some helpful practical details regarding how small groups and the apprenticeship model function within their adult evangelization and catechesis.

While this isn't the only way to structurally build a parish culture of apprenticeship, perhaps Tyler's experience will help us envision what such a model could be like:

At St. Thomas Aquinas, we've made small groups and one-on-one discipling the core of our adult faith formation. Our small groups are places of prayerful encounter with Christ through Scripture, providing support and accountability. The content is Scripture (and associated Church teaching), and the goal is that people grow in relationship with Christ, namely through further developing their own prayer and sacramental life.

How does the small group accomplish this tall task? In sum, our groups are a time to study the Word prayerfully within a close community of friends. The resource we use contains the Scripture reading, some well-prepared questions, and a suggested "homework" assignment that focuses on how we can live out what we have experienced in the small group.[12] However, small groups only take a person so far, and it's with that in mind that we seek to foster a one-on-one discipleship culture in conjunction with small groups.

In small groups, participants are opened to discipleship, to a new way of seeing the world and living within it by intentionally applying Scripture to all of life, by being challenged and supported by their fellow seekers and disciples. One-on-one discipleship then allows the small group participant to go further, to delve into the heart and habits of a disciple and to address particular successes and failures, hopes and discouragements, obstacles and opportunities. This is where St. Thomas Aquinas' quote comes to its deepest fruition within our community, "To convert someone, go and take them by the hand and guide them."

What does one-on-one discipleship look like? Simply put, it is, as our pastor Fr. Jon says, putting people in touch with saints, with disciples. In essence, those who are discipling others meet people where they are, accompany them, and along the way share how they walk with Christ. Material is prepared to share with the one being discipled. For instance, they could discuss how to establish a prayer routine. Then they gather in a casual environment, like a coffee shop, and talk. This is all predicated on an authentic friendship. We are not seeking to turn people into projects, to objectify them. Instead, we are finding people who show a desire for more and then guide them. We help them to become aware of the people within

---

12. Materials are provided by the Evangelical Catholic organization in Madison, WI. More information available at https://www.evangelicalcatholic.org/.

their world who could benefit from such a ministry. I then "walk" with the leaders as they "walk" with others, providing support and care for them.

A great challenge to our one-on-one ministry is that it is an extremely difficult culture to establish. This culture is not familiar within the current Catholic paradigm for most of our parishioners. The process can be scary and parishioners can feel inadequate. This new culture isn't established through a workshop or program but through the extremely inefficient work of discipling others (and experiencing being discipled), one person at a time.

My role then, as director of faith formation, is to form, train, and equip parishioners to be missionary disciples. Specifically, I form them to be small group leaders who are able to do one-on-one discipleship. We do this through what we call training groups that I lead, after which, they launch their own small group and seek individuals within their sphere of life who are ready for one-on-one apprenticeship. From this, everything else flows. Thus, I focus most of my attention on only twenty-three people (the ten training group participants and the thirteen current small group leaders). I seek to reach the whole parish, the whole community of Ames, by putting my efforts into a deep and lasting formation of these twenty-three people God has placed in front of me. While many might wonder at whether this is an efficient use of my time, we are following the example set by Christ himself, who sought to reach the world by deeply investing himself in just twelve disciples.

PART II

Liturgical Catechesis for the Transformative Encounter with God

What must it have been like to be with them as they were departing Jerusalem (see Luke 24:13–35)? They were leaving the community of disciples, the Church as it was moving through the birth canal. They were walking away, disillusioned and crushed by loss. All of this they verbalized to one another—word after difficult word. After all the miracles, the teaching, the time he invested in them. . . . After being known personally by him and growing into friendship with him. . . . After settling into unconquerable convictions. . . . And after being deeply moved upon hearing of those final hours he spent with the Twelve, when he had wrapped the towel around his waist, washed their feet, and said to them, "I have given you an example, that what I have done you also must do . . . " and most astonishingly how he had celebrated the Passover meal, uttering those words, "take and eat, for this is my body . . . " He had even spoken of a union they would enjoy with him—as a branch is united to its vine. These words were spoken, but then he was taken from them, seized and crucified. After all that he had given them, how could all of this have collapsed so abruptly and so completely?

It was at this moment that the stranger joined them as they walked. He asked a simple question that drew from them an incredulous answer: "Are you the only visitor to Jerusalem who doesn't know?" They recounted detail after dizzying detail to him who quietly listened. Then it was his turn to speak. What words they were! "Oh, how foolish you are! How slow of heart to believe all that the prophets spoke." As they listened, as they began to see everything about the Master—about his life and his death—in a new light, they felt something begin to change within them. Who was this man who walked at their side? They had finally reached their destination, the house at Emmaus, but he was continuing on. They couldn't let him go, not just yet. "Stay with us." His explanation of the Scriptures, his way of seeing the events of the last week, had brought them to a new vista. But they were struggling to make sense of what they were seeing. They wanted this man to remain. His words had stirred in them again—even in their acute suffering— the deepest of desires for the Master, the One whom they loved above all else.

"And it happened that, while he was with them at table, he took bread, said the blessing, broke it, and gave it to them. With that their eyes were opened and they recognized him, but he vanished from their sight. Then they said to each other, 'were not our hearts burning [within us] while he spoke to us on the way and opened the scriptures to us?'"

It was his presence and his teaching—with the light he brought to the scriptural prophecies and to the Passion, Death, and now (clearly!) Resurrection of the Master from the dead—that caused their hearts to be set aflame with desire. And this desire of theirs propelled them to the table where they recognized him in the breaking of the bread.

Luke's account of this meeting with the Risen Christ reveals how desire for Christ in the sacramental encounter is best brought about. The Master accompanies them (even as they are moving away from the Church). He forms a relationship, a friendship with them. On account of his questions, his genuine interest, his empathy, and his clear grasp of the true way of seeing things, they are drawn towards him. Their hearts are opened—indeed they begin to blaze—as they take to heart his teaching. He speaks with boldness. He speaks with authority of what is true and real. He teaches from the Scriptures. He offers them a kerygmatic way of seeing, a way that had eluded them, unable without his assistance to see the divine pattern undergirding his passion and death. Through his words and his presence with them, their hearts were kindled with a desire to meet their Divine Master once more. And this desire was utterly satisfied when they recognized him in the breaking of the bread.

How, we might ask ourselves, is sacramental desire "learned" today? What would liturgical catechesis need to be if it is to cause just such a fire to burn in the hearts of those entrusted into our formative care?

As we turn now to the primary proposals of this book, we keep before us this conviction: only by cultivating a desire for God in his uniquely powerful sacramental presence can there be a new genesis in sacramental practice today. The most important questions facing pastoral leaders revolve around how our catechetical approaches can evoke and deepen desire for God in the sacraments. From this place of desire, and only from this vital position, will each of us assume personal responsibility to discover how the sacramental encounter can be all that the Church says it is.

CHAPTER 6

The Liturgy: Entering the Eternal Exchange of Love

I would like to quote a relatively unknown theologian. She lives in my house, is eleven years old, and her name is Grace. Three years ago, after returning from parish catechesis one morning, I was looking with her through her textbook. I closed the book and asked, "Grace, who is God?" She paused thoughtfully and then responded, "God is a waterfall . . . and we are all his thirsty flowers."

Taken aback, I have frequently now pondered and prayed with this metaphor. It illustrates for me the energy, the outward movement, of God's perpetual and total gift of himself in love—and at the same time the beauty and dignity of every human being, with our deep poverty to receive what only God can give. God has made us so that we might freely enter into communion with him, receive his divine life as pure gift, and share his splendor with others. This is never more real and true than it is in the Mass and in the whole of the sacramental life.

Jeremy Duo from Gibraltar expresses this well, in describing his experience of his son Álvaro's Baptism.

And so the big day arrived—the day for our son to be born anew.

The moment came when my wife Stephanie and I stood next to the baptismal font and Fr. Derek called down the Holy Spirit on the waters. Images were evoked from the Spirit hovering over the waters at the creation of the world, the flood and Noah, the Israelites crossing the Red Sea, the Israelites crossing the Jordan into the Promised Land, and the Holy Spirit descending on the Lord Jesus as he himself was baptized, simultaneously sanctifying the waters for us.

Just a moment later, as I was increasingly welling up inside with joyful anticipation, Fr. Derek brought little naked Álvaro, in the hands of my wife, to the baptismal font and prayed those beautiful words, as creative and sanctifying as when God had said "Let there be light" and brought the world into being: "Álvaro José, I baptize you in the name of the Father, and of the Son, and of the Holy Spirit." In an instant, I truly encountered the power of God as He spoke his Word into my son and brought unfathomable light into him and made him into a new creation. The entirety of Salvation History suddenly converged within my son and lo, Jesus had bound the strong man of my son's soul, plundered his house and triumphantly claimed my son as his own by the power of his Cross. This was the day that my son became my brother. Blessed be God.

We turn our attention now to the sanctifying power of the liturgy. As we catechists come to truly understand its transformative potential, our own worship will become more conscious and fruitful and those we mentor in liturgical prayer will approach the liturgy with the eyes they need to truly see.

The Liturgy as Divine Encounter

One of the twentieth century's most important liturgical theologians, Cyprian Vagaggini, OSB, described the liturgy as "the privileged place of encounter between man and God." The bishops of the United States explain that this encounter with God is an experience of what is at the living center of Christianity: "Through the Eucharist, the People of God come to know the Paschal Mystery ever more intimately and experientially. They come not simply to the knowledge of God—they come to know the living God" (NDC, 110). And St. John Paul II reminded catechists aiming for transformational teaching that "it is in the sacraments, and especially the Eucharist, that Christ Jesus works in fullness for our transformation" (CT, 23). While catechesis can change hearts and minds, there is no substitute for how this happens in the sacramental life, with the Eucharistic presence at its center.

Above all else that might be said of the liturgy, it is an opportunity for an especially concentrated encounter with God. Significant conversion of life—yielding the fruit of love, joy, peace, patience, kindness, generosity, faithfulness, gentleness, and self-control (Gal 5:22–23)—will be the eventual outcome seen in every person who approaches with understanding and humble desire. How can the true weight of this meeting be best understood?

The idea of meeting God (who we know is omnipresent to every person) might not strike many today as remarkable. If we are confident that God is real and that he loves us and wants to draw close to us, then it does not require a great stretch of the imagination to believe that any time we reach out to him can be an opportunity for encounter, whether in focused prayer, thinking of him while driving on the freeway or meeting him hidden in a person in need.

An important distinction is helpful here. As we enjoy varying levels of connection with other human beings, there are also different depths to how we experience contact with God. With human beings, we exchange texts and "like" social media posts, and we also take pleasure in sitting down with friends and family to share long conversation over a good meal. We also know that encounters with others can unfold into moments of exceptional significance when love is exchanged in ways that bind us closely.

In the life of Jesus as he walked the earth, those who knew him and lived with him must have relished every moment. Certainly, though, there were times of particularly intimate connection. We can think of such events as Peter's confession of faith in Jesus "the Messiah, the Son of the Living God" and Jesus' response to him: "Blessed are you, Simon son of Jonah. For flesh and blood has not revealed this to you, but my heavenly Father. And I say to you, you are Peter, and upon this rock I will build my Church . . . " (Mt 16:16–18). Or, at the request of those grieving parents, entering the home of that little girl, tenderly taking her lifeless hand in his own and saying, "Little girl, I say to you, arise!" (Mk 5:41). Or the woman who opened her jar of precious oil, reserving nothing as she poured it, anointing his feet and drying them with her hair (Jn 12:3). How these experiences cut right to the heart! As resplendent as these moments are, no experience with the Lord rivaled that of the few who were present with him in his sacrificial self-offering on the Cross. It was in that encounter that they received each of his "last words"—with all the love that could be summoned from their breaking hearts—and the offering of himself unto death on the Cross.

Even with God, then, there are gradations in the depth of our encounters with him—acknowledging, of course, that these different levels of contact are due to our limited capacity to give and receive and not to the infinite capacity for both which may be found in the Blessed Trinity. How, then, do we describe the depth of the encounter possible in the liturgical life?

"Through Him, with Him, and in Him . . . "

The sacramental encounter is a connection of *supreme intimacy* with God, both *to whom* and *through whom* we offer worship. Liturgical prayer is not merely the private prayer of individual persons, who could—as individuals—pray just as well while walking the beach or in a quiet place within the home. The liturgy is not merely *our prayer*. It is always first the prayer of Christ Jesus, "our great high priest," who ceaselessly intercedes for us from the right hand of the Father (Heb 7:23–27).

Such an acknowledgement requires us to take into account the heavenly dimension of liturgical prayer. What we see with our eyes is not all that is happening. Indeed, Christ Jesus is the Divine Liturgist, the One who from heaven re-presents his Paschal Sacrifice to the Father in praise, making an atoning supplication for the sanctification of the world. When we join ourselves to the God-man in his liturgical offering of this sacrifice, as the assembled members of his Mystical Body, we are intimately united to Christ our brother in this great work. And, because he enjoys perfect unity with the Father in the Holy Spirit, so too are we brought into this unity as we give ourselves to this prayer, which is the very life of the Church.

In the liturgy, then, it is the whole Christ—Head and members— who prays. When we join ourselves to this priestly prayer, the most extraordinary of divine encounters takes place. There is, first, the union enjoyed by each member of the Body with Christ the Head as individuals assemble for liturgical worship. Second, liturgical prayer is a beautiful sacrificial offering of praise to our Heavenly Father, an offering which—through Christ who is "the one Mediator between God and man" (1 Tim 2:5)—is pleasing to him and effectively brings us into his fatherly embrace.

In liturgical prayer, through Christ and in the Spirit, perfect worship is offered to the Father. At the same time, through Christ and in the Spirit, the Father lavishes his sanctifying life upon us. Christ is, indeed, "the ring which weds man and God."[1]

How else might we understand this union we enjoy within the liturgy? While he is our teacher, friend, and brother, the Christ we are joined

---

1. Vagaggini, *Theological Dimensions*, 301.

to sacramentally is Christ in the event of his supreme love on the cross, rising from death and definitively conquering sin, ascending to his Father in glory and bringing everyone who is joined to his Mystical Body with him. This means that the Lord Jesus we meet in the liturgy is not distant or inaccessible. As the Paschal Mystery is made present, we join those few disciples two thousand years ago gathered at the foot of the cross and see that he wishes to give everything to us, to hold nothing back. And in that Paschal Event, the power of perfect love is unleashed, which becomes the source for the world's transfiguration in every generation. All this has been done that we might enter fully into the "eternal exchange of love" that is the unending life of Trinitarian love. Such an unthinkable destiny becomes possible only through the sheer generosity of the God whose essence it is to give everything of himself away.

In the sacraments, then, we are put into contact with God's total and complete gift of self. There is nothing better he could give us and there is no more intimate union possible. With great joy, we who accept this gift of divine grace can make Paul's exclamation our own: "I live, no longer I, but Christ lives in me!" (Gal 2:20). This is the depth of intimacy into which we are invited! Even our most personal encounters with one another—including the highest expressions of love between devoted spouses—are but a shadow and anticipation of the love for which we were made. "What eye has not seen, and ear has not heard, and what has not entered the human heart, what God has prepared for those who love him!" (1 Cor 2:9).

The divine encounter in the liturgy is a real encounter. As we learn to better perceive it in our own experience, it can be helpful to hear how others recognize the movement of God in the celebration of the sacraments. As an example from the unique perspective of a priest, let's consider the testimony of Fr. Michael Berry, OCD, from Hubertus, Wisconsin.

> In my experience as a priest, I am regularly awed and consequently humbled by the *particularity of encounter* in the sacraments, whether in celebrating the Mass or when hearing a confession. St. John of the Cross says, "In giving us His Son, His only Word (for he possesses no other), [God] spoke everything to us at once in this sole Word. . . ."[2] Yet within the Sacraments, this one Word speaks powerfully in a personally relevant way to such a variety of needs and

---

2. St. John of the Cross, *The Ascent of Mount Carmel*, nos. 2, 22, 3–5, in *The Collected Works of St. John of the Cross*, trans. K. Kavanaugh, OCD, and O. Rodriguez, OCD (Washington, DC: Institute of Carmelite Studies, 1991), 230.

the diverse experiences of His people. In my daily experience of the Sacrament of Holy Orders, I know myself as an agent of "this sole Word" instrumental in a moment of unique encounter between Christ and His people.

Even while I experience my weakness and personal limitations in the work of ministry, I repeatedly discover anew—and with delight!—the faithful, actively solicitous presence of Jesus Christ, supplying what is necessary for His son or daughter in the moment (and speaking to His priest in the process). How often following a daily Mass one of the faithful will tell me concerning a homily (and often a seemingly forgettable one at that), "Father, your words were spoken directly to me!" Or when in the confessional, as I pray to the Holy Spirit for wisdom, a particular word from Scripture or the writings of a saint will come to mind and I am impelled to share this insight with the penitent. I never cease to be amazed and grateful for the particular relevance of these insights and the power of God's word to liberate and to refresh those I encounter in the confessional. And this occurs often enough when subjectively I feel exhausted or otherwise uncertain.

As a priest, I love the Sacraments because I *know* by faith the real presence of Christ encountering His people as unique individuals. And what I come to appreciate with ever deepening awareness is how I, as a priest, am not simply a witness to Christ's saving action in the lives of others, but that in these ministerial encounters with others Christ is saving me.

While God gives himself to us for the sake of forming an intimate communion, we must consciously and intentionally *receive* this gift from him. Pope Francis frequently describes the experience of Eucharistic adoration as a time of allowing the Lord to gaze upon us. Certainly he is always "gazing upon us" whether we are aware of him or not, for "even the hairs of your head have all been counted" (Lk 12:7). Becoming aware of his gaze, which requires a deepening of the interior life, can be the most penetrating of experiences in life and is central to Christian conversion. In this experience, we begin to see clearly—through our attunement to God who looks upon us with love, as he did the rich young man (Mk 10: 21)—how great is our dignity, how our immeasurable value is not earned, how *infinitely we are loved*. In becoming truly conscious of this gaze and welcoming it in gratitude and humility, we are able, with the full investment of ourselves, to return this loving gaze.

" . . . All Glory and Honor Is Yours, Almighty Father"

Sacraments are not merely experiences of receiving from God, though this is indeed primary. We, too, bring ourselves into an important work within the liturgy: giving our loving praise and worship to God.

For members of the liturgical assembly, expressing adoration to God is the very essence of the worship we offer. Joining ourselves to the Son's adoration of the Father in the Holy Spirit means uniting ourselves to the words and gestures of the Mystical Christ, making them our own.[3] The worship we give also consists in sacrificially elevating every dimension of our lives to God, making an encompassing gift of ourselves to him. Ever called through such worship to ongoing purification of life, we are able to offer lives to God which are progressively more consistent with our words and actions in the liturgy.

In short, we love by giving everything. Offering such a gift does not change God, who is perfect and unchangeable; it doesn't somehow make him feel better about himself. He does not *need* the praise of his creatures. Rather, the experience of divine worship changes us. The *Catechism of the Catholic Church* teaches us how adoration and worship turn us fundamentally towards God in love, which frees us from being enslaved within the constricting confines of a life centered on self:

> To adore God is to acknowledge, in respect and absolute submission, the "nothingness of the creature" who would not exist but for God. To adore God is to praise and exalt him and to humble oneself, as Mary did in the *Magnificat*, confessing with gratitude that he has done great things and holy is his name. The worship of the one God sets man free from turning in on himself, from the slavery of sin and the idolatry of the world. (CCC, 2097)

As we lovingly give ourselves away in worship of God, we are sanctified by his gift of grace that he has poured out first, without which true worship would not be possible.

The liturgy is, then, a loving exchange of gift, a participation in *the* eternal exchange that is life in the Trinity.

---

3. Christopher Carstens and Douglas Martis, in *Mystical Body, Mystical Voice: Encountering Christ in the Words of the Mass* (Chicago: Liturgical Training Publications, 2011), describe the liturgical expression of word and sign as the "mystical voice" of the Mystical Body of Christ. Liturgical participation, then, consists in joining our own individual expression of adoration and sacrifice to the one mystical voice of Christ, through whom the Church's prayer rises to the Father in the Holy Spirit.

What is it, precisely, that *we give to God* through the sacramental life? There are many answers to this question. Let's consider just a few.

First of all, at the most basic of levels, our mere presence at Mass or in the confessional or at the baptismal font is a kind of gift, isn't it? By being present, we have cleared time and space in our life for God—and the very act of doing this has value. When we take the next step and *deliberately* offer our time to him—rather than mindlessly, mechanically being present—it becomes an intentional gift of self that is pleasing to God. And if we choose to invest ourselves into the words and actions we pray, this forms the highest personal gift that we can offer to God in the liturgy, worshipping as we do in union with the whole Mystical Body.

The Sacrament of Reconciliation also involves a deeply personal gift of self. As we present to him, in sorrow, our sinful actions and patterns, we are freely revealing the most sensitive aspects of our fallen humanity. On a purely natural level, when I confess my own weaknesses to my wife and ask her forgiveness when I have hurt her in some way, vulnerability and love are reintroduced into our relationship and new beginnings become possible. When we approach God in this same way, something marvelous opens before us. In this trauma wing of what Pope Francis likes to call the "field hospital" for the sick, we entrust God with our brokenness, with those parts of us we keep hidden from others. There is unquestionably an opening of the person to the Divine Other—and is this turning to him in our absolute weakness not an act of loving self-donation? The Church wisely encourages us to frequently enter into this loving exchange with God in the confessional, for the opportunities to root ourselves in the ground of infinite joy are breathtaking. The person who chooses not to follow the prodigal son in his return to the Father (Lk 15:11–32) withholds a uniquely beautiful gift of self that could be given to God. He consequently misses the homecoming longed for by every person: the incomparable embrace of the Father of Mercies.

When a man and a woman are married sacramentally, a gift to God is also perceptible in their action. Not only do they give themselves unreservedly to one another, but they also turn to God in their need, in their poverty as finite man and woman. They offer to him the love that they have for one another. They put into his hands their commitment to lifelong union with one another. They entrust him, too, with the gift of their fertility. In this sacrament, they place the totality of their marriage and family life at his service that his glory might shine through.

The sacraments, then, are a marvelous exchange of self-gift with God. We enter into God's profound act of self-emptying, and in this encounter with the One who is perfect Love, the gift we make of ourselves is elevated and divinized. Our gift of self becomes more and more like his gift of self. We become, by grace, capable even of Christ-like, supernatural love. We can see how such a transformative exchange is the foundation of a truly joyful missionary Christian life, for the Lord meant it when he said, "I came that they might have life and have it to more abundantly" (Jn 10:10).

This exchange is best seen in the Mass, which is the great dialogue of divine and human love: deeply revelatory of God's self-emptying gift as well as that of every person intently united to the Mystical Body of Christ. By beginning with the sign of the Cross, we place ourselves under the saving presence of God, remembering in these words how the Father has given the Son to us and how the Holy Spirit is also given us for the sake of love. The very first words spoken after this expressive gesture are words of gift: "The grace of our Lord Jesus Christ, and the love of God, and the communion of the Holy Spirit be with you all." This is followed by a humble and loving response on the part of the assembly, who "confess to almighty God and to you, my brothers and sisters, that I have greatly sinned." Immediately after this admission of sin, we are absolved of all venial sin: "May almighty God have mercy on us, forgive us our sins and bring us to everlasting life." And the Mass continues in just this way: God gives and we receive. Our words and gestures express a gift of ourselves, which God lovingly gathers to himself. Such a ritual exchange of love—which happens through, with, and in Christ—is transformative for us, drawn as we are into the dynamic exchange of Trinitarian life and love. "The ultimate purpose of this meeting of above and below . . . is the divinization of the created, the perfection of the fallen, and the consummation of restored communion."[4]

Today's Indifference: A Crisis?

Many today, sadly, have no conscious awareness of the liturgy's language of dialogue or how to invest themselves into this exchange. As a result, the

---

4. Carstens and Martis, *Mystical Body, Mystical Voice*, 27.

sacraments become one-sided, blandly anesthetizing rituals that often do not speak in earnest to the contemporary person.

Without a vivid sense for sacramental living as the life of divine encounter and loving exchange, it is small wonder that so many today are bored! St. John Paul II diagnosed well the sacramental crisis of our times when he wrote, "sacramental life is impoverished and very soon turns into hollow ritualism if it is not based on a serious knowledge of the meaning of the sacraments" (CT, 23).

However, we could ask: *Is it a terribly big deal that so many today are bored with the sacraments?* We might frankly remember many periods in our own childhood and beyond when we ourselves were indifferent. If we think about our faithful forebears several generations ago, our grandparents and great-grandparents, it certainly seems conceivable that even they, for at least a few moments on every fifth Sunday, may have been elsewhere intellectually and disinterested in the divine encounter unfolding before them. So, is today's widespread liturgical boredom truly problematic?

The bishops of the United States incisively answer this question, speaking more generally about the Church's broad formative work, with these words: "Young people are taught both by the excitement generated by technology and by the effervescence of popular culture to reject something if it bores them—and often the only things that do not bore them are those that seduce or titillate" (NDC, 12). *That which is boring is rejected!* This is a new sociological response that would have been unthinkable two generations ago in religious practice. If today we are uncomprehending, unconvinced, and consequently unengaged, we simply won't return. And whereas a few decades ago many young people left the Church but later returned to get married and settled back into sacramental practice when it was time for their own children to receive the sacraments, that predictable (and encouragingly consistent) pattern is far behind us. According to a 2015 study by the Pew Forum on Religion and Public Life, approximately 52 percent of American Catholics have left the faith of their childhood at some point and only 11 percent have left and returned.[5]

---

5. Pew Research Center, "America's Changing Religious Landscape," May 12, 2015, available from www.pewforum.org/files/2015/05/RLS-08-26-full-report.pdf, accessed on Jan. 3, 2016.

Indeed, if we join the Council Fathers in teaching that the liturgy is the "summit" of the Christian life, what do today's Catholics conclude about Catholicism if they find our high point *uninteresting*?

For these reasons, liturgical boredom is the watershed issue of our time within the Church. If many of us today are sinking into a dislike for a liturgy that we no longer understand, desire, or desire to understand, it is quite possible that the objective graces conveyed to us through this privileged place of encounter are received in a fruitless way (CCC, 1128). It is also likely that, for most, receiving sacramental grace fruitlessly is not a compelling concern.

Therefore, the more we become convinced that the sacraments are transformative encounters with God—real exchanges of love with the One in whom all true love originates—and that these encounters have supernatural effects, the more *interesting* they will become for people today. This is an assertion that concerns both *the liturgy* and *catechesis*—and must begin to shape the pastoral priorities of both liturgists and catechists.

We must beg God for a passion (if we don't yet have it) to mentor others in how to find Christ where he may be supremely found, so that this most important truth rises to the forefront of all the other things we learn about the sacraments. We must also be able to speak of this in a convicting way from our own experience, always complementing the communication of our true, good and beautiful doctrinal content with our testimony to its veracity. Perhaps it would be helpful to read such an account from a fellow catechist. Elizabeth Siegel, of Ann Arbor, Michigan, shares her own experience of an early encounter with God at the Easter Vigil.

> "The power of this holy night . . . " Forty years later, I still hear these words of the Easter Exsultet in the deep, resonant voice of gray haired Abbot N. at the Norbertine Abbey in PA. I was 9 or 10 when my parents, who had grown up before the reform of the Easter Vigil rite, began taking all four of us children, ages 6–11, to the nearby abbey for the entirety of the Triduum. I was affected by all of the great three days, but most of all by the vigil.
>
> I do not remember receiving any catechesis on the vigil, and perhaps that allowed me simply to witness the liturgy with totally fresh eyes. The waiting was long—we had come early to get seats, but I did not get sleepy. I loved the hushed darkness, for I could sense a shared anticipation in the people gathered, who waited too. And when the towering abbey doors swung open, revealing the first light of the Paschal Candle, I was spell-bound. The light danced as

the acolyte moved, casting strange shadows on the plain white abbey walls. We responded in loud unison, "Thanks be to God," as the candle was lifted high. Strangers passed on to us the light of the Easter fire, and we held it each in our hands.

Then the abbot began the Exsultet, and my heart trembled within me. I heard power. I heard majesty. I heard nobility. I heard the proclamation of something radical and definitive. I felt myself drawn up into something far greater than I. The world was being changed. I was being changed. I could not speak. The poetry of the words seared into my memory. "Night truly blessed when heaven is wedded to earth"; "the morning star which never sets." Oh, not even Christmas had this power to touch the depths of my soul. I listened as the past great event of the Exodus was fused into this present night when Christ was rising. The proclamation spoke of Christians everywhere, and I knew that I was one of many, of a whole host of people, of that beautiful thing called the Church. I felt proud, newly dignified, by this inclusion in such a tremendous whole, and such a tremendous happening. I was being raised up, as He was. I grew that night, and every vigil since. And all the places I have heard the Exsultet . . . chanted in Latin in the twelfth-century Cistercian monastery in Fribourg, Switzerland, or at the Dominican House of Studies in Washington DC, and in parish churches everywhere . . . my heart always swells and I become more.[6]

Theological Reference Points for Liturgical Catechesis

To sum up this theological content most essential to liturgical catechesis, we can identify the following six helpful reference points for catechists. Returning to these truths frequently and creatively in our catechesis will help those we teach approach the liturgy with a depth of understanding and desire.

First, *the liturgy is an action of the Blessed Trinity.* To enter into the liturgy is to unite ourselves to the sacrifice of praise which is offered to God the Father, through God the Son, and in the power of God the Holy Spirit. Every liturgical act of the Church has God the Father as its source and ultimate aim. The Lord Jesus is the Divine Liturgist in his mediatorial identity as Son of Man and Son of God. And the liturgical act is carried out and effected in the power of the Holy Spirit, who is the artisan of

---

6. The quotations included here are from the previous translation of the Exsultet.

God's sacramental masterpieces (CCC, 1091). In the economy of salvation, the Father sends the Son and the Father and Son send the Holy Spirit for the sake of the redemption of the world, and the redeemed return to the Father through the saving work of Christ in the power of the Holy Spirit. This Trinitarian dynamic is reflected in the Church at prayer.[7] It is important for the faithful to understand that the liturgy is a participation of the people of God in God's work (CCC, 1069), in his very life—and coming to see the presence and action of God in this great work is of highest importance.

Second, *the liturgy is an action of the Mystical Body of Christ.* The liturgy assembles the members of the Mystical Body, in union with Christ the Head; it is therefore "a sacred action surpassing all others" (SC, 7). Liturgical catechesis reinforces the corporate-Christic nature of our experience in the sacraments. In particular, understanding the sacraments as acts of the Mystical Body helps us see how closely united we are to Christ, so much so that he shares his work of worship and sanctification with us. It is, then, the case (for instance in Baptism) that "when anyone baptizes, it is really Christ himself who baptizes" (CCC, 1088). The Mass is not a gathering of isolated individuals who are arbitrarily joined in their pursuit of personal inspiration and greater purpose. Rather, it is an assembly of one body, united in Christ, who offers the Paschal sacrifice to the Father for the sake of giving glory to God and for the salvation of the world. The unity of the body is ultimately realized by this prayer of Christ's unifying salvific action, which is the summit and font of the whole Christian life.

The third essential reference point reinforced by liturgical catechesis is that *the liturgy makes accessible the saving Paschal Mystery of Christ.* While the Second Vatican Council recentered all aspects of liturgical ritual on the Paschal Mystery, today's Christians must come to grasp how this is so. The redemptive event of the Death, Resurrection, and Ascension of Christ into heaven is the turning point in the great drama of human history and the Church makes it sacramentally present to us today. As the CCC states:

> His Paschal Mystery is a real event that occurred in our history, but it is unique: all other historical events happen once, and then they pass away,

---

7. A clear description of the work of the Blessed Trinity in the liturgy may be found in CCC, 1077–109.

swallowed up in the past. The Paschal Mystery of Christ, by contrast, cannot remain only in the past because by his death he destroyed death, and all that Christ is—all that he did and suffered for all men—participates in the divine eternity, and so transcends all times while being made present in them all. The event of the Cross and Resurrection abides and draws everything toward life. (1085)

It is from this mysterious event that is drawn all the power needed for worship and the sanctification of the whole world.

The fourth theological reality discernible in any liturgical act is *the twofold aim of every liturgical action: "human sanctification and God's glorification"* (SC, 10). Liturgical catechesis must prepare people who are capable of and longing for the worship of God. The reorientation of vision and life that is the fruit of divine worship is an important balm for the tendency towards self-centeredness that afflicts each of us. Catechists can also prepare us to eagerly seek the sanctifying gift of grace "which is poured forth upon us as from a fountain" (SC, 10). A lack of understanding and conviction regarding this two-fold purpose of the liturgical experience undercuts our ability to fruitfully participate in the Mass and sacramental life.

Fifth, we understand the liturgy *to be a participation in the priesthood of Christ.* In respectively distinct ways this is true of the ordained minister and of all the baptized (CCC 1546–47). With these different priestly roles operating in concert, the action, then, of the Mystical Body at prayer is a priestly action, for the greatest of sacrifices is offered. As Christ's sacrifice on the Cross is offered to the Father in the Holy Spirit, we join our own sacrificial gift to this offering. The offering of ourselves and the content of our lives to God through Christ—this is the principal ability needed if we are to participate in the liturgy fully, consciously, and actively. This ability is at the heart of sanctifying corporate worship. The Council Fathers described this priestly offering of the baptized with compelling words:

> For all their works, prayers and apostolic endeavors, their ordinary married and family life, their daily occupations, their physical and mental relaxation, if carried out in the Spirit, and even the hardships of life, if patiently borne— all these become "spiritual sacrifices acceptable to God through Jesus Christ" (1 Pt 2:5). Together with the offering of the Lord's body, they are most fittingly offered in the celebration of the Eucharist (LG, 34).

These sacrifices, ordinary and representative of every aspect of life, are offered in union with the sacrifice of the High Priest of the New

Covenant, and they are lovingly received by our Heavenly Father. Timothy O'Malley describes well the ordinary splendor of the assembled people's priestly offering:

> Consider a Sunday assembly and the sheer range of human affections, desires and narratives included there. A widow enters the sanctuary, devastated by the loss of her husband. A soon-to-be high school graduate is overjoyed by news that he has been accepted to the university of his dreams. Many couples enter this assembly worried about the burden of bills and the fearful possibility of losing a job. When the Eucharistic prayer is offered, these joys and desires, these sorrows and disappointments become part of that sacrifice of praise offered by the priest and the assembly alike. Our entire selves are joined to Christ's sacrifice to the Father, as we give ourselves away in prayer in response to the God who first loved us.[8]

And, finally, *liturgical catechesis focuses upon the effects of active participation in the liturgical life of the Church.* Once we begin to see liturgical prayer as a participation in the life of Trinitarian love, such a meeting with God becomes supernaturally transformative. This encounter always has objective supernatural fruits, which we learn of from the Tradition.[9] The catechist can—with imagination and reverence—unfold this compelling panorama of the supernatural effects of the liturgy. When those we teach learn of the effects and fruits of this meeting with God, and begin to cooperate with his work of love in them, those gifts objectively given by God become subjectively received and actualized. Great things become possible! As these fruits begin to take root, we can begin to understand the unmistakable responsibilities that accompany liturgical living. The Mass and the other sacraments, then, become causes of heroic virtue and the establishment of justice in the world.

These six truths about the liturgy are integral to a fruitful catechesis in the sacramental life. With these convictions—along with an accompanying desire stimulated by the testimony of catechists who can speak as living witnesses before the sacramental encounter—comes an exponentially greater potential for a transformative experience of the sacraments.

---

8. Timothy O'Malley, *Liturgy and the New Evangelization* (Collegeville, MN: Liturgical Press, 2014), 26.

9. One very helpful feature of how the CCC treats each of the Seven Sacraments is found in each section where either the "effects" or the "fruits" of the sacrament are delineated. For catechists, these sections are absolute gold.

Empowering liturgical catechesis with a theologically rich vision of the liturgy is not to suggest a reactionary return to the purely theoretical or conceptual approaches of the preconciliar period. On the contrary, this proposal is made for the sake of drawing attention to those precise fundamental aspects of the Mass and other sacraments that, if better grasped today through a process of apprenticeship as described in chapter 5, have immense potential to stir up a new curiosity and desire for God. Certainly such a movement would provide, by the grace of God more consciously received, a new moment in the life of the Church.

CHAPTER 7

The Trajectory of Liturgical Catechesis: From the Visible to the Invisible

The *Catechism of the Catholic Church* begins its treatment of the sacramental life by reflecting on a Christian work of art, a fresco originally painted at the beginning of the fourth century on the walls of the Roman catacombs of Saints Marcellinus and Peter.[1] As early Christians secretly gathered in this resting place of many martyr-saints, they would have looked upon this image of the hemorrhaging woman's healing. This radiant fresco captures the very moment when she reaches out her trembling hand to touch the cloak of Jesus. It is in that moment, we know, that her twelve years of suffering came to an end.

Taking a step back, we can ask ourselves: Why is this image a starting point for the *Catechism's* treatment of the sacramental mystery?

The woman's healing was effected not by being spoken to or approached by the Master himself, but by merely touching "the tassel on his cloak" (Mt 9:20). As it is in her encounter with the God-man, so it is with the rest of us. God has chosen to give us his healing power, his divine grace, his supernatural life, by way of the physical, sensible, and earthy materials he has designated for this purpose. The Lord's own choice, when he physically lived among us, to confer his healing power through the mundane stuff of saliva and mud, the waters of a pool, the physical touch of his hands, and by human words spoken through his human body reveals to us the characteristic way that his healing power would be dispensed to the end of time: by way of what can be seen, heard, touched,

---

1. Not every edition of the CCC includes what the early hardcover editions did: the four color images inaugurating each of the four parts of the text.

tasted, and smelled. In this, we can recognize that God has chosen to communicate his grace to us in ways perfectly suited to human beings.

While we identified six theological reference points for the *content* of liturgical catechesis in the last chapter, we will focus here on how our liturgical theology influences our *method* of helping others see the divine encounter awaiting them in the liturgy.

Cyprian Vagaggini, OSB, and the Law of the Incarnation

We turn now to an important idea described for us by the great Benedictine liturgical scholar Cyprian Vagaggini, OSB. Vagaggini is a twentieth-century theologian of the liturgy worth reading. Born near Siena, Italy, in 1909 and raised in Belgium, in 1921 Vagaggini became a monk of St. André, near Bruges. In addition to having earned doctorates in philosophy (1931), theology (1938), and oriental ecclesiastical sciences (1940), he also possessed a keen competence in pastoral issues. Vagaggini's most significant work was undoubtedly his *Theological Dimensions of the Liturgy*, tremendously influential in twentieth-century liturgical thought and rightly considered one of the great modern classics of liturgical theology. Vagaggini was honored with the request to serve on the preparatory commission on the liturgy for the Second Vatican Council and also served as an expert consultant at the Council regarding liturgical matters.

Vagaggini's helpful insight in this matter could be summarized in this way: it is only in the revealing light of the Incarnation—that is, in the act of God's eternal Son assuming human nature for the sake of our salvation—that the logic of God's decision to employ the liturgy in his plan of salvation may be correctly understood.

Vagaggini articulates this principle with these words: "By freely choosing the way of the incarnation, what [God] has done is in substance, to take into account the nature of man and to treat man, spirit-incarnate, in the style of man."[2] The liturgy's characteristic way of giving that which cannot be verified by human senses (invisible, supernatural grace) *by way of those very senses* (through what we can hear, see, touch, etc.) is but an extension of the divine consistency underpinning the Incarnation itself.

---

2. Cyprian Vagaggini, OSB, *Theological Dimensions of the Liturgy*, trans. Leonard J. Doyle (Collegeville, MN: Liturgical Press, 1976), 305.

The Invisible God, the One who is Pure Uncreated Spirit, becomes visible, hearable, touchable out of love for his creation. In establishing a *visible/sensible* Church, he provides a way for the *visible/sensible* sacraments he instituted to be offered to those *visible/sensible* human beings desperately in need of his supernatural grace, but dependent upon the medium of *visible/sensible* communication in every other aspect of life. Vagaggini contends that this sacramental system is a perfectly logical way for creatures consisting of a physical body and a spiritual soul to receive divine life. This was true historically in the life of Christ on earth as divine grace was given by way of his human nature. It is also the way in which he wills to communicate the divine life through the sacraments of his Mystical Body, the Church. Vagaggini explains:

> This way in which God has willed to appear in the world and to communicate Himself to men, truly astonishing to human comprehension, is of inestimable importance in allowing us to gain some understanding of the ways of God's working among men and to show us the way which we must take in order to reach Him. In fact, for arriving at God the way of the incarnation was imposed not only upon the contemporaries of Jesus, but remains even today the only way that leads to the Father. It is a law. In a certain way it can be said that what the humanity of Jesus was for his contemporaries, the sacraments are for us. . . . We are not able to go to God except by passing through these realities, sensible and spiritual at the same time, which are the sacraments, through which the divine sanctifying power is operative.[3]

While this "law" can be clearly seen in many facets of Catholicism, its operation is most vividly seen in the liturgy. "The liturgical world, more than any other aspect of the life of the Church, is the world of the incarnation prolonged, made present, and participated in by men, in the sanctification which God works in the Church and in the worship which the Church renders to God."[4] Divine life is communicated to human beings through such earthly, tangible, and creaturely things as water in the Sacrament of Baptism, the oil of chrism in the Sacrament of Confirmation, and bread and wine in the Eucharist.

To many, it is precisely these incarnational intermediaries that present a stumbling block. *How can bread and wine be the Body and Blood of Christ?* Of course, not only does the incarnational economy embrace things,

---

3. Ibid., 302–3.
4. Ibid., 305.

but also human beings and the very Word of God itself. Therefore, additional questions are asked by many: *Why do I have to confess my sins to a priest? How is it possible to believe, in our modern scientific age, that a process of transmission riddled with complexities and intrigue has inerrantly given us God's Word?* Without hesitation, Vagaggini acknowledges that the liturgy's dependence upon the law of incarnation is deeply challenging, even as it is logically appropriate:

> [T]here remains in the liturgy always the threat of the scandal of the Incarnation: *Nonne hic est filius Ioseph?* Beneath all this humanity does there really lie hidden something divine? Is it really necessary to bind one's own interior freedom to this externalism, this materialism? And if so, what happens to adoration in spirit and in truth? Anyone who so reasons, had the choice been his, certainly would not have chosen the incarnation as the way to redeem the world, and at any rate, not the way of incarnation in the *forma servi*, by which God did in fact appear on earth *in similitudinem hominum factus et habitu inventus ut homo* (Phil 2:7).[5]

Without the ability to see through the sensible elements to the reality within the liturgical life, we can understand the tendency of many to dismiss all things sacramental as centuries-old constructs of the Church hierarchy, *impediments* to coming to know Christ and freely enter into worship of God.

There are clear implications here as we consider our strategies for apprenticing others into a rich sacramental life in Christ. Catechists who desire to help people understand and participate in the Mystery made present by way of earthy words, signs, and gestures must begin with those very words, signs, and gestures! Therefore, the *Catechism* gives us this helpful statement of the method most appropriate to this task: "Liturgical catechesis aims to initiate people into the mystery of Christ . . . by proceeding from the visible to the invisible, from the sign to the thing signified, from the 'sacraments' to the 'mysteries'" (CCC, 1075). Initiation into the mystery of Christ (the aim) is accomplished in liturgical catechesis through the study of sensible sacramental signs (the methodology). The distinctive *modus operandi* of this form of catechesis is always a movement *through* the various ritual elements to a deeper understanding of the divine presence and action.

---

5. Ibid.

Lost in Translation: The Crux of Today's Challenge

If the primary objective of the "liturgical catechist" today is to help guide the faithful into seeing what God is doing in the sacramental action, then our fundamental axiom must become: *from the visible . . . to the invisible!*

Note that we do not begin with a doctrinal statement about transubstantiation or divinization or substance and accidents and then offer examples from sacramental experience to bolster doctrinal teaching. Rather, the catechist must begin concretely with the sacramental experience itself because the signs, symbols, words, and gestures of the liturgy are the door through which we must pass in approaching the mystery. Liturgical catechesis parallels the inductive process employed by any believing liturgical participant, teaching others how to make this important journey "from the sign to the thing signified."

A starting point, then, could be the words of a Eucharistic Prayer, the ritual enveloping the lighting of the baptismal candle, the prayer of absolution in sacramental confession, the action of genuflection, or a tour of the church building that highlights the liturgical art and architecture. Whichever avenue we choose to travel, we move from a reflection upon this concrete and earthy starting point into the reality which is accessible to us by virtue of the sign, word, or gesture.

Yet a serious challenge presents itself. In making this movement "from the sacrament to the mystery" in our catechetical process, we need to make sure to actually arrive in our catechesis at the invisible mystery. There can be a *natural* tendency today to remain on "our side" of the veil of signs and never, or inadequately, move our catechesis into the sphere of the "work of God" on the other side. If we remain in this decidedly *unsupernatural* position regarding the sacraments, those we catechize will not receive what they most need. They also will lose interest quickly and thoroughly.

To illustrate this point, British scholar Petroc Willey invokes a memorable image from the Scottish Presbyterian fiction writer George MacDonald, who wrote:

There is nothing in the outer fact by which man can live, any more than by bread; it needs the poetic eye, illuminating with polarized ray as it pierces, to reveal in the heart of fact its life, that is, its eternal relations.[6]

The problem with some contemporary approaches to liturgical catechesis, explains Willey, is that they have become entrenched in the purely natural dimensions of the sacraments and move only cursorily—if at all—into the divine mystery. He explains that when liturgical catechesis turns away from its properly theological considerations:

> We can remain on the level of what MacDonald has called the "outer fact." But, as he said, there is no life for us there. Neither is there life for those we catechize in such a catechesis. We have been called to proceed from the visible to the invisible, to catechize about the mystery, about the eternal relations, beyond the outer fact.[7]

We remain in this purely natural position when we spend an inordinate amount of time describing what liturgical signs (water, bread, wine, etc.) might mean in our human experience without proceeding to their properly theological meaning. We can also fail to shed light on the supernatural dimension of the liturgy when we attempt to so exhaustively teach the Eucharist (for example) in a brief period of time, that there just isn't enough time to experience what Pope John Paul II called "Eucharistic amazement" (EE, 6).

Making this move from the visible to the invisible in catechesis is a way of immense potential. With conviction and imagination, catechists teaching about the liturgy can lead people into what is most needed for living in the grace of God: a real contemplation of the invisible, supernatural mysteries made accessible in the sacraments.

Is This Too Theological? Two Accounts of How Children Can Teach Us

Some catechists might be tempted to dismiss such an emphasis on divine mystery as being beyond the capacities of today's uncatechized or under-catechized people. Sofia Cavalletti, with her decades of direct catechetical experience with children, would assuredly disagree. She believed the ability

---

6. Petroc Willey, "Editor's Notes: Liturgical Catechesis," *the Sower* 32, no. 4 (October 2011): 4, referencing words from MacDonald's novel *Castle Warlock*, which is cited in A. H. Hyatt, *The Pocket George MacDonald* (London: Chatto and Windus, 1907), 164.

7. Ibid.

to see the invisible by way of the sacramental sign can be acquired by very young children. She writes,

> It is a fact that the child seems capable of seeing the Invisible, almost as if it were more tangible and real than the immediate reality. . . . [C]hildren penetrate effortlessly beyond the veil of signs and "see" with utmost facility their transcendent meaning, as if there were no barrier between the visible and the Invisible.[8]

Such a confident statement about the innate religious capacities of children to see in this sacramental way may strike some as surprising. Isn't this truth about children verifiable in the experience of most of us who spend time with little ones? Cavalletti provides the following two fascinating examples of the profound sacramental vision of which children are capable:

> Bianca (five and a half years old) was mixing flour with yeast, as an exercise relating to the parable that compares the kingdom of God to the yeast that leavens the dough. The catechist asked her to explain to a woman who had come to visit the center what she was doing; Bianca responded: "I am watching how the Kingdom of God grows." A group of children between the ages of six and seven were meditating together with the catechist on Baptism as the participation in the life of the risen Christ. All the children were holding little candles in their hands that had been lit from the paschal candle, symbol of the risen Christ. The catechist wanted to help the children's meditation and spoke about the beauty of that "light" they had received, but Agnese constantly corrected her, saying: "It isn't light; it's goodness," as if the goodness were more visible to her than the light itself.[9]

In another work, Cavalletti suggests that the liturgy's incarnational language is accessible to all—not just the child—and her reasons for this assertion are quite intriguing:

> The language of liturgy—signs or symbols—is one that speaks to the learned and to the unlearned, to adults and to children. It is a language that one both hears and sees; it invites us into an immediate and living contact with the reality presented. It is an allusive language that does not pretend to enclose the Christian mystery within the limits of an enunciation and respects the level of growth of each individual believer. It is a language that attracts us,

---

8. Sofia Cavalletti, *The Religious Potential of the Child: Experiencing Scripture and Liturgy with Young Children*, trans. Patricia M. and Julie M. Coulter (Chicago: Liturgy Training Publications, 1992), 43.
9. Ibid.

I could even say seduces us (Jer 20:7), drawing us to ponder—with eyes, heart and mind —what it is expressing and to marvel in seeing how its content opens onto ever deepening and widening horizons.[10]

For Cavalletti, then, sacramental reality is intelligible (and impactful!) by virtue of its accommodation to the senses, the immediacy in which it places the person into contact with the signified reality, its meaningfulness to people at every developmental level and its profoundly attractive quality, always inviting us to deeper contemplation of the divine mysteries.[11]

Cavalletti is not the only Catholic thinker to carefully consider the potential of the youngest members of the Church to penetrate deeply into the realities signified by sign and symbol. Blessed Marie-Eugene of the Child Jesus, OCD, the founder of the Notre Dame de Vie secular institute in Venasque, France, also expressed confidence in the child's capacity to see through the visible sign into the invisible mystery. His conviction arose from his theological understanding of the baptismal gifts of faith, hope, and charity as well as the gifts of the Holy Spirit, graciously entrusted to the baptized person by God. What happens, he wonders, when these supernatural gifts are engaged by the baptized child, unobstructed by sin—original or personal? This is precisely the graced state of the baptized child who has not yet reached the age of reason.[12] Reflecting

---

10. Sofia Cavalletti, *Living Liturgy: Elementary Reflections*, trans. Patricia M. Coulter and Julie Coulter-English (Chicago: Liturgy Training Publications, 1998), 4–5.

11. It is notable that Cavalletti was familiar with the theological work of Vagaggini. And Vagaggini had such an appreciation for the pioneering catechetical work that Cavalletti was carrying out with children that he wrote the preface to an early book she coauthored on the topic of the liturgy's influence in the catechesis of children (Sofia Cavalletti and Gianna Gobbi, *Teaching Doctrine and Liturgy*, with a preface by Cyprian Vagaggini, OSB [Staten Island, NY: Society of St. Paul, 1964]). Vagaggini's esteem for Cavalletti and Gobbi can ultimately be measured by how he singles them out in his preface for the "excellent contribution" they have made to understanding how best to educate children, naming their contributions in the same paragraph as he identifies the importance of the contributions of Jungmann and the Center of Pastoral Liturgy in Paris on the pastoral-catechetical dimension of the liturgy and Johannes Hofinger, SJ, on the formative value of the liturgy in the missionary context (ibid., Vagaggini, preface, 16–17).

12. Of course, these little ones are not preserved from the *temporal effects* of original sin. The USCCB describes this well: "[By Baptism] though all sins are removed, there remains, as an effect of Original Sin, the inclination to sin that is called concupiscence. This inclination to sin shows itself in what is sometimes referred to as a darkening of the mind and a weakening of the will, that is, the inability to know clearly the right or wrong of an action and/or the lack of strength to resist temptation and always do the right thing no matter how hard this is" (USCCB, *United States Catholic Catechism for Adults* [Washington, DC: USCCB Publishing, 2006], 192). Yet, much remains possible, when it comes to union with God, as Blessed Marie-Eugene points out, for one who is freed from original sin and incapable of personal sin.

upon the seemingly ordinary occurrence of a child being introduced to a visible sign of God's presence in a church and the responsiveness that can sometimes be seen in little ones, Blessed Marie-Eugene describes this reaction in the child as something infinitely more than what it appears to be on the surface.

Here is a little child who is carried to church in his mother's arms. He has been baptized; he is already two or three years old. His intelligence is awakening. His mother shows him the tabernacle and tells him, "Jesus is there." Or, she leads him to the crèche. What does this little one do? He uses his senses. He opens his eyes; his mind is at work. He believes what his mother has told him, he believes that Jesus is there. What will he do? He will put his faith in action. He will blow a kiss to the tabernacle, he will smile at the infant Jesus in the manger. Do you think that this prayer is somehow inferior? He may never pray better in his entire life. He has the grace of baptism and the theological virtues. More than that, he has the gifts of the Holy Spirit. The use of his theological virtues and the gifts of the Holy Spirit is not hampered by all the layers that will come later, caused by selfishness and all the rest, all the sins. We could almost say that his theological virtues and gifts of the Holy Spirit are within easy reach, only skin deep. . . . So in this smile there can be communication with God that is all the more intimate as there are no obstacles, nothing to hinder the free use of the theological virtues, since the child's heart is pure and uncomplicated.

And in response to this smile of the child at the Nativity scene or the tabernacle, a torrent of divine life flows into his soul. This little child has touched the divine fire, the burning bush, the fountain of living water. And this fountain of living water overflows. Why? Because faith has touched it. Just as the sick woman who followed Jesus in the streets of Capernaum found a healing grace simply by touching the hem of his clothing, so will this little child find grace and a singular increase of divine life through this clearly supernatural contact.

Let us not say that this little one's prayer is inferior. His human activity may be limited, for he is doing what he can at his age, but the activity of the life of grace in his soul is already very elevated.[13]

---

13. Marie-Eugene of the Child Jesus, OCD, "La Priere: Contact avec Dieu," (public lecture given to the Religious Sisters of the Cénacle, Bordeaux, France, January 10, 1959), trans. Teresa Hawes. Published in *the Sower* 35, no. 3 (July 2014): 32.

We notice in this remarkable description that a profound exchange takes place precisely through visible, sacramental things such as a tabernacle or a statue of the infant Jesus. The natural instinct of the child to express affection to Jesus through a material intermediary is the starting point of what becomes a supernatural encounter. *By faith, the child moves from the visible to the invisible, through the natural to the supernatural.* And it is important to acknowledge that this contact with God is real; it is truly effected. It is the result of the love of God for the child—and the child's engaging of the theological virtues and the gifts of the Holy Spirit given in sacramental Baptism.

In the mind of Blessed Marie-Eugene, it is precisely this instinct in the child to express love and confidence in God which ought to be recognized, cultivated, and strengthened, beginning at a very young age, through the work of catechesis. He explains: "This education of the youngest, this catechesis given to children, is extremely important. Why? So as to create spiritual reflexes and also because at that age the supernatural life can develop, blossom and act in complete freedom."[14] Blessed Marie-Eugene would certainly concur that a sustained apprenticeship process is needed for the child, and also of course for the child's parents—and any adult! The "spiritual reflexes" needed for encountering God can be learned well in the home and reinforced through the loving presence of catechist-mentors.

These examples from Cavalletti and Blessed Marie-Eugene are provocative. Perhaps the ease with which children see through sign into reality is one reason why the Lord said, "Unless you turn and become like children, you will not enter into the kingdom of heaven" (Mt 18:3). Learning to discover the invisible mystery by way of the sacramental sign is learning a supernatural way of seeing, hearing, speaking, offering, and receiving. This is in deep continuity with the incarnational character of the entire divine pedagogy.

---

14. Ibid. In order to study Marie-Eugene's insights into the exercise of the theological virtues and the gifts of the Holy Spirit as a means of making oneself receptive to God, it is particularly helpful to read chapters 4 ("Mental Prayer") and 5 ("The Good Jesus") of part 1 and chapter 2 ("The Gifts of the Holy Spirit") of part 3 of his text *I Want to See God: A Practical Synthesis of Carmelite Spirituality* (Chicago: Fides Publishers Association, 1953).

The Implication of the Liturgy:
We Are Opened to Others

What about life after the liturgical encounter? How is life's trajectory altered by the transformation God wishes to bring upon us through our participation in the liturgy? Entering into sheer divine love has consequences. The *National Directory for Catechesis* tells us that those living a sacramental life need assistance to "discern the implications of their participation in the liturgy" (110). Pope Francis describes these implications in this way: "The more that you unite yourself to Christ and he becomes the center of your life, the more he leads you out of yourself, leads you from making yourself the center and opens you to others."[15]

The liturgical experience, then, has the potential to reorient us, to change the way we see and live. This encounter with God isn't merely for the sake of being "fed," consoled, or inspired, but ultimately is meant to change our mode of being, so that we will, through our worship and cooperation with grace, "love one another as I have loved you" (Jn 15:12). The liturgy, then, becomes the source for the establishment of a civilization of life and love not only within ourselves but in our homes and parishes—and ultimately in the world.

Therefore, while liturgical catechesis apprentices us into more conscious and active liturgical participation, it also equips us to live a life intensely influenced by the sanctifying act of divine worship. *If we move from the visible to the invisible in liturgical catechesis, we then move back from the invisible to the visible conditions of living the Christian life in the world.* An indispensable objective of mystagogical catechesis, in the mind of Pope Benedict XVI, is "bringing out the significance of the rites for the Christian life in all its dimensions—work and responsibility, thoughts and emotions, activity and repose." He went on to explain, "The mature fruit of mystagogy is an awareness that one's life is being progressively transformed by the holy mysteries being celebrated" (SCa, 64).

Liturgical catechesis, then, places primary emphasis on the encounter with God and the transformative effects of the sacraments. Additionally,

---

15. Pope Francis, *Address of Holy Father Francis to Participants in the Pilgrimage of Catechists on the Occasion of the Year of Faith and of the International Congress on Catechesis*, September 27, 2013, http://www.vatican.va/holy_father/francesco/speeches/2013/september/documents/papa-francesco _20130927_pellegrinaggio-catechisti_en.html, accessed on 11/4/16.

the well-catechized person comes to understand how to integrate the sacramental encounter and graces into the rest of life, ultimately moving into a life of missionary apostolic witness and service.

Pope Francis gave us a helpful image at the 2013 International Catechetical Congress at the Vatican. The Holy Father was describing the connection between centering ourselves in Jesus and taking up our mission to others, which he describes as a characteristic mark in the life of the catechist. These words are certainly applicable more widely to every Christian who, by Baptism, has a vocation to holiness and a call to evangelical mission:

> The heart of a catechist always beats with this systolic and diastolic movement: union with Christ—encounter with others. Both of these: I am one with Jesus and I go forth to encounter others. If one of these movements is missing, the heart no longer beats, it can no longer live. The heart of the catechist receives the gift of the kerygma and in turn offers it to others as a gift. . . . That is the nature itself of the kerygma: it is a gift that generates mission, that compels us to go beyond ourselves. . . . And so it is: love attracts us and sends us; it draws us in and gives us to others. This tension marks the beating of the heart of the Christian.[16]

Life in Christ is distinguished always by these two yearnings in the heart of the Christian: a desire for encounter with God in the sacraments and a longing to express the implications of that divine encounter. Both of these integral movements can be learned through the school of discipleship that is liturgical catechesis.

---

16. Ibid.

CHAPTER 8

Liturgical Catechesis as a School of Discipleship: Apprenticing Skills for Sacramental Living

The day had finally arrived. Our twin daughters were ready and enthusiastic, if admittedly a bit nervous. Frequently over the past two months, they both had expressed longing to know the joy of sacramental reconciliation. By watching the rest of their family frequent the confessional, they knew that this would be a new and beautiful way to meet God.

When we found our seats that April day, the children and their families were presented a choice: go to one of the priests sitting in the sanctuary up front or join a line to go to the priest in the confessional. Mairen jumped enthusiastically into the sanctuary line—even though this meant she would have to go second or third with little preparation time—and Monica made her way to the queue forming outside the confessional, desiring the familiar voice of our pastor and the anonymity of the screen. My wife and I had the great honor of praying very hard for them both and (of course!) peeking at them as they waited in line. Mairen was up first. For the first time that day, she seemed to experience some slight uncertainty as she made the long walk up the steps, behind the altar, to the waiting priest. Soon after, Monica entered the confessional. My wife and I joined hands and prayed earnestly for them both.

Mairen finished first, nearly bounding across the sanctuary to us with an enormous smile. Her sheer joy and excitement overwhelmed us. Monica came out some moments later with a different reaction: her sweet little seven-year-old body was shaking as she sat with us and knelt quietly to pray her penance. As soon as she was done, Mairen looked at us and loudly whispered, "When can we do that AGAIN?" Monica, still a bit shaken from how she had summoned herself for this first confession, smiled and courageously nodded her agreement.

Twin sisters: alike in so many ways and yet clearly distinct in personality and temperament. In taking in their noticeably different reactions, both so lovely to their parents, we were immediately struck by their utter individuality. Their need was also present before my wife and me: with such uniqueness comes a corresponding need for *personal* accompaniment—for mentoring approaches that would resonate with each of them—if they are to enter deeply into a life of sacramental mystery.

Some months earlier, my oldest daughter had just departed the confessional and knelt down beside me. As she was praying her penance, she looked unsettled. After what seemed to be some sort of interior struggle, she leaned into me and said, "Daddy, my penance was to pray three 'Our Fathers.' I can't go three or four words without my mind wandering. What can I do?" Such a great question—and an opportunity for her two primary catechists to step up and offer encouragement based upon our own similar battles.

Assisting others into rich, life-giving experiences of sacramental encounter with God is an awesome privilege and responsibility. As we take on this role—either as parents or catechists—it is helpful to call to mind precisely what they will most need over the course of life. Consciously entering into the sanctifying worship of God in Mass, in each respective sacrament, requires three particular skills. These three—gradually learned through a consistent and patient mentoring process—are vital to liturgical practice becoming personally and communally transformative.

The First Skill: Attuning Ourselves to God

So many great masters of the Christian spiritual tradition have been convinced of this truth: before entering into the place where God is to be encountered, we must quiet our inner distractions and focus ourselves on the Divine Other. Renowned twentieth-century liturgical theologian Romano Guardini wrote:

> Stillness is the tranquility of the inner life, the quiet at the depths of its
> hidden stream. It is a collected, total presence, a being *all there*, receptive,
> alert, ready. There is nothing inert or oppressive about it. . . . If someone
> were to ask me what the liturgical life begins with, I should answer: *with*

learning stillness. Without it, everything remains superficial, vain. . . . [It is] the prerequisite of the liturgical holy act.[1]

As we approach God in the liturgy, we follow the example of Moses, figuratively taking off our sandals in recognition that we are entering "holy ground." Moving into a place of stillness and turning ourselves towards God shows loving respect to God and is spiritually helpful for us, especially those of us with short attention spans!

Back in 2001, I had the extraordinary opportunity to meet St. John Paul II at the end of a Wednesday audience in St. Peter's square in Rome. My heightened anticipation before this meeting was not a disposition that had to be especially willed from within. It came naturally and easily, so that in the hours leading up to this meeting I could think of nothing but what was about to happen. As I stood in line and drew closer, all became still, moving almost in slow motion. I was completely focused on this man who was such a hero to me—to the point that I could not remember whatever eloquent words I had planned to say to him in this once in a lifetime meeting! As a result, I was able to soak up as much of his presence as I could and make a simple expression of my gratitude for his life of sacrificial love. (He responded by putting his hand on my head and giving me a playful—and fatherly—rub of the head!)

With the Unseen God, it can be more challenging. I frequently notice how turned in on my distracted self I can be when approaching God in liturgical prayer. One writer who also admits to struggling against this malady explains the interior struggle in this way:

> My mind is racing and I'm distracted by a thousand little preoccupations.
> By the time the Gospel is finished being read, all too often I realize that
> I hardly heard a word. My response "Praise to you, Lord Jesus Christ,"
> sometimes elicits a silent chuckle as it comes at the end of a stream of
> thoughts that had nothing at all to do with Jesus.[2]

Certainly being overwhelmed in one's own thoughts during the liturgy is a common challenge for most of us today. Something is required of us before the liturgy begins if we are to reach beyond our distractions: a movement towards stillness, towards God. St. Anselm of Canterbury, the great medieval theologian, describes well the twofold action needed

---

1. Romano Guardini, *Preparing Yourself for Mass*, with a foreword by Henri J. M. Nouwen (Manchester, NH: Sophia Institute Press, 1997), 11–12.

2. Robert Kloska, "My Mind Wanders at Mass," *The Catechetical Review* 1, no. 4 (October 2015): 9.

whenever God is approached. While he suggests this way of humble approach to God as important for the study of theology, it also is a useful antidote for today's distracted liturgical participant:

> Come now, insignificant man, fly for a moment from your affairs, escape for a little while from the tumult of your thoughts. Put aside now your weighty cares and leave your wearisome toils. Abandon yourself for a little to God and rest for a little in Him. Enter into the inner chamber of your soul, shut out everything save God and what can be of help in your quest for Him and having locked the door seek Him out (Mt 6:6).
>
> Speak now, my whole heart, speak now to God: "I seek Your countenance, O Lord, Your countenance I seek." (Ps 26:8)[3]

These words encapsulate well what is required of us before the liturgy begins. First we fly from our "affairs" and the "tumult of [our] thoughts" so that we can finally abandon ourselves to God and turn ourselves completely to him. We become smaller so that God might become greater in this encounter with him.

Through the sacraments, it is the God of the universe who is being met, and we "see" him through the gift of faith and through the language of signs by which he communicates. Being able to see in this way is both a gift from God and the result of hard work in training ourselves to look through the signs into the mystery. Perhaps it is on account of this veil of signs that the sacraments require much more inner willpower to move ourselves out of our distractedness and into a place of presence. If we don't take that preliminary step to prepare ourselves for this meeting, it is entirely possible to remain in a position, as Daniella Zsupan-Jerome puts it, of "continuous partial attention"[4] throughout the sacramental encounter. Most of us find ourselves today in a perpetual state of multitasking, and in our worst moments (or even more frequently!) we are only partially present to others. The work of the liturgy, of "seeing" God by way of ritual words and signs, requires our full, conscious, and active attention. If we

---

3. St. Anselm, "Proslogion" in *Anselm of Canterbury: The Major Works*, ed. Brian Davies and G.R. Evans, Oxford World's Classics (New York: Oxford, 1998), 84.

4. Daniella Zsupan-Jerome is, to my knowledge, the first to employ this term within the context of pastoral and liturgical theology. Dr. Zsupan-Jerome's presentation at a symposium sponsored by the University of Notre Dame's Center for Liturgy in 2016 offers some helpful reflections on this reality in the context of liturgical participation. See "Daniella Zsupan-Jerome–'Digital Media and the Liturgical Capacity of the Christian,'" YouTube video, 1:17:57, posted by "ICLnotredame," July 6, 2016, https://www.youtube.com/watch?v=UxbH4y4pt-w.

remain partially immersed in our own inner worlds at the very time when he is fully revealing himself to us and offering us his grace, we run the risk of missing God in the place where he is most present. The potential for transformative liturgy becomes much diminished.

As a gardener does not move too quickly to plant a seed, but is rather first concerned with making the soil fertile and receptive to the seed, so we must first attend to the sometimes infertile soil of the heart, that it becomes a place where the encounter with God may be well received and grow deep roots.

Cyprian Vagaggini, OSB, explains that the liturgy actualizes the whole person, body and soul, directing us to the worship of God and to the reception of God's gift of sanctification.[5] While this is what the liturgy *objectively* does, on the *subjective* level of the individual person, each of us must intentionally allow our full selves to be "actualized" into this great work. We must give ourselves to it. Vagaggini introduces the very helpful idea that we must first "attune" ourselves to the liturgical action into which we enter.[6] Just as a musical instrument must first be tuned to the right pitch before a performance, so we must do the work of attuning ourselves: bringing ourselves into harmony with God's unique presence and gift in the liturgy. Vagaggini warns that "without a certain degree of this attuning, participation in the rites would be empty of any fruit of salvation."[7]

---

5. Cyprian Vagaggini, OSB, *Theological Dimensions of the Liturgy*, trans. Leonard J. Doyle (Collegeville, MN: Liturgical Press, 1976), 312. The author explains it in this way: "It is, in fact, precisely in this perspective of unified totality that the liturgy views man and vitalizes him, in its own way, in the concrete unity of his many-faceted existence; as an individual and social being; body and soul; with all his faculties and activities directed, in the organic unity of the whole, towards being sanctified by God and towards rendering worship to Him under the veil of sensible signs."

6. Because the human person is composed of a body and a soul, there is always both a spiritual and bodily attunement important to the work of liturgical catechesis. Vagaggini's description of how the liturgy attunes the body to the sanctifying act of worship is quite interesting. He suggests that the fulfillment of the obligation to be present at Mass on Sundays and Holydays of Obligation is the first level of bodily attunement. Secondly, the conforming of the body to the various "bodily attitudes" suggested by the liturgical action (such as "genuflections, prostrations, bows, standing erect, striking one's breast, elevating the eyes, joining or elevating one's hands") (313) is another form of acclimation. Vagaggini explains, "It is the whole man who must attune himself to the liturgical action; the attunement of the body is a substantial part of the attunement of the man, in the same way that the body is, along with the soul, a substantial part of the man. Besides, in accord with the laws of psychology, the body and the soul exercise in turn a reciprocal action, so that the bodily attitude is the connatural expression of the internal attitude of the soul" (ibid., 313). This idea of how the body participates in the liturgical prayer which a person offers to God, in union with the Mystical Body of Christ, is important to communicate in the liturgical-catechetical endeavor.

7. Ibid.

Learning to become present to God is not a skill that the liturgy, in itself, teaches. It is, rather, presumed. Beginning a sacramental celebration with the sign of the Cross "calls on the Savior's grace which lets [the Christian] act in the Spirit as a child of the Father" (CCC, 2157), but this first sacred liturgical action is unlikely to have our attention if we are still thinking about other things.

Where, then, is this intentional movement of mind and heart learned? This is a skill that is almost always "coached" outside of the liturgy and "practiced" within it. The coaching happens within the environment of the family and (secondarily) within the catechetical setting. Of course, if a child comes from a family that is not living a vibrant sacramental life—frequently the case today—then the need for developing this ability may fall almost entirely to the Catholic schoolteacher or parish catechist. In these cases, what is intended only as peripheral support sadly takes the primary position of influence. Every catechist in such circumstances can attest to how great today's need is for adult evangelization and lifelong catechesis, for the sake of both parents and children.

Many catechists today might not assume that they should be teaching skills such as these, that their work is more informational than a mentoring process. If the Christian life isn't being apprenticed at home, the catechetical setting in school or parish may be the only remaining opportunity to help children develop the abilities needed to genuinely encounter God both inside and outside of sacramental celebrations.

For catechists, there are many ways we might strengthen these capacities in those we teach. This task must, however, be approached intentionally and strategically. We arrive now at the important question: *What can the catechist do to help participants become increasingly attuned to God?*

The catechist can certainly tell them the significance of this first step before the liturgical encounter, but we can do more by also assisting them *in developing this habit for themselves.*

The instinctual action of attuning ourselves to God's presence in the sacraments is also the exact habit needed within the catechetical setting. God in his Mystery is also accessible (though in a different way) in catechesis. We can be confident in his presence with us every time we enter into catechesis because he is present in his Word and he promised that "where two or three are gathered together in my name, there am I in the midst of them" (Mt. 18:20). Helping our learners recognize God's presence and make contact with him will open them up to his voice and inspiration inside and outside the place of catechesis. In this way, catechesis becomes a training ground for truly encountering God in his unique presence in the sacraments.

Regular practices can be established within the first ten minutes of every catechetical meeting that will move this ideal into a conviction and then into a way of life *whenever* God is approached. I suggest to catechists wherever I go (and they readily agree) that our bedrock conviction should be this: most catechetical participants, as they come through the doors, either don't want to be here or are busy with their own thoughts. Msgr. Francis Kelly describes the essential first objective within catechesis, therefore, to be creating "the conditions for the possibility of a deepening of God's Word in the hearts of those being served."[8] The first ten minutes are vital to establishing the conditions for this possibility. This time must be spent helping them transition from wherever they are as they enter the room to a new position of curiosity (about what you're teaching) and desire for God who is present to them. While games and icebreakers might sometimes be employed with children and teenagers, the purpose of these must be realized: we are helping them be truly present and interested. After helping participants into this place of presence, the climactic movement of any catechetical introduction is the opportunity to enter into prayerful contact with God.

My university students gradually grow in confidence as they learn how to guide others to make this transition. I suggest to them that we not only dedicate the first ten minutes to making this possible, but we additionally help participants attain the habit of doing this for themselves. Therefore, if we take the lead in helping them to prayerfully open themselves to God at the year's beginning, there has to be a gradual weaning process so that catechetical participants become more and more responsible for making this inner movement on their own, independent of the direction and ingenuity of the catechist. The one being apprenticed eventually must come to possess the new ability and have ample opportunities to put it into practice so that it becomes a confident habit.

---

8. Francis D. Kelly, *The Mystery We Proclaim: Catechesis for the Third Millennium*, 2nd ed. (Huntington, IN: Our Sunday Visitor, 1999), 138.

What we do in catechesis is then easily transferable to the liturgy. As our students become more and more confident in exercising their ability to attune to God in catechesis, it becomes a real opportunity to introduce how this skill will serve them well in the liturgy. We can inspire them with our own victories and motivate them towards practicing and strengthening this ability at Mass and in the sacraments. We can discuss with them concrete strategies for how we prepare ourselves for the liturgy. Perhaps we might inspire and motivate them to prayerfully read the Scriptures from the Liturgy of the Word before Mass, spend time in an examination of conscience before going to confession, or turn off the music in the car on the way to the church and spend that time asking God for the gift of sacramental desire and focus. Following such a process, we mentor them towards a less distracted gift of self to God in the liturgy, helping them to be present to God in this new way.

Action Steps for the Catechist

- How can I strengthen *within myself* the habit of cultivating interior stillness and consciously turning myself to God in the moments before the liturgy begins?
- What needs to be done to help those I catechize become less distracted and more focused at the beginning of my catechetical time with them?
- What can I do to give my best to planning prayer, so that we all might encounter God regularly as we begin catechesis?
- After participants become comfortable with regularly transitioning to a place of stillness and presence to God in catechetical prayer, how can I mentor them in developing these abilities themselves?
- What specific opportunities can I give them to practice and strengthen this habit specifically at Mass and in the Sacrament of Reconciliation?

The Second Skill: Uniting Ourselves to God

We might remember from earlier chapters that liturgical catechesis begins with the concrete, with what we receive through our senses in the liturgy, and from there we seek to understand the mystery of God's sacramental presence and action. This new knowledge of the mystery is not meant to be merely theoretical—it ought not remain "at a distance" from our lived experience. Rather, liturgical catechesis prepares us—with this richer vision of the liturgy—to enter more consciously and actively into the divine worship that sanctifies us.

Practically speaking, then, each of chapter 5's theological reference points becomes, through liturgical catechesis, embodied in how we participate in the liturgy. Let's examine how this is so. Good liturgical catechesis shows us (1) how to recognize the presence and action of the Blessed Trinity, (2) that we are "working" as Christ's Mystical Body, (3) that Christ's saving Paschal Mystery is made accessible and is an available source of transformative power, (4) that through Christ we enter into divine worship and that we are being sanctified in this encounter, (5) that we are able to offer something which is tremendously pleasing to God: a priestly sacrifice of every aspect of our lives, and (6) that we depart this encounter with supernatural gifts that can propel us into holiness and a more dynamic living of our respective vocations. Each of these truths about the liturgy, if grasped well in the catechetical context, makes "full, conscious, and active participation" possible and deeply transformative.

In liturgical catechesis, this depth of understanding is reached by way of concrete and "earthy" starting points. The GDC states that the first task of liturgical catechesis is to "explain the contents of the prayers (of the liturgy)" (GDC, 71). This directive provides us some sense of our tangible point of departure, though great care is needed. If those we teach are already bored and disinterested in the liturgy, few words could be spoken by a catechist that would be *less curiosity-inducing* than "I will now spend the next two hours explaining the words of the Mass." The content of liturgical prayer must instead be introduced in a passionate, interesting, and convincing way, in shorter segments rather than all at once, and with primary emphasis on how the liturgy facilitates a transformative encounter with God.

During every catechetical session, the catechist has the opportunity to make frequent liturgical connections. We can recall from chapter 3 Joseph Jungmann's image of the hub and the spokes of the wheel. It was suggested earlier that the kerygma be placed in that central position as the connecting point of each of the spokes, but we also remember that the kerygma is not an abstract formula. The Good News of Christ is made *present* and *accessible* to us most especially in the Mass and other sacramental celebrations—and this is important to the content of Christ's Good News. The catechist who teaches for transformation operates from this kerygmatic-liturgical center. The entire content of teaching is seen through this lens. This means that, no matter what aspect of the faith we are teaching, we can make frequent connections to the celebration of the Paschal Mystery, which is the axis around which revolves the work of the whole Church.[9]

In this light, we can see just how important the sacred words, signs and gestures contained in our liturgical rites are to catechesis. This is particularly true for every kind of sacramental preparation. To be ready to meet the Blessed Trinity, the person preparing to receive a sacrament for the first time needs a robust contact with the language of the rite.

When I first began working as a parish catechetical leader in 1989, there was a notable omission in our confirmation preparation process, a problem that I came to see only many years later as I began to study the connections between the liturgy and catechesis. We prepared our sixteen-year-olds to understand what Confirmation is and to learn more about Christ and the Church more broadly. However, when it came to the actual Confirmation rite, this was our approach: On the Wednesday before the bishop came to confirm them, we would arrange a rehearsal of the cere-mony. After lining everyone up and showing them where they were to sit, we would "practice" every segment of the rite where they had to say or do something, so that they would be comfortable with their "parts." And so, we rehearsed the reading of the Scriptures during the Liturgy of the Word and the renewal of baptismal promises. We then practiced what would happen when they processed forward to the bishop: after receiving the anointing with sacred chrism on the forehead with the words, "N., be sealed with the Holy Spirit," the bishop's hand would be received in a hand-shake, responding to his "N., peace be with you" with "And with your spirit." As we walked through all of the externals of the rite—all the words to say and gestures to do—we spent no time at all explaining the sacred meaning

---

9. A similar argument was advanced in SC, 16, regarding the liturgical connections which ought to be made in the teaching of other theological subjects in seminaries and religious houses of study. The Council Fathers wrote, "Those teaching other subjects should expound the Mystery of Christ and the history of salvation in a manner which will clearly set forth the connections between their subjects and the liturgy. . . . " If this is true for the formation received in seminaries and religious houses of study, would not it also follow that such a liturgical connectivity within the Christian message also be preserved and practiced in the catechesis of the faithful, whether in parishes or Catholic schools?

of these words and actions. We stayed completely at the level of the sign, without any real movement into the mystery. We had thought it sufficient to teach what Confirmation is and left no time to help them understand the meaning of the ritual and *how* it is an encounter that strengthens.

The same scenario unfolds at many wedding rehearsals today. It is of course important that bride and groom are familiar with where they are to stand and kneel, and what words they say during the ritual. However, if the wedding rehearsal is the first time that they hear the words of the vows they are to exchange the next day—and if no real attention is drawn in their preparation to the language of the Nuptial Blessing which is the epiclesis of the sacrament—this is a very real problem. The wedding Mass may end up being beautiful and stirring, but if bride and groom aren't prepared to understand the sacramental meaning of the wedding Mass and the unique gift that God makes of himself through this sacrament, the language of the full rite of marriage will remain at arm's length, not embraced and intelligently willed by those entering the sacrament. The Rite of Marriage, then, risks being understood on a purely natural level—as a public celebration of natural human love. Human love is, of course, beautiful and profound, but something *infinitely* marvelous is available here.

The words of the Nuptial Blessing, in fact, reveal to us the most significant reason why men and women who choose marriage ought to seriously consider joining themselves in *sacramental* marriage. A portion of the Nuptial Blessing reads:

> Look now with favor on these your servants,
> joined together in Marriage,
> who ask to be strengthened by your blessing.
> Send down on them the grace of the Holy Spirit
> and *pour your love into their hearts,*
> that they may remain faithful in the Marriage covenant.
> (*Roman Missal*, Nuptial Blessing; emphasis added)

Many today, if they are even paying attention to the words of the Nuptial Blessing, might see these ritual words as pretty embellishments, flowery ornamental language intended to lend an air of sacredness and dignity to a religious ceremony. In fact, we know that the language of the liturgy beautifully expresses the meaning of what is effected in the sacrament. In the words of the Nuptial Blessing, we see that God's life-giving love enters into the love between husband and wife. Their human love becomes (on the objective theological level) accompanied and transformed by divine love. They become capable of drawing not only on their own natural resources for love and fidelity to one another, but they can now depend upon the infinite power of pure divine love. The *Catechism of the Catholic Church* luminously describes this divine gift given to man and woman in this sacrament:

> Christ dwells with them, gives them the strength to take up their crosses and so follow him, to rise again after they have fallen, to forgive one another, to bear one another's burdens, to "be subject to one another out of reverence for Christ," and to love one another with *supernatural*, tender and fruitful love. (CCC, 1642)

Sacramental preparation, then, is a singular opportunity to be equipped with "eyes to see and ears to hear," so that we can enter consciously into the sacramental encounter with God—to give and receive in the ways that each respective sacrament makes possible. The catechist who prepares others to receive sacraments—no matter if parents are being prepared for their child's Baptism or seminarians are being instructed on what they will experience as they receive the Sacrament of Holy Orders—must see the sacramental rite itself as a primary catechetical source. Often this will mean moving beyond a provided textbook or lesson plan and accessing resources that contain the words of the sacramental rite. The rite can then be explained in such a way that the core ability they come to possess is this: the skill of seeing, touching, speaking, tasting, and even smelling in a sacramental way. Their liturgical catechesis prepares them so that this axiom has settled into their bones: what we perceive through the senses indicates what is taking place spiritually, invisibly, supernaturally. Our objective is that they come to affirm that (even if they wouldn't use these particular words):

> In the supernatural world of grace, our human faculties lead us to a mystagogical encounter with Christ. With our physical eyes we see bread, and yet with our mystagogical sight we see the body, blood, soul and divinity of Christ. With our bodily ears we hear the choir, and yet on account of our mystagogical hearing we listen to the choir of angels. With our mouths we speak to God, yet with our mystagogical voices we join the Mystical Voice in praise of God. The mystagogical encounter begins with what is perceptible

and leads us deeper into the invisible reality, which is Christ. In order to listen and speak with the Church we must acquire supernatural faculties, so that we can be led [*agogue*] into the mystery [*mystes*].[10]

As necessary as this liturgical-catechetical mindset is for sacramental preparation, it is equally important for every other form of catechesis. As the summit and font of the Catholic faith, the re-presentation of the Paschal Mystery cannot be confined to those content units specifically dedicated to the liturgy. Rather, we catechists, teaching whatever catechetical subject, can ask ourselves: how can I make apparent the connections of what I am teaching to the sacramental life? How is this truth expressed and empowered through God's gift of himself in the liturgy?

For example, if we find ourselves teaching about sin and grace, we might choose to catechetically "unpack" the words of an act of contrition or the prayer of absolution from the Rite of Penance. We could also teach from the Scriptures and collects from the Ash Wednesday Mass or Divine Mercy Sunday.

Presuming our learners participate in these sacramental celebrations, how could teaching from the language of the rites be to their good? Catechetical participants will experience two immediate benefits to this liturgical-catechetical approach. First, if they have some familiarity with the sacramental language from which we draw, we will be helping them to better understand something with which they are already familiar. Every educator knows the value of helping learners more deeply comprehend what they already know. These are tremendous "light bulb moments" where we really "get it" for perhaps the first time.

There is a second and even more important benefit. The next time they participate in this sacrament, they will remember what they've learned and the sacrament will more likely become accessible to them, an encounter. As they hear those beautiful words of absolution wash over them in sacramental confession, they can increasingly give and receive in the sacrament because they will remember the marvelous unbinding and restoration these words indicate. A transformative encounter with God in His mystery has become much more likely. This sacrament will then assume its full conversion-inducing power in the lives of our students as they become more confident in what they've learned: the ability to unite

10. Carstens and Martis, *Mystical Body, Mystical Voice*, 67.

themselves to God through a deeply personal embrace of the language of the liturgy.

While the language of the rites—expressed in both word and sign—is an important source for liturgical catechesis, we can immediately see how dependent we are upon other resources. The Word of God remains primary to liturgical catechesis, as we can only understand liturgical actions in their important relation to the *narratio* of salvation history. Magisterial sources are also useful to us in their unique ability to authoritatively convey the mind of the Church regarding the meaning of sacramental rites. The introductory documents that accompany each liturgical rite—such as the *Rite of Christian Initiation of Adults* text or the introduction to the *Rite of Confirmation*—offer helpful theological insights for the catechist. In addition, this generation of catechists possesses a great gift in the *Catechism of the Catholic Church*, which is characterized by, among other qualities, a liturgically oriented style of communication.

While every person might be able to partially interpret the liturgy through his or her own subjective experiences, there is objective meaning to liturgical words and signs. Drawing upon those sources which authoritatively articulate the faith of the Church in regards to the liturgy is eminently valuable.

Of course, the twentieth and twenty-first centuries have produced theologians of the highest caliber, whose historical and biblical studies of the liturgy have richly complemented magisterial reflections on the meaning of the liturgy. So many works have been written that can help catechists grow in their own understanding and love for the liturgy, thereby helping them become better teachers at the same time.[11]

Action Steps for the Catechist

- How can I draw from the content of liturgical rites—through concrete words, signs, symbols, and gestures—as a source in my catechetical planning? How can I move "from the visible to the invisible," that is, from what we can perceive through the senses to the unseen reality?

---

11. My favorite titles, wonderfully accessible even if just beginning one's theological education, include: Jean Daniélou, SJ, *The Bible and the Liturgy* (Notre Dame, IN: University of Notre Dame Press, 1956), Blessed Columba Marmion, OSB, *Christ in His Mysteries* (Bethesda, MD: Zaccheus Press, 2008), Romano Guardini, *Sacred Signs* (St. Louis: Pio Decimo Press, 1956), and Scott Hahn, *The Lamb's Supper: The Mass as Heaven on Earth* (New York: Doubleday, 1999).

- What frequent connections can I make to the Eucharist and the sacraments, so that those I teach come to see what is the summit and font of their Christian life?

- What can I do to give testimony, from my own experience, to how the actions of God in the liturgy are revealed by what we perceive with our senses? How can I introduce the testimonies of others in the parish? The witness of the saints?

- If I help prepare people for receiving a sacrament, how can I dedicate time to helping them actively and intelligently participate in the ritual celebration?

The Third Skill: Cooperating with the Grace of God

Today's Catholics must come to see that the eternal exchange of love in which we participate has accompanying supernatural effects. These effects are what the sacrament objectively accomplishes, and they are worthy of our wonder and close consideration.

St. John Paul II once told young people, in his 2001 World Youth Day message, that "through baptism, our whole being has been profoundly changed."[12] We can discover the nature of this change that God wishes to accomplish in us by turning through the pages of the *Catechism of the Catholic Church* in its description of the effects of Baptism. All of our sin is forgiven. We are reborn, becoming adopted children of the Heavenly Father. We become "partakers of the divine nature" (2 Cor 5:17), members of Christ's Mystical Body and temples of the Holy Spirit (CCC, 1263–65). With creativity and passion, catechists can help contemporary people marvel before the work that God is doing in us through this sacrament. Each of these effects may be pondered and unpacked, to the great benefit of those we catechize.

What is God doing in the sacrament, and how is it coming to fruition in us? These questions absorb those engaged in mystagogical reflection. Those weeks immediately following the reception of a sacrament are the particularly important time to consider the reality of what we have received. The sacraments are not magic, and their effects do not

---

12. John Paul II, "Message of the Holy Father to the Youth of the World on the Occasion of the XVII World Youth Day," July 25, 2001, 2.

automatically impact how we live. For these effects to be fruitful for the person and the world, the sacramental recipient must knowingly receive and cooperate with sacramental grace. This important aspect of each person's fruitful reception of grace is, unfortunately, rarely spoken of today. Sherry Weddell puts it well:

> In recent decades there has been little or no serious discussion at the parish level about how an individual receiving the sacraments can prepare his or her heart, soul, and life to do so fruitfully. Nor do we dream about the amazing things God would do in our midst if the lives of our people were characterized by great spiritual fruitfulness. A Church that understands itself as possessing the "fullness of the means of grace" must yearn for the fullness of the manifestation of that grace.[13]

Such a manifestation will come about only as we recognize that something of immense value has been imparted in the sacrament—a share in God's life and power—and as we then summon ourselves to will its purposes. Following the way of the One who calls us into his reckless generosity is a great adventure. By the grace of God and each person's *fiat*, sacramental living becomes a transformative process in which we are working with God in us, growing towards the perfection of love.

Through liturgical catechesis—and in particular, mystagogy—we are invited to become what we have received, to embrace the sacramental momentum that will see us conformed more and more to our Model of Holiness, Christ our Lord. The catechist serves those receiving sacraments by apprenticing them into a divinely empowered living of their Christian discipleship in the world.

The great work of fashioning our lives into the new creation we are becoming through the sacraments is God's work in us and our work in God. This deeper configuration to Christ is not only an effect—it is also at least implicit in the very logic of sacramental participation. Cyprian Vagaggini helps us to see that liturgical participation presumes a certain willingness not only to enter into the worship and sanctification of the Mystical Body of Christ, but also to live in ways that are consistent with the liturgical encounter. In the liturgical action, we conform ourselves to the prayer of the whole Church—the Head and members of Christ's

---

13. Sherry Weddell, *Forming Intentional Disciples: The Path to Knowing and Following Jesus* (Huntington, IN: Our Sunday Visitor, 2012), 98–99.

Mystical Body—so that in this act, our own wills gradually align with the will of Christ. Vagaggini explains that this alignment of our wills also contains within it a certain "moral obligation for the future." Liturgical participation first presupposes that we intend to live in a way which "corresponds to the requirements of the new mode of being received in the sanctifying act." Second, we freely oblige ourselves, *by the act of worship itself, to live* "as God's pre-eminence and our submission require." In summarizing this idea of the liturgy's moral obligation, Vagaggini writes, "Every liturgical act, therefore, in which man receives sanctification and renders his worship to God, involves an engagement, an obligation freely assumed for the future, an implied oath."[14] How we live becomes deeply affected by what we do—and what God does—in the liturgy. Just as the marriage rite has implications for the lived relationship between man and woman (and also their relationship to God) so too does the Mass and every other sacrament have implications for how we love God, love other people, and understand every facet of our lives.

The whole point of full, conscious, and active liturgical participation is our holiness of life. If a parish does not offer postsacramental mystagogical reflection, a great inconsistency is evident. We have, in this situation, a group of people who have received supernatural gifts—but there is no structured assistance for them to learn how to employ these gifts, how they might become fruitful. They are left to their own devices to try to figure out how to live this new life in Christ. Of course, without an insistence by catechists and liturgists that something is different as a result of receiving the sacrament, that they have new supernatural capacities, many will presume that nothing has actually changed. The reception of the sacrament becomes in these cases a ceremony with no accepted theological meaning, only the meaning derived from their subjective familial and cultural experience. In the case of the Sacrament of Confirmation in particular, the sacramental celebration then becomes for young people a "graduation" from catechesis.

Very few parishes today offer postsacramental catechesis, due to a lack of resources and catechists. Choosing to offer mystagogical catechesis for neophytes receiving any of the sacraments is a courageous decision, as it runs contrary to the accepted culture in most parishes. The

---

14. Vagaggini, *Theological Dimensions*, 71.

transformative experience of such a neophyte process that emphasizes the divine encounter and newly received objective supernatural gifts creates an opportunity for increased evangelistic flourishing. With a greater possibility of a life-changing liturgical-catechetical experience, every other dimension of parish life will be positively influenced.

If a parish were to accompany sacramental neophytes through this "sensitive period" in the life of grace, two sources would be particularly important. First, mystagogical catechists can draw from the language of the sacramental celebration, as it is this exact experience that is to be more deeply pondered and understood. Second, mystagogy is a place where neophytes must hear from those who have experience identifying and living in sacramental grace. Much rests here on the testimony of real people who can give voice to what it looks like to live from the grace of the sacrament. In a mystagogy for matrimony, for example, there is no substitute for very real married couples (representative, ideally, of different stages of married life) sharing how they are able to draw upon matrimonial grace during arguments, crises, temptations, sorrows, general busyness, and great joys. It's one thing to be taught that the love of Christ is present in a new way through this sacrament; it's another to have numerous concrete examples of what this looks like in real people's lives. With such testimonies, we can begin to envision it in our own unique circumstances. This is a form of catechesis that would be compelling—and potentially quite effective in apprenticing couples through the first years of marriage, which can be challenging for many. In postsacramental catechesis, therefore, we can confidently root ourselves, and our fellow brothers and sisters in parish life, within Pope Paul VI's timeless wisdom: "modern man listens more willingly to witnesses than to teachers, and if he does listen to teachers it is because they are also witnesses" (EN, 41).

Action Steps for the Catechist

- How can I both teach and bear witness to the life-changing effects of the sacraments?
- How can I emphasize the need to cooperate with sacramental grace, so that God's gifts may become fruitful and transformative?

- What can I do to become a mentor for those I teach so that they can see the real-life implications of sacramental grace for how we live, especially for how we love God and love other people?

- How can frequent testimony be provided—from my experience, that of other parishioners, and the lives of the saints—to the wondrous fruits of the Holy Spirit which come from consciously living out of our sacramental grace?

These three skills, learned in liturgical catechesis, can deeply influence the quality of our liturgical experience. The skill of preparing ourselves helps us to be attuned to the presence and action of God. The art of uniting ourselves to the words and signs of the liturgy enables us to offer true worship to God and to be sanctified through his gift of divine grace. And, finally, that ability to identify and cooperate with the supernatural effects of the sacraments empowers us to grow in holiness and to reach out to others in acts of evangelization and loving service.

As we grow in our mastery of these abilities, something extraordinary begins to take place. We become less dependent on the homilist's ability to inspire us, the musician's ability to move us, and the congregation's capacity to befriend us. These features of the liturgical experience are, of course, terribly important and worthy of our greatest investment for the good of our people. But if we are strong in these three liturgical skills, we can worship God and experience his sanctifying power, even when these sometimes unpredictable aspects of how the liturgy is celebrated are less to our liking. The problem of Catholics falling away once a beloved pastor retires, or upon moving to a new parish that "just isn't the same," becomes less prevalent because of such apprenticeship. We become more active in the liturgical encounter—becoming responsible agents whose transformative encounter with God depends less and less on the personal qualities and talents of our liturgical ministers and more on our seeking out the presence and action of the Divine Liturgist.

In my own experience when I was a teenager, I loved attending our vibrantly engaging Sunday evening Mass, with inspiring and relevant homilies and music that spoke to my soul. But it was only when I began also attending simple daily Mass that I learned to take more personal responsibility for praying the Mass. I tried to arrive five minutes early to prepare myself. I strove to keep my mind focused on the words I heard and those I spoke. I worked to allow those words to move in and out of my heart so that I really meant them and received them with my full being. Throughout this important period in my sacramental formation, the mentoring I received from kindly people experienced in the art of liturgical prayer has ended up making all the difference.

As we can see, when liturgical catechesis is envisioned as an apprenticeship, helping people to both see and participate in the sacramental life in new ways, it becomes a school in the way of discipleship. These three abilities—important to how we prepare for, enter into, and depart the liturgy more responsive to our missionary vocation—form the most vital "content" of this school. We move now into the third part of this book, featuring chapters written by four experienced catechetical leaders. These next four chapters will shed light on how children, teenagers, and adults can grow in these abilities through how we conceptualize and carry out our age-specific liturgical catechesis.

PART III

Emerging Practices:
What It All Means for
Parish Liturgical Catechesis

In drawing this book to a conclusion, it would be helpful to envision in concrete terms how liturgical catechesis can be a school of transformative discipleship for people of different ages. I have asked four catechetical leaders, widely respected for their dedicated work in the field, to describe how they see fruitful liturgical catechesis unfolding today. You will hear ringing through their reflections a confidence in the presence of God in the sacraments, deep respect for those in need of catechesis, and a commitment to accompanying learners as they discover the divine encounter possible in the liturgy.

Sr. Hyacinthe Defos du Rau, OP, and Come Follow Me. It was in 2011 that I first witnessed a demonstration of a new method of children's catechesis, Come Follow Me, created by several members of the French secular institute Notre Dame de Vie (Our Lady of Life). I found it deeply stirring. Perhaps it was their reverence for Scripture, using it so beautifully and wisely with children. Or maybe it was the profound respect shown for the freedom of children—offering choices to them at important catechetical moments—which so delicately allows desire for God to flourish. The way that these catechists prayed with children demonstrated absolute confidence that God is present and wants to encounter both children and catechists in the communion of prayer.

In 2013, I was able to visit Notre Dame de Vie in Venasque and observe ten-year-old children in a French school learning about the angels through Come Follow Me. I was amazed to see their depth of silent prayer and the penetrating conversation that ensued as their catechist taught the children about angels by opening the scriptures to them.

Sr. Hyacinthe Defos du Rau, OP, who has translated the catechist guides into English, has graciously written chapter 9. Born in France and now living in the United Kingdom, there is no English-speaking person who knows this method better than Sr. Hyacinthe. In this chapter, she describes many important connections between the themes we have examined thus far and the sacramental approaches in Come Follow Me. Every catechist of young children wants to stimulate desire for prayer and the sacraments in today's learners. Come Follow Me has a unique charism for precisely this vital work.

Mary Mirrione and the Catechesis of the Good Shepherd. I first experienced this striking method of children's catechesis in my home parish where I worked as a youth minister in the early 1990s, when we transitioned our children's program to Catechesis of the Good Shepherd. Many years later, my wife Kate and I were blessed to take the first week of level-one training (for children aged 3–6) with Mary Mirrione. We were both taken aback not only by the richness of the method, but the holiness and kindness of our training leader.

I highly esteem the ideals of Sofia Cavalletti, the Italian founder of Catechesis of the Good Shepherd. She has taught us how to create a catechetical environment where wonder and awe can be cultivated in children. In what is called "the atrium," the Church's doctrinal depository is deeply reverenced and studied in age-appropriate ways, with scripture and the liturgy receiving particular emphasis. This method helps children to *contemplate and enjoy* the beautiful riches of what we all have received from Christ through the Church, meeting a deep need in their souls.

With wonderfully concrete language, Mary explores how Catechesis of the Good Shepherd sees catechesis, as Sofia Cavalletti described, as the meeting of two mysteries: the Mystery of God and the mystery of the child. This vision for catechesis beautifully influences how the sacraments—and so many other aspects of the faith—are presented to children.

Jim Beckman and Youth Discipleship. When it came to a chapter focused on liturgical catechesis and teenagers, knowing how the broader book would value the importance of apprenticeship, I was so pleased when Jim Beckman agreed to write this chapter. Jim is one of today's foremost trailblazers in articulating a Catholic discipleship process for teenagers through relational youth ministry. For many Catholic pastoral leaders today, this concept of apprenticeship is new territory and a daunting enterprise. For those beginning or persevering in this process, Jim Beckman is a reliable guide. He draws upon over thirty years of experience in youth ministry, many of them as an important voice in the youth ministry movement in the United States. His understanding of how to disciple teenagers is rooted in his own familiarity and success in establishing discipleship-based youth ministries in parishes.

Jim explains well what a mentoring process looks like that accompanies teenagers towards fruitful sacramental participation. For those who know Jim or have heard him speak, you will not be at all surprised that he places enormous importance on encouraging parents in their role as primary mentors for their children in the faith. Youth ministers and most other catechists know well the Church's assertion that parents are their children's primary catechists. Perhaps one of Jim's greatest contributions to this book is how he describes what can be done to empower parents to take up this most decisive responsibility.

William J. Keimig and the RCIA. In addition to being an exceptional writer, Bill Keimig brings with him a wealth of experience with the RCIA. Bill spent fifteen years investing himself into one parish community in southern Maryland as director of religious education. In that capacity, he guided many candidates and catechumens through the rites and into mystagogy. At the same time, having served for nine years as director of the Association for Catechumenal Ministry, he also had the opportunity to work with numerous RCIA leaders and catechists on an international level. Drawing upon this varied background, Bill is uniquely positioned to describe the potential of liturgical catechesis within today's catechumenal process.

Bill's chapter fits well at the end of this third section of the book not only because he is writing about the oldest age group. His compelling wisdom regarding our personal witness of the liturgy is among the most helpful convictions that could be remembered from this book. He writes: "In my experience, the only effective way to do liturgical catechesis in an RCIA context is as a *personal witness*." He then describes how necessary it is for RCIA catechists to see clearly their deep need for what the liturgy gives—and to live from this need. It is when adults find other adults living from the Paschal Mystery that liturgical catechesis is most likely to be welcomed and desired. This supremely important idea forms the many other helpful insights of his chapter, whether he is describing how RCIA catechesis can best prepare for the threshold ritual celebrations along the way or that the liturgy is the "glue" of conversion within the process. No matter what age group you serve, Bill's chapter will be both challenging and encouraging.

One note is perhaps in order, particularly with chapters 9 and 10, as they are based on specific catechetical *programs*. No program or approach is flawless, and the quality of a program's implementation will sometimes widely vary from parish to parish. When catechists are trained to employ particular methods, much depends upon the level of the catechist's understanding and receptivity to what is heard. Additionally important is the specific trainer's embrace of the vision and content of the founding writer(s) and the trainer's ability to communicate it well. These issues are potentially more relevant with Catechesis of the Good Shepherd as the program's content is not set down in a published text, opting instead for a beautiful oral transmission process in training sessions. I have a depth of respect for both of these approaches to children's catechesis and believe they have much to recommend to us. The authors of chapters 9 and 10 are exceedingly conversant with the ideals underpinning their respective methods. They have done a wonderful job describing and applying these methods as they were originally set forth by their visionary architects.

It is my hope that all of these four chapters prove helpful and energizing to readers no matter their background or which catechetical models they currently employ. Each writer shares incredible insights that are constructive across a broad spectrum of catechetical models and even age levels. I want to express my deepest gratitude to Sr. Hyacinthe, Mary, Jim, and Bill for all that they've poured into these chapters. I am excited for readers, who have an opportunity to reflect with them on the great potential of liturgical catechesis today.

CHAPTER 9

Come Follow Me: A New Model for Children's Catechesis

Sr. Hyacinthe Defos du Rau, OP

"I want to be baptized!" "I want to receive the forgiveness of Jesus!" "I want to receive Jesus in Holy Communion!" These are the beautiful and compelling words of real children who have experienced deep sacramental desire in their parishes and schools through the Come Follow Me catechetical program.[1] These little ones have been helped to understand the truths of the Faith and enter into the life of the Church. More than this, Come Follow Me has also awakened in the children a personal desire for communion with God, opening the way for the movement of God's grace. These children are able to freely develop, at an individual level, their own interior life of prayer and intimacy with God.

Come Follow Me was born in France, from within the Notre Dame de Vie Institute based in Venasque, in the heart of Provence. Over the past thirty years, members of Notre Dame de Vie, priests and lay persons, have devoted themselves to the catechesis of children in the light of their own Carmelite spirituality and under the inspiration of their founder, Blessed Marie-Eugene of the Child Jesus, OCD.[2] In 2007, the fruit of their labor, the Come Follow Me program, began to be published in French. The program is used throughout France and is spreading to other parts of the world for the catechesis of children aged seven to eleven. The catechists' guidebooks

---

1. As evidenced in the research I conducted in 2009–2010, asking twenty-eight catechists and teachers from France and abroad to evaluate the impact of Come Follow Me in the children's sacramental, moral, and prayer life: Sr Hyacinthe Defos du Rau, OP, *How Can Catechesis Awaken Desire for God*—master's dissertation submitted for Maryvale Institute, United Kingdom, 2010. Subsequent quotes from French catechists will be taken from this research.

2. In particular, Noëlle Le Duc, who first designed and refined the pedagogy over the course of many years, and Fr. Benoit Caulle and Anne-Marie Le Bourhis, who authored the complete program for seven- to eleven-year-old children between 2007 and 2011.

are currently being translated into English and are beginning to be used in England, Ireland, and the United States.

During four essential years of ongoing catechesis, Come Follow Me aims to awaken and nourish the children's interior life of faith, hope, and charity in communion with Jesus, under the breath of the Holy Spirit, in the family of the Church. This comes about through the following essential elements: (1) the proclamation of the Word of God understood in and through the Church's faith, (2) the centrality of prayer, (3) a respect for the freedom of the children, and (4) a systematic doctrinal and liturgical structure. After briefly describing these four elements as a general orientation to the program, we will discover several important liturgical features of Come Follow Me. While this catechetical model is not a sacramental preparation program, it integrates a rich liturgical vision into how children are formed in the Faith. We will finally consider three distinct pastoral settings in which this program has been utilized in order to better understand its potential amidst today's challenges in catechizing children.

The Proclamation of the Word of God

In the Come Follow Me program, Holy Scripture does not merely provide an illustration of the teaching, or even an introduction to prayer. It is the essential, unadulterated text of each catechetical session. The catechist's role is to proclaim the Word of God from the Bible, explain it from the faith of the Church, and help the children enter into its life-giving depths.

After providing a clear and simple introduction and then inviting them to turn their hearts and minds to God in prayer, we open the Word of God. The catechist does not read the entire Scripture passage all at once, but rather pauses after certain words or sentences to enter into dialogue with the children about the literal and spiritual meaning of the text. This allows the children to keep their focus and to grow in their own understanding of Scripture by giving them time to ponder and freely ask questions related to the text. Through this approach, the children receive the content of the Catholic Faith through the Scriptures themselves. The richness of Catholic doctrine becomes, in this way, *scripturally driven*. This preparation and proclamation of the Word of God, including the doctrine taught alongside the Scriptures, is all presented in the catechist's guidebooks.

An accompanying visual component is also vital to the program, helping the children to "see" the Scriptures by way of beautiful card silhouettes (see figure 9.1) that have been designed to accompany the catechesis. Each session's silhouettes are presented on a wooden stand—with horizontal and vertical features that help the children gain a sense of the transcendence of God and of his action in the world. This visual arrangement is one of the most immediately striking aspects of Come Follow Me. As Scripture is proclaimed, the catechist often carefully moves the silhouettes with the story, helping the children more deeply take in and ponder what they are hearing. These silhouettes also serve as signs and symbols of an interior attitude that the children are invited to adopt, rather than as mere illustrations of the Bible narrative.

Once a group of children entered a room where the silhouette of Moses—praying before the burning bush—was displayed. The children had never before experienced a Come Follow Me session. Some of the children stayed, faced the silhouettes, and adopted the same attitude as Moses, bowing to the ground and spending some time in worship of the name of God displayed above the bush. The silhouettes used in this program are powerful visual tools that invite the children to openness of heart and interior receptivity.

Below is an example taken from a Come Follow Me catechist's book for seven-year-old children, which includes guidelines and suggestions for the catechists, integrating visual learning and moments of silence to give the children time to interiorize the Word of God. This extract shows the opening sentences for session 22, on the Our Father, and illustrates the prayerful, experiential setting for the proclamation of the few words of Scripture which the children are invited to receive and ponder in faith.

"Let us prepare our hearts. Let us listen to the Word of Jesus."

Moment of silent prayer

The catechist will have prepared the figures of the apostles and the name "Lord."

Then the figure of Jesus praying is put in place, without explanation. This is done with quiet background music. After a moment of silence, the catechist reads:

Figure 9.1: Our Father silhouette

"One day, Jesus was praying in a certain place."

Moment of silence, and then "When he had finished, one of his disciples said to him,"

The catechist places the sentence: "Lord, teach us to pray" and asks the children:

"Do you understand what is happening?"

Let the children reflect.

"Why do the apostles ask Jesus to teach them to pray?"

"They already know how to pray to God! But when they see Jesus praying, the apostles understand that this is something new. They would like to be ableto pray like Jesus."

Jesus is going to fulfil their great desire.

The catechist turns the music on again and places the word "Father" on top of the word "Lord."

Then the words of Jesus are read:

"When you pray, say this: "Father . . ."

The catechist stops the music and leaves a moment of silence in order to allow the children to read the name "Father" and to take it in.

The apostles never imagined that we could call God *"Father."*

The session continues with a doctrinal lesson on God our Creator, who is also our Father and invites us to become his children in Baptism. The first notions of interior prayer are then presented from Scripture to the children, who are invited to remain silently in prayer, in the presence of their Father, at the end of the session.

The Centrality of Prayer

Since the aim of the program is to awaken the children's interior life, prayer is at the heart of Come Follow Me. A dearly held conviction on the part of Come Follow Me catechists is that children are capable of genuine prayerful contact with God. This is no pious platitude; rather it may be seen in the opportunities accorded to prayer in each session.

We begin every session with a quiet moment of recollection and invocation of the Holy Spirit before listening to the Word of God. When encountering deep mysteries in the Scriptures that are difficult to understand, the catechist may pause and invite the children into prayer so that we can gain insight into the mystery. The period of discovery and understanding of the Word then ends with common prayer, which is always prolonged in a free time of silent, personal prayer. Children may remain in this place of prayer as long as they wish.

The care and time devoted to prayer in this methodology are substantial. The time we spend in prayer allows the proclamation of the Word to bear fruit in a free, interior encounter with God.

Respect for the Interior Freedom of Children

The pedagogy used in Come Follow Me emphasizes respect for the interior freedom of the child. Come Follow Me gives the children the necessary education and the time to make their own free response of faith and love in receiving the Word of God, in approaching the sacraments, and in living, through grace, the life of the children of God. This education in freedom and responsibility is all the more crucial in a context where adherence to Christian faith and morals cannot rely anymore on the influence of culture, society, or even the family. This adherence has to be personal, even on the part of children and at their own level. This aspect is what makes Come Follow Me not merely a catechetical program, but an opportunity for evangelization as well.

This respect is particularly evident in how we pray with the children. Sessions take place in two distinct areas: a "place of meeting with each other" and a "place of meeting with God." If it is not possible for these areas to be located in separate rooms, then two spaces within the same room can be created. While the "place of meeting with each other" is an area arranged with tables and chairs, facilitating group work and exchanges in small groups around a table, the "place of meeting with God" is arranged simply and beautifully, focused on a display of silhouettes and candles around which the children are invited to sit silently. Each session ends with a time of common prayer led by the catechist and provided in the book. This time of prayer leads into silence. It is then that the catechist quietly invites the children: "Now you can spend as much time with God as you want, and when you have finished, you can quietly make your way into the 'place of meeting with each other' to work on your activity without disturbing the others who are praying." When possible, the catechist remains in prayer, giving an example the children are invited to follow. While some children immediately return to the "place of meeting with each other" to work on a practical activity related to the theme, others freely choose to remain in prayer, sometimes for up to ten minutes.[3] We have found that offering this free choice in every session

---

3. As a catechist myself, I sadly have had to stop some children in their silent prayer in order to clear the room at the very end of a Come Follow Me session. This means that the children had remained ten to fifteen minutes in silent prayer. These sessions were held in St. Joseph and Our Lady Catholic School, Lymington, UK, in 2013–2015, as part of their religious education curriculum. About half of the group of children catechized were unbaptized.

gives an opportunity for each child to respond to God in a personal way, by choosing to spend time with Him—and such a free choice is important to growing in communion with God. The whole of the methodology builds up toward this moment of grace.

Systematic Doctrinal and Liturgical Structure

This emphasis on respect for the children's freedom is never opposed to the program's carefully crafted doctrinal structure, but is rather helped by it. Each session is organized according to a recurrent pattern, which becomes familiar to the children and allows them to freely grow in the four dimensions of the Christian life and faith: (1) the reception of the Faith through Scripture, (2) the awakening of the liturgical sense, (3) the embrace of the moral life (each session includes a section: "Your Word is a light for my life today"), and (4) prayerful encounter.[4] The whole four-year program deepens these themes in ways adapted to the psychology of each age-group, covering the four Gospels, with a specific focus on faith (seven years old), charity (eight years old), hope (nine years old), and freedom in the Holy Spirit (ten years old). Focusing on the theological virtues in this way nurtures the baptismal grace of the children and so helps them grow in Christian life.

Liturgical Elements in Come Follow Me

The Liturgical Year

Come Follow Me is structured according to the liturgical cycle, renewing and deepening the same Trinitarian and liturgical themes throughout each year. In the Figure 9.2, the overall thematic progression corresponding to the liturgical year is shown. This same structure is used for each year group, but the passages of Scripture used to cover the themes (in column 3) are different each year, from the more simple (seven-year-olds) to the more difficult (ten-year-olds). This cyclical structure provides security and order while it also allows the children to gradually enter into and so fully receive the proclamation of the Gospel.

---

4. These four dimensions follow the structure of the *Catechism of the Catholic Church*: the Profession of the Faith, the Celebration of the Liturgy, Life in Christ (moral life), and Prayer.

Overarching Themes	Liturgical Year	Theme of the Sessions Each Year
God, Creator and Father Welcoming the love of God	September to All Saints Sessions 1 to 6	God our Creator The Angels The Human Person Prayer Sin and Mercy The Conscience
	All Saints Session 7	Celebration of All Saints The Happiness of the Saints
	November Sessions 8 to 11	Abraham Moses (2 sessions) The Prophets
Jesus Christ, Master and Savior To live in Communion with Jesus	Advent / Christmastide Sessions 12 to 16	The Incarnation Celebration of Christmas The Infancy narratives (5 sessions)
	Ordinary Time / Lent Sessions 17 to 23	Public Life of Jesus Miracles Teaching / Parables (7 sessions gradually introducing the Paschal Mystery)
	Holy Week Session 24	Celebration of the Passion of Jesus (1 or 2 sessions)
	Eastertide Sessions 25 to 27	The Resurrection The Church (3 sessions)
The Holy Spirit, Giver of Life To live as a Child of the Church with the Holy Spirit	The Ascension Session 28	The Ascension
	Pentecost Session 29	Pentecost
	May to June Sessions 30 to 33	Call to Holiness Life of the Church Sacraments Mission / Vocation (4 sessions)
	June Session 34	Eternal Life Second Coming (1 session)
	End of June / Beginning of July Session 35	Our Blessed Mother Mary Celebration with Mary

Figure 9.2 Overall Thematic Progression Corresponding to the Liturgical Year

In addition to the catechesis following this cycle, the liturgical year is marked by five times of celebration in the parish church. Parents are invited to gather together with the children: a celebration to mark the beginning of the year, All Saints, Christmas, the Passion of Jesus, and a celebration to mark the end of the year with Mary, the Mother of God. These liturgically oriented celebrations gather families together in parishes and schools and are great opportunities to evangelize the parents and welcome them more closely into the communion of the parish. These celebrations can also include social times to grow in friendships, which the parents appreciate. It is often the children who are keen to bring their parents along and are becoming, through the program, agents of evangelization within their families. A few years ago, a mother and her three daughters were all baptized during the Easter Vigil. It was the youngest one, a six-year-old, who had started Come Follow Me, who had brought her two sisters along, until their mother, touched by the witness of her girls, came herself to the faith.

Liturgical Aspects of the Methodology

Come Follow Me helps develop the children's liturgical awareness and sense of sacramental mystery. Influenced by the teachings of Maria Montessori and by a balanced anthropology that takes into consideration the various dimensions of the human person, the pedagogy employs gestures, silences, physical reverence for the Word of God, singing, candles, and visual symbols to educate the children in faith.

The structured unfolding of each session also recalls the movements evident in the Mass. Once they arrive in the "place of meeting with God," the children enter a recollected silence as they prepare to listen to the Word of God, read from the Bible itself. The proclamation of the Word is followed by the understanding of the Word, then by communion with the Word of God in prayer, finally ending with a sending out into mission. The whole time spent in the "place of meeting with God" is one of attentive listening and prayerful encounter. Many catechists using Come Follow Me have remarked on the attentiveness of the children, whose intelligence is captivated in the loving dialogue with the Word of God and whose physical senses are engaged by the beauty and movements of the visual display and singing.

Introduction to the Sacraments

As mentioned earlier, Come Follow Me is not a program dedicated to the sacramental preparation of children, but a program of fundamental catechesis, which aims at rooting the children into communion with God and life in the Church. It is in this light that the sacraments are introduced and explained as signs and causes of the grace which the children come to experience in their encounter with Jesus Christ within the family of the Church.

Moreover, each year has a particular sacramental focus, with frequent reinforcement of important aspects of the sacrament for the Christian life of the child. A detailed example of this focus may be helpful to see the many sacramental connections made in a year of catechesis. Figure 9.3 is taken from the program for seven-year-old children, which focuses on the Sacrament of Reconciliation.

This sacramental emphasis is similar each year, introducing different sacraments from the Scriptures: At eight, the children will focus on the Eucharist. At nine, they enter into the historical perspective of Israel and the Church and discover the Sacrament of Holy Orders. At ten, a year dedicated to freedom under the Holy Spirit, the children discover the Sacrament of Confirmation. Throughout the program, the sacraments are always accompanied by the proclamation of the Gospel.

It is from this integral, organic presentation of the faith that the children begin to respond and express for themselves the desire to receive the sacraments so as to enter more fully into communion with Jesus in the Church.

Inviting Children to Sacramental Desire

Consistent with the rest of its pedagogy, Come Follow Me's approach to the liturgy respects both the integrity of Revelation and the personal freedom of each child. As the Mass and the sacraments are introduced, the children, at their own level, are able to perceive how the liturgy connects with their own lives and are able to offer their own free response of faith. This beautiful response is expressed by the children in so many ways: in their own adherence to God in faith, in their free decision to remain in prayer at the end of the catechetical session and build their own prayer corners at home, in the moral transformation that can be observed in

Come Follow Me—7-yr.-old children "Live as Children of the Light"	Focus on the Sacrament of Reconciliation
Session 3: The Human Person	The children explore their ability to know (the age of reason), with an emphasis on self-knowledge and knowledge of God, who can be known with certainty although he is not tangible to the senses.
Session 4: Prayer—The Virtue of Faith	The children discover a relationship of love and friendship with God through faith.
Session 5: Sin and Mercy	The children understand that sin is a rejection of God's friendship and love. Yet God continues to reach out to us in mercy and never abandons us.
Session 6: The Conscience	Through a simple exercise, the children discover their own ability to discern what is right and what is wrong: their conscience
Session 18: The Healing of the Leper	This account provides a first introduction to the power of Jesus to heal us outside and inside and his desire to do it.
Session 19: The Healing of the Paralytic	Jesus is revealed as God, with the power to forgive sins. The Sacrament of Reconciliation is first explained, very simply.
Session 20: The Raising of the Son of the Widow of Naim	Jesus has power not only over illness (leper) and sin (paralytic) but even over death. Through his words, Jesus brings life where there is death.
Session 21: The Woman who had Sinned	Jesus teaches us in words and action about the mercy of God. Here there is an explicit teaching on the Sacrament of Reconciliation. The children who desire it can receive the sacrament.
Session 24: The Celebration of the Passion	The "good thief" and the forgiveness of Jesus extended from the Cross to all sinners.
Session 27: The Church	Simple explanation of Baptism.
Session 31: Life in the Church	Focusing on Peter's speech after Pentecost, the teaching on baptism is deepened with an explanation of "repentance."
Session 32: The Sacraments—Reconciliation	This session is an explicit and detailed explanation of the sacrament of reconciliation, with an examination of conscience and an invitation to receive the sacrament if the children desire it.

Figure 9.3 Focus on the Sacrament of Reconciliation in the program for Seven-Year-Old Children

their behavior, but above all in their explicit request to receive the sacraments: Baptism, Confession, Holy Communion, Confirmation.

A catechist working in school saw a little boy coming into school one morning all dressed up in a suit and tie. Asked whether he was attending a wedding afterwards, the little boy answered, "No! Don't you know that today is the day I am going to receive the forgiveness of Jesus for the first time?!" He had decided himself to dress up for his first Confession, which would take place, at his request, after his Come Follow Me session in school.

Many parishes and schools in France now use Come Follow Me as their standard, ongoing, catechetical program. A few of these have made the courageous decision to move away from automatic sacramental preparation for all children reaching a certain age at a certain time, regardless of their personal circumstances and maturity in faith. Instead, those parishes now rely on Come Follow Me to provide for the children the fundamental evangelization and catechesis they need, and from this solid foundation in faith, to offer the sacraments as and when the children freely ask for them. Because the children are receiving an evangelistic, scripturally rich catechesis and also have a well-defined space (in dialog and prayer) for their own free personal response to this revelation, the result is that children begin to experience deep desire for the sacraments. Parishes using Come Follow Me typically have concurrent sacramental preparation programs, available as needed, with children entering these as they express their desire to receive the sacrament. When a child explicitly asks to receive a sacrament, we have found that such a request is indicative of a certain understanding of faith and Christian maturity, reducing the needed preparation to its minimum. Other parishes and schools combine Come Follow Me with a traditional and fixed sacramental preparation process but are still able to discern the fruits of the ongoing catechesis in the quality of the children's understanding and receptivity when it comes to sacramental preparation.

As Come Follow Me awakens the children's desire for the sacraments, the tragedy of those who are unable to receive them because their parents refuse their request is all the more vivid. Faced with this situation, little can be done. One eight-year-old boy in our group asked for Baptism but his non-Christian parents wouldn't allow him. Another

Muslim boy told his teacher in school that he would ask for Baptism once he became an adult. A little girl, unable to go to church, told her teacher that she had a little ceremony in the prayer corner of her bedroom, reading Scripture and thinking about Jesus on her own during Easter. However, these situations also demonstrate that the evangelization and catechesis of the children is taking place and is bearing fruit in spite of their cultural and family circumstances. By using Come Follow Me, catechists, working under the breath of the Holy Spirit, are able to sow enduring seeds of faith in the hearts of children coming from all backgrounds and environments.

Catechists have reported some of the words children use to express their desire to receive the sacraments. These little ones have asked to receive "the forgiveness of Jesus" (confession) and "the Body of Jesus" or "Jesus in Holy Communion" (Holy Communion). These words show that the children have already made a connection between the sacraments and their personal relationship with Jesus, and that they understand the sacraments to be a means for that relationship to grow. Once the children's faith has been awakened into a relationship with Father, Son, and Holy Spirit, their understanding of the sacraments grows in this context. Desire is expressed, and sacramental preparation need not be offered through the "automatic," age-related model so prominent in our parishes. Reception of the sacraments can now become the "natural" outcome of a long and patient encounter between the Holy Spirit and the children's freedom through the ecclesial proclamation of the Word of God. The children's desire for the sacraments now grows and endures beyond "first" Confession and "first" Holy Communion. This has been the experience, both in Europe and the United States, of the catechists who have taken up Come Follow Me.

Come Follow Me: Models from Parishes and Schools

How is Come Follow Me adapted into various parish and cultural situations? Let's examine several examples.

Strasbourg, France: An Innovative Model of Parish Catechesis[5]

Our first model is from the largest urban parish in the Strasbourg diocese. In 2004, the parish pastoral team faced with honesty the reality that many of the First Communion children and their families were not going to Mass on Sundays. This realization started a process of catechetical reflection and renewal in the parish.

The Eucharist is not only communion with Christ but also and inseparably communion with the Church, with the concrete assembly of the People of God (cf. CCC, 1331). Yet here was a complete lack of religious practice among the young families approaching the parish for their children's First Communion. Most of these were families living at the margins of the Church. For years, the parish had tried to attract and retain these families during the period of the children's preparation and celebration of First Communion, with no success. The parish pastoral team realized that their mission, considering these circumstances, was primarily to cultivate within children and their families *the desire to live with Jesus*, "to live in communion" or "to enter into communion." The desire to listen to him and follow him needed to be awakened so that they could come to know him in the Church.

For seven- to eleven-year old children, the pastoral team specifically chose Come Follow Me, which, thanks to its cyclical structure allowed them to welcome any child at any time of the year. The program has now been running for almost ten years, and is combined with a parents' group, which meets five or six times a year.

The Experience of Sunday Mass

The parish combines Come Follow Me with an emphasis on welcoming and including children and families during Sunday Mass. A few months after having started Come Follow Me, the lead catechist realized that the children had become more attentive during Mass. With no explicit introduction to the Mass yet in the catechesis, they were able to enter into it thanks to the preparation they had implicitly received in catechesis. She found herself sitting in the midst of more than thirty children who were listening attentively to the homily, happy to be there, with no need for

---

5. This account is based on the testimony of Elisabeth Clement, lead catechist in Strasbourg city center parish.

discipline. Moreover, families would now remain together after Mass for a drink or a shared meal, building a living community.

A children's Liturgy of the Word is offered every Sunday, with the exception of the monthly Sunday "families Mass." This Sunday children's program has been adapted to the pedagogy of Come Follow Me and facilitated by a larger team of catechists and volunteers. During this time, the children hear and ponder the Word of God—the Sunday Gospel—just as they do during their catechetical sessions. Encountering the Word, then, twice a week, nurtures well their communion with Christ.

Desire for the Sacraments

Through an ongoing personal dialogue with the catechist over the year, the children can examine their own hearts and decide whether they are willing and ready to receive the sacraments of Baptism, Reconciliation, and Eucharist. It is only once they have freely asked to receive a sacrament that a short preparation is undertaken. By then, the children are already familiar with prayer and with the life of the faith community. As a result, each Come Follow Me year group includes children who are preparing for Baptism, for Reconciliation, and for Holy Communion, while others may not feel ready to do so or may already have received these sacraments.

Baptismal preparation takes place over a year, alongside the normal Come Follow Me curriculum. This preparation gathers children from all age groups who meet together twelve times a year and culminates with the celebration of their Baptism during a parish Sunday Mass.

Preparation for the Sacrament of Reconciliation takes place over two afternoons (a total of four hours), for all the children who desire to receive it, across age groups. Most of the children ask for this sacrament at the end of the first year (seven-year-olds), or sometimes at the beginning of the second year (eight-year-olds). Catechists plan three times of preparation during each year: November, March, and May, to which children can freely sign up. This preparation for confession offered alongside Come Follow Me allows for a full explanation of its meaning and ritual. The children receive the Sacrament of Reconciliation during a penitential celebration opened to everyone: to those who receive it for the first time as well as to all those who have already received it. Three such celebrations take place every year. It is a joy to see the children coming regularly. In one instance, the lead catechist reminded the children of the next penitential celebration, and a little boy clapped his hands with joy, saying "Oh! This is when we receive the forgiveness of Jesus, when we go and see the priest! . . . Great!" It is wonderful to see children receiving the sacrament for the first time surrounded by the others who have been receiving it for some time: the community of faith is alive and active.

Preparation for Holy Communion is offered on a similar model to the children who freely express their desire for it, across age groups (seven to eleven). Most of the children will receive First Holy Communion at the end of the second year (eight) or in the course of the third year (nine). Once children, in informal personal conversation with their catechists, express their desire to receive Holy Communion, and the catechists can confirm their spiritual readiness, preparations can begin. There are no dates planned at the beginning of the year for a parish celebration of First Communion. These dates are chosen according to the children and their family as and when they ask for it. First Communions can take place in October, November, February, March, April, May, and June. In this way, the child has the space and time to freely express his desire to live with Jesus and to make room for Jesus in his life.

After discussion with the parents and catechist, the child publicly expresses his desire to receive Communion during a monthly Sunday family Mass, asking for the prayers of the community. This is a crucial moment for each child, who comes to realize that he or she is not alone and is called to experience communion not only with Jesus, but also with the Church. It is also an important moment for the ordinary parishioners, who often express their joy in being involved through prayer in the children's preparation, and who have a chance to get to know the children and their families. The direct preparation which follows allows the children who already desire this sacrament to discover its full meaning. The children meet six times in a small group for a more specific teaching on the liturgy of the Eucharist. Their First Communion is celebrated during a family Mass. During the Mass, they are simply called to stand in front of the altar to pray the Our Father. They remain there, facing Jesus, until their Communion. Once they have received Jesus, they go behind the altar, at the back of the sanctuary, for a time of personal prayer. Afterwards, they pray together in thanksgiving. Since this process has begun, the church on Sunday is continually filled with ordinary parishioners, with the children making their first Holy Communion and with their families, integrating these groups into one community of faith. One grandmother, who had been a catechist, shared her joy to see her grandson setting off on a genuine spiritual journey rather than conforming to a ritual mostly irrelevant to his personal and family life.

The Fruits of the Program

Many children in this parish are now freely pursuing catechesis beyond their First Communion. Living with Jesus gives meaning to their lives. Through the faithfulness and enthusiasm of the children attending Come Follow Me and the catechesis offered beyond, many more families come to Mass regularly. During catechesis, the children show high levels of attentive listening, personal reflection, and deep questioning. They are able to make connections in their understanding of the truths of the faith and between the biblical accounts. Most of all, they show real depth and quality in their prayer, which is entered into seamlessly, in a personal encounter with the Lord. They learn to appreciate silence and they love to sing and pray together. Through the spiritual growth of their children, many parents start afresh in their own faith journey and come to adult formation. The catechists themselves grow in their own personal faith as they prepare the sessions together in prayer and common study of the Word of God. Come Follow Me has influenced the whole parish as a means of renewal in faith, centered as it is in the celebration of the Church's liturgy.

Dunsford and Ardglass, Northern Ireland: A New Approach within a Traditional Structure[6]

The parish priest of this small community gathering two churches and two Catholic primary schools decided to start implementing Come Follow Me for the children of the parish in 2014. After a successful training weekend led for a group of nervous, retired volunteers (with mostly no previous experience in catechesis) and four enthusiastic teachers from Dunsford primary school, the first year, for seven-year-old children, was introduced in September 2014. The program is held both in the school and in the parish.

---

6. This account is based on the testimony of Fr. Gerard McCloskey, parish priest of Dunsford and Ardglass, and on the testimonies of some of his catechists and teachers.

After only a year, the parish priest, catechists, and teachers were already able to identify areas of great progress and spiritual growth for the children. Catechists and teachers also witnessed to their own growth in faith as a result of preparing for and leading Come Follow Me. As the work of implementing Come Follow Me continues in Ardglass and Dunsford, the parish priest was able to identify the effect it had on the liturgy and sacramental preparation of the children. He noticed most of all the children's heightened sense of awe and wonder, and their sensitivity to the sacredness of God and therefore to liturgical acts. For example, at the end of session nine on Moses and the burning bush, the children all prostrated themselves in front of the tabernacle with no prompting from anyone, but copying Moses and their parish priest in prayer.

Although the children of the parish continue to be prepared for the sacraments all together at a certain age and time of year, their approach to the sacraments has been transformed thanks to Come Follow Me: they are more open, more willing, and there are no behavior problems. The children all eagerly approached the Sacrament of Reconciliation. During the celebration of their first confession, the priest was sitting in the church's sanctuary, and the children were grouped at the back of the church, free to go as and when they wanted. Instead of nervously walking the length of the nave, priest and catechists saw them running in haste, one after the other, eager to receive the forgiveness of Jesus. One little boy even went twice. The children's desire to receive the sacraments is noticeable.

Unfortunately, only 10 percent of the children are able to come to Mass every week, as their parents do not take them regularly. The children's sadness in not being able to attend Mass is noticeable. Some children do succeed in bringing their own parents to Mass. On the other hand, parents who do practice their faith have expressed their delight in seeing their children visibly grow in faith and eager to go to Mass with them.

Stoke-on-Trent, England: Come Follow Me as a Model of First Evangelization for Children[7]

In a much more secular environment than Northern Ireland, where cultural Catholicism is still very strong, a parish priest adopted Come Follow Me in 2013 in the three Catholic schools which he oversees in

---

7. This account is based on the testimony of Fr. Julian Green, Parish priest of Biddulph, Kidsgrove, and Goldenhill, Stoke-on-Trent.

Stoke-on-Trent, Staffordshire. Fr. Julian runs an after-school club for the children in each of the schools, using Come Follow Me. The children are evangelized and catechized through the program. Most of the children do not attend Mass because their parents refuse to take them, yet they express their desire to be there, to receive the sacraments and to live in communion with Jesus. Most of them also build themselves a prayer corner in their bedroom at home to meet personally with the Lord.

Within the first year of running Come Follow Me, Fr. Julian acknowledged that he had heard the best first confessions of his priestly ministry. The children were eager and ready. For the first time, he organized a penitential service where the children were free to go as they wished, and not in a line. He noticed in particular the joy of the children approaching Confession. One little boy said: "I'm really glad I went. I know it's all true." He also noticed a great change in the children's approach to their First Communion, showing greater understanding and eagerness to receive Jesus, as well as efforts of interior preparation. Inevitably however, because of the children's absence from Sunday Mass and the parish community, the full potential of Come Follow Me is stunted. It nevertheless contributes to the children's evangelization and catechesis in the context of a first encounter with the Lord through the Word of God and the person of his priest.

Conclusion

These three models demonstrate the adaptability of Come Follow Me in different settings and circumstances, whether in schools or parishes. They also show that it can be implemented at different levels, either in keeping with a more traditional approach to catechesis and religious education (Dunsford and Ardglass), as a first proclamation and preparation for ecclesial life (Stoke-on-Trent), or as the means of full integration within the Church (Strasbourg). Perhaps the remarks of a catechist from the United States who has only started to implement Come Follow Me in her parish in September 2015 for second, third, and fourth grades can confirm the European experience so far:

> Come Follow Me is a very natural way of introducing the children to the liturgy and the sacraments, and they are able to understand them as they hear the Word of God and see the figurines. Our children have gone from

having Come Follow Me during the school year, into having four weeks of intense sacramental preparation. And Come Follow Me has laid a strong foundation for them. The children are more ready to participate and are engaged and asking questions. This program uses several methods of learning that cater to the different styles of learning of each child. It is a tremendous tool.[8]

In a great variety of religious and cultural contexts, Come Follow Me awakens within children the desire to receive the sacraments, to belong to the family of the Church and to participate in her liturgical worship, summit of the Christian life and faith.

---

8. Lead catechist from the parish of St. Joseph, Modesto, California, June 2016.

CHAPTER 10

The Liturgical Encounter and the Child: Insights from Catechesis of the Good Shepherd

Mary Mirrione

The experiences narrated by Sofia Cavalletti and Gianna Gobbi are capable,
I think, of unfolding unsuspected horizons to many educators. The marvel
lies in the rediscovery of the natural harmony which exists between
the psychological laws governing the spiritual development of children
and the "method" possessed by the Church in her liturgy.

Cyprian Vagaggini, OSB[1]

Sofia Cavalletti viewed Cyprian Vagaggini's *Theological Dimensions of the Liturgy* as a foundational work on liturgy. So much so that when she began her work with the Catechesis of the Good Shepherd (CGS), she sought his advice for the course she developed for adults and for her first publications regarding CGS. She said, "He affirmed that the liturgy . . . is a most important source of theology; it is a source that does not speak in the language of abstract theology, but rather by signs—the universal, concrete language that is grasped not only with the mind, but with the eyes, by looking and touching."[2]

In the Catechesis of the Good Shepherd we recognize the power of these liturgical signs that "speak to us" both through our senses and our spirit. Signs speak a language that is rich in meaning, and children need

---

1. Sofia Cavalletti and Gianna Gobbi, *Teaching Doctrine and Liturgy* (New York: Pauline Fathers and Brothers, 1964), 15. Vagaggini wrote the preface of this book and went on to say that "It is hoped that many mothers and Christian educators will become familiar with this work so that such great treasures will not remain hidden."

2. Sofia Cavalletti, *Way of Holy Joy: Selected Writings of Sofia Cavalletti*, trans. Patricia Coulter (Chicago: Liturgy Training Publications, 2012), 70.

to be introduced to this language as they would to their mother tongue or other languages. Therefore, we help the children to become aware of the sign and to look closely at it, and then we offer them assistance in "reading" these signs in their ongoing discovery of their deeper meaning.

The children have shown us that their relationship with God is largely built through concrete, sensory experiences. Such experiences, in fact, reflect

> a deep, vital need of the human being, and God honors this need by communicating with us through what is perceivable: through creation, through events in salvation history, through the Person of the Son, the Word, and God's continued presence in the sacraments. Thus, a concrete, perceivable "material" is always involved in God's self-communication to us.[3]

In the Catechesis of the Good Shepherd, this need of every person for receiving the spiritual in concrete form is met in the environment of the atrium.

The Place of Encounter

Monica is nine and in her first year of a level-three atrium.[4] The seed of faith, alive in her heart, has been deeply sown and nurtured in her since she first came to the Catechesis of the Good Shepherd when she was three years old. Entering the atrium, she carefully chooses a sheet of colored paper and the perfect calligraphy pen. She silently sits down at a small table. In peace and with enjoyment she writes:

> There's a place where I can be myself;
> a place with treasures on every shelf.
> A place to learn about God and pray;
> A place where I'd like to be all day.
> It's just called "atrium," quite a short name,
> but it's still a wonder all the same.
> I just love that little room where I can be myself,
> and I can explore as I please,
> those treasures on the shelves.

---

3. Gianna Gobbi, "The Meaning, Importance and Limitations of our Catechetical Materials," *The Journals of the Catechesis of the Good Shepherd 1998–2002* (2003): 106.

4. There are three levels and environments for the children. There is an atrium for three- to six-year olds, six- to nine-year-olds and nine- to twelve-year-olds. Each environment is prepared to serve the vital religious needs and developmental stage of the child.

Such poetry from the heart of a child! It is easy to see she enjoys her work. The Gospel has been sown lavishly in her heart through the announcement of a catechist who has studied long and hard to serve the children in their religious needs. The catechist has prepared an environment filled with simple, handmade materials for the child to use, which Monica calls "treasures." She finds this little room, the atrium, "a wonder."

The word *atrium* is an ancient term for the entry porch of a basilica, where catechumens were prepared for Christian initiation. In CGS, it continues to have that meaning. It is a place between the world and the Church where the child can be mystagogically initiated into the life of faith. Monica loves the freedom found in this place, lovingly prepared, where she can truly "be herself" before God. Her experience is the heart of the Catechesis of the Good Shepherd—and is common in many children throughout our nation and our world. This experience is the abundant fruit of those seeds sown with care by catechists who share a particular commitment to nurture and support the religious dignity of children.

If our aim is to help children, like Monica, enter into and enjoy their relationship with God, we must consider what kind of environment will best respect and cultivate the child's needs and capacities at their developmental level, and give special attention to their spiritual life. The atrium, as an intentionally prepared environment, is an environment where children can learn more from interaction with materials than they would from any direct instruction from a teacher. The atrium is not a classroom, it is not a place of religious instruction; it is a place of religious life.

The slow and thoughtful development of the hands-on materials present in the atrium—materials which invite the children into contemplative activity—began in that first atrium of Sofia's in Rome in 1954. It was there—and in later atria—that children could reflect on a scriptural passage, or a moment from the liturgy, by working with materials—like placing small sheep in a sheepfold of the Good Shepherd, setting a small altar with articles used in the Holy Mass, or positioning figures within a dioramic representation of the Last Supper. (These activities undertaken by the children on their own are called "works.") Older children, with the ability to read, could work quietly and contemplatively at copying the scriptural maxims of Jesus, laying in order the written prayers from the Rite of Baptism, or labeling the long timeline depicting the history of the Kingdom of God.

God and the Child

In the development of Catechesis of the Good Shepherd, we have continually seen a confirmation that God and the child are already in relationship and that children possess a unique capacity to respond to God's loving invitations to deepen that relationship. For close to fifty years, Sofia Cavalletti and Gianna Gobbi collected the children's drawings, recorded their briefly uttered insights and prayers, and observed their joyful, prolonged, and repeated work with certain materials. With this research and study, they developed the materials that we now use in the atrium. Sofia and Gianna were delighted and astonished to find that the children, without prompting, had selected the materials which spoke to the core of Christian belief, omitting nothing that is essential.

Maria Montessori, a Roman Catholic pedagogue, found that children pass through "sensitive periods" which heighten their ability to choose what they need for their growth and development from a complex environment. The three- to six-year-old child is in a "sensitive period" for movement, language, and order. In this period, the young child has a special affinity to the rites of the Church which, of course, present all three in a significant way. During this period they also have the extraordinary capacity to receive and give love unconditionally. In God, children find a suitable partner, one who can truly love them unconditionally and to whom they can respond with love and gratitude.

Children of this age can readily "see" the invisible and delight in the Church's signs, gestures, and symbols. They can, for example, "see" the presence of the Good Shepherd who gives all he is and all he has to his sheep in the holy sacrifice of the altar. This understanding can be seen in in a drawing by a seven-year-old boy, from the original atrium in Rome (see figure 10.1). This child began attending the atrium at the age of three and has had ample time for reflection and contemplation in an environment prepared for his religious needs. One day, without any prompting from the catechist, he spontaneously drew the elements of the parable of the Good Shepherd and the Eucharist on two parallel lines, writing: "This" (the parable) "is equal to this" (the liturgical celebration).

At this age they are filled with wonder and awe, which is a hallmark of their spirituality. Drawn to what is most essential and beautiful, they enter into self-development through the repetitive work of their hands

Figure 10.1: "This. . .Is Equal to This"

and the joy they take in their developing relationship with God. They are capable of experiencing the deepest aspects of communion with God. We have come to know that their silent plea is: "Help me come closer to God by myself."

Around the age of reason, the child undergoes great changes physically, socially, emotionally, and intellectually. The eyes of the child are open to new and wider horizons; they seek the friendship of others and want to collaborate in groups. They begin to judge what they see in the world and are held responsible for their actions. They are fearless in the challenge of adventure and develop a deep sense of justice. They actively seek a moral code and are goal-oriented. They search for heroes and develop a love for knowledge. In Christ, their Good Shepherd, they find the perfect model for living a loving and merciful life. With, through, and in him, they seek to collaborate in the Kingdom of God in justice and peace.

Often when an adult asks about the Catechesis of the Good Shepherd we will respond: "Come and see!" In these words is an invitation to encounter the hidden religious life of the child. We have found that the prayer of the children remains the most mysterious aspect of their relationship with God, and as such, must be approached with the deepest respect and care.

While as catechists we do have a part in the prayer of the children, we must always remember that prayer is made up of two moments. The first moment is of primary importance: this is the moment in which God speaks to his creatures, and it is the time of listening. This is the moment when we proclaim to the children what God wants us to know about him, the announcement of the kerygma. We are present in this moment as fellow listeners, and we hold dear this insight from the apostolic exhortation *Catechesi Tradendae*:

> [The catechist] will not seek to keep directed towards himself and his personal opinions and attitudes the attention and the consent of the mind and heart of the person he is catechizing. Above all, he will not try to inculcate his personal opinions and options as if they expressed Christ's teaching and the lessons of his life. Every catechist should be able to apply to himself the mysterious words of Jesus: "My teaching is not mine, but his who sent me" (Jn 7:16). Saint Paul did this when he was dealing with a question of prime importance: "I received from the Lord what I also delivered to you" (1 Cor 11:23). . . . [W]hat detachment from self must a catechist have in order that he can say, "My teaching is not mine!" (CT, 6)

Sofia Cavalletti often reminded us that this text establishes a principle of the utmost importance in catechesis: the need for the catechist to be rigorously objective in the transmission of the message. We must allow the Word itself to speak.

The second moment of prayer is that of the personal response to God. It is the point in prayer which actualizes "people's most secret core and their sanctuary. There they are alone with God, whose voice echoes in their depths" (GS, 16). This is holy ground for the children, where we must tread lightly and silently. In this moment we can offer the peripheral assistance of the prepared environment, which is easily accessible to the child and free of adult interruptions. It is in this environment that children can deepen within themselves the desire for Divine Love and their response to it. Ultimately, this is God's work in them.

What We Have Seen and Touched

Allie is seven years old. She has had time in this prepared environment to experience what the psalmist proclaims, printed on a beautifully illuminated card displayed on the prayer table: "Your word is a lamp for my feet, a light for my path" (Ps 119:105). Tenderly, she contemplates the light of the Word and then she writes, "God, thank you for keeping me in your light, and feeding me with your food, and your wisdom. Amen." Her prayer beautifully expresses her relationship with God and comes forth from her time in contemplation. Already at her young age she is profoundly encountering the light and love of God.

We readily see the child's capacity for contemplating and enjoying the liturgical signs when we ponder with him or her the signs of Baptism. There are a number of presentations given to the children in the Easter season just after the Easter Vigil. These presentations foster a deep connection to the Paschal candle as a sign of the Risen Christ. The youngest children are fascinated by the light of the Paschal candle and captivated with the light of the small, baptismal candle which is lit from the Paschal candle and handed to them. They also joyfully associate the light of the candle with another kind of light they have received in Baptism. As the lit candles are presented to the little ones, the catechists ask a meditative question: "Is the light given to us by the Risen Christ just in a candle? Where do we carry his light?" "In our heart" is most often the response.

As they grow spiritually, we introduce the other signs of Baptism, and with each of these signs, our principal goal is simply to provide an opportunity for the child to linger over the sign, to look at it closely, and enjoy it in an unhurried way. The "baptismal corner" contains a small baptismal font, a Paschal candle, a San Damiano crucifix, a Bible on a small lectern, and a cabinet containing a small, simple, white garment, as well as some individual baptismal candles and small containers of oil. The oil symbolizes the Oil of Catechumens and Sacred Chrism. As understanding deepens, so too does their enjoyment of the gifts of this sacrament.

Blaize is four years old. He has been in the atrium for one year and is the oldest of three cousins. Upon entering the church for the baptism of one of these cousins he stands before the Paschal candle and with great joy proclaims: "Wow!" His attention is very concentrated on the hands of the priest throughout the liturgy imitating the gestures with his own little hands. When he returns to the atrium the next week, he places three small candles very close to the Paschal candle found in the baptism corner, telling the catechist that, "they like to snuggle."

Ari is eight years old. After working with a card work that depicts all the gifts of Baptism, she draws a picture filled with light that includes a person standing in the baptismal font with a Paschal candle on his garment. Rays of light beam from this person. She has also illustrated a chalice and paten and the two sheep at the base of the baptismal font with rays of light beaming from them as well. Michael, who is six and has also worked with the same material, proclaims: "Let me do something like a bath in your light!" (see figure 10.2).

Claudia is ten years old. After working with a card work that depicts the complete Rite of Baptism she draws a self-portrait. In this portrait, her hands hold a large heart, colored yellow. The text over the portrait reads, "I want to have a very brilliant light." Around the image Claudia writes:

> God has given me many gifts and I need to make the most of them. I do not know if I am more than others, but I would like to know for sure that in front of God and my neighbors I would be a good, noble, respectful woman, with a light that cannot be extinguished, as the light God has given me in baptism which I reinforce in Communion. I know that someday, when God calls me, with my effort I will be a messenger of peace. [5]

Reflecting on the Mass and Preparing for Holy Communion

"The Parousia will be like the mixing of the water and the wine: 'God all in all,'" as the water and the wine become one.[6] This statement was proclaimed in peace and in joy by an eleven-year-old child. How is it that one so young could understand and articulate something so deeply profound? Only one who has the time and opportunity to study and contemplate the signs and the meaning of the liturgical celebration in an environment carefully prepared for their religious needs can come to such a conclusion. In the Catechesis of the Good Shepherd, the child finds the time and place to do such interior work in contemplation and enjoyment in the presence

---

5. Maria Christlieb, "A Celebration of Light," *Journals of the Catechesis of the Good Shepherd 1984–1997* (1998): 129.

6. "The Children Speak to Us about God," *Journals of the Catechesis of the Good Shepherd 1984–1997* (1998): 149, quoting 1 Cor 15:28. Many of the children's responses can be found in this and other publications of CGS found at www.cgsusa.org.

Figure 10.2: Ari's Image of Baptism

of God. We have found these to be two of the most essential spiritual values of childhood.

With the youngest children, we isolate the gestures the priest makes during Mass, so that they can ponder their meaning. Children are naturally fascinated by movement, and these gestures of the Mass are rich liturgical signs worthy of their wonder. These gestures speak a language that is too great for words.

The first gesture the youngest children work with is the preparation of the chalice. This might seem a difficult task for a three-year-old, and it would be if not for the great care the catechist takes in preparing the child first through various exercises in pouring and carefully handling sacred objects. Once the child has had practice and success with that task, the gesture of the Mass is then presented slowly and with few words. At the beginning of this presentation, the child is invited to remember that we sometimes speak with our bodies rather than with our words. The child is then helped in recalling the special movements or gestures the priest makes during the Mass. The child is invited to drape a white cloth over a small table and then place the prepared cruets, one holding water, and the other wine, as well as a small glass "chalice." Glass is used so the child can "see" what is happening. The catechist states simply, "This is wine; at Mass it will be used to help us know Jesus." All of the wine from the cruet is poured into the glass. She continues: "The water will help us think of all of us." Then a single drop of water is placed into the chalice. The child is then asked what they see and if there is a way for us to remove the water from the wine. Together we ponder what this gesture can mean. Only at a later time are the words of the prayer prayed by the priest shared.

Sofia recounts the story of Massimo, who continued to repeat this exercise for a very long time.[7] In fact, he worked with this exercise for so long that the catechist, thinking he might be doing this work out of simple laziness, invited him several times to do other work. Nonetheless, it was Massimo's countenance of concentration and contemplation, carefully observed by the catechist, which showed that he was working with something very important, something that he was searching for a way to understand and to express. It was only at the end of the year that Massimo

---

7. Sofia Cavalletti, *The Religious Potential of the Child: Experiencing Scripture and Liturgy with Young Children* (Chicago: Liturgy Training Publications, 1992), 92.

could finally say: "A few drops of water because we must lose ourselves in Jesus."[8] For an entire year Massimo pondered this great mystery of our union in the offering that Christ gives to the Father in the liturgical celebration. What would have happened if he had been interrupted?

Today, in atria all over the world, children like Massimo ponder these mysteries as he did. They show us they are capable of understanding what Sofia called "elements of the highest theology."[9] The essential aspects of our Christian life come naturally to children, and they receive them in a spontaneous manner. Gestures like the "mingling" penetrate them to their core, not because of the words of the catechist, but rather because of their personal meditation and the depths of the sacred sign. The "mingling," in fact, can be traced back to the first centuries. The wealth of its meaning, and the meaning of many other liturgical signs, symbols, and gestures, may be discovered in reading the Fathers of the Church. For example, St. Cyprian, the third-century Bishop of Carthage writes:

> Divine Scripture declared in the Apocalypse (1:15; 14:2; 19:6) that the waters represent the people. And this we obviously see also in the sacrament of the chalice. In fact, as Christ carried all of us and carried our sins, so we see that in the water the people are signified, and that in the wine the blood of Christ is signified. Therefore, when the water is mixed with the wine in the chalice it is the people that unite with Christ, it is the throng of the faithful that conjoin and unite with him who they believe in. This union, this mingling of the water and the wine in the chalice of the Lord is something that is inseparable. Thus nothing could ever separate the Church from Christ, nothing could separate from him the people who are in the Church and who faithfully and firmly persevere in the faith, so as to be always united with him by a love which, of the two of them, will make one, unique whole. When the chalice of the Lord is consecrated, water alone cannot be offered, just as wine alone cannot be offered. Indeed if wine alone is offered, the blood of Christ is present without us; and if there is only water the people are present without Christ.[10]

Today, the children continue to remind us of the beauty and deep meaning of this gesture. They "see" from the gesture what the Fathers of the

---

8. Ibid., 92.

9. Sofia Cavalletti, "The Water and the Wine of the Eucharist," *Journals of the Catechesis of the Good Shepherd 1984–1997* (1998): 34.

10. St. Cyprian, *Letters*, 63, as quoted in Sofia Cavalletti, "The Water and the Wine of the Eucharist," *Journals of the Catechesis of the Good Shepherd 1984–1997* (1998): 34.

Church describe.[11] They have a boundless ability to unite their hearts, minds, and souls to the gestures which join bodily prayer with the spoken word during a liturgical celebration. Truly we see in the children an immense capacity for "full, conscious, and active participation in the Mass" (SC, 14).

It has been my privilege, in those children I have served, to witness their response to this gesture at the celebration of First Communion. Every group of children, for over twenty years, has done the same thing.[12] Although the contemplation of the mingling of water and wine happens three years earlier in the atrium, at that moment of the First Communion Mass, every child leans forward toward the altar in rapt attention, in contemplation and joy. In experiences such as this, it is wondrous to see how the children are our teachers. They remind us of what is essential, preserved in the heart of the tradition of our Church.

A most significant moment in the Catechesis of the Good Shepherd is the celebration of First Communion. The children are prepared with great care; it is a time of serenity and peace. There has been first the indirect preparation, beginning with the moment the child enters the atrium and finds these words on a card situated on the prayer table: "Taste and see the goodness of the Lord." We talk about what it means to taste something new and what we will discover together during our time in the atrium. Then for three to six years, depending on the child's readiness to begin their work, we, together, ponder our Good Shepherd, who calls us each by name. During five weeks of intense prayer, preparation, and contemplation, and the three days of the retreat leading up to the First Communion, part of our time is spent reflecting on the Sacrament of Reconciliation as an encounter with the Good Shepherd, who carries the found sheep on his strong and loving shoulders. The Sacrament of Reconciliation brings us into communion with God through his gift of tender mercy. Celebrating the Sacrament of Reconciliation just before First Communion brings into focus the joy-filled character of the sacrament and its celebratory nature.

---

11. Also see Irenaeus, bishop of Lyons, *Against the Heretics*, vols. 1, 3, and St. Thomas Aquinas, *Summa Theologica*, III q. 74, art. 6.

12. St. Anne in Gilbert, AZ, has grown into a very large parish. The author has prepared and observed more than 5000 children receive their First Communion in the past twenty years. It is always the same: the children always deeply attend the Mass.

Their time in the atrium has taught the children the tremendous importance of the personal conversation we have with the Lord in prayer. As we look at the Sacrament of Reconciliation, we invite the children to focus on their gratitude for the gifts God has given them. Only then can we look to our own inability to respond to the gracious generosity of God embodied in the maxims of Jesus found in the Sermon on the Mount: "Love your enemies." "Let your yes be yes and your no be no." "Do not sound a trumpet when you give alms." "Why do you notice the speck in your brother's eye and ignore the log in your own?" "When you pray, go into your inner room and pray to the father in secret." These maxims help the children see how to follow their Good Shepherd when preparing for this sacrament.

The children are always radiant after the encounter with the Lord in the Sacrament of Reconciliation. Their joy is tangible and abundant. At this vigil of their First Communion they renew their baptismal promises, and as on the day of their baptism are clothed once again in the white garment they will wear for the Holy Mass the next day. It is a precious time, all the more so when they take their place at the Eternal Banquet. Having been educated in the language of signs, given time for silence, they are now prepared to participate with dignity and solemnity in procession and prayers of celebration. They have come to know and understand that the Mass is the time and place in which the Good Shepherd calls his sheep so that he can be with them and give himself to them in a most particular way.

The Movement through the Signs

The development and growth of the Catechesis of the Good Shepherd was a continual source of joy and amazement for Sofia:

> We had followed the method that departs from the sign to arrive at the theology, and the message, without losing any of its greatness, was received with wonder and joy. Great was our joy when we catechists realized that in working in this way we did not invent anything at all; but rather that the children had conducted us to nothing less than the catechetical methods of the great catechesis of the fourth century, of which Enrico Mazza writes: "In the second half of the fourth century the great mystagogical catechesis constructed the theology of the salvific event, commenting on the rite enacted in the sacramental celebration and transmitting it to the faithful as catechesis." We had just discovered riches that were always present in the life of the

Church. Great was the joy of feeling ourselves inserted, together with these children, into the great river of faith and hope of the most authentic tradition of the Church, receiving within her, and from her—as a marvelous gift—the Christian message.[13]

Fourth-century catechesis was mystagogical in nature, with the bishop reflecting with the newly initiated on the meaning of the words and signs experienced at the Easter Vigil. We find the same catechetical method to be beneficial with children. *Mystagogy* literally means "interpretation of the mystery" or "teaching the mystery." It is a way of aligning what we hear in scripture and doctrine with what we celebrate in liturgy and discovering at the heart of this the God of all. The task of mystagogy consists in leading that attention and the active participation of the faithful from the rite to the mystery, from what is seen to what is unseen. Originally its function was to help its hearers enter into the liturgy in such a way that they could walk through the doors of the sacred and experience sacred space, time, and meaning—so that they could live out its vision. Mystagogy is lifelong, a commitment to learning and deepening our relationship with God and with each other and celebrating that through, with, and in Christ.

The celebration of the sacraments of initiation are not intended to bring our formation as Christians to an end, but rather to begin a process of continuing education and formation that is lifelong and that gradually unfolds the mystery of God's love and our response as we grow and mature. All of the sacraments are generous gifts from our loving God. Mystagogy invites us into a never-ending process of cherishing the gifts of the sacraments of initiation and continuously growing in our understanding of the power of God working in us as a result of our initiation into his Church. Understood in this light, Confirmation and Eucharist are not seen as an end, but rather as a beginning. They are gifts of the Father that strengthen and support us in living faithfully our life in Christ. They are gifts to be continuously meditated upon and studied. Our understanding of them is meant to deepen as we grow and mature.

We in the Catechesis of the Good Shepherd who assist the involvement of children and adults in a common religious experience in which

---

13. Sofia Cavalletti, "The Catechesis of the Good Shepherd as Gift," *Journals of the Catechesis of the Good Shepherd 2003–2008* (2005): 72, quoting Enrico Mazza, *La celebrzione eucaristic* (Edizioni Dehoniane: Bologna 2003), 143.

the religious values of childhood, primarily those values of contemplation and enjoyment of God, are predominant, have come to celebrate the meeting of the mystery of God and the mystery of the child in a continual song of praise. In our choir there is a particular place for the soft voices of the children, and together we sing with our Lord who raised his eyes to heaven and proclaimed: "I give praise to you, Father, Lord of heaven and earth, for although you have hidden these things from the wise and the learned you have revealed them to the childlike. Yes, Father, such has been your gracious will" (Mt 11:25–26). We sing recognizing that every choir has the need for a maestro, a master. And who is the master of the choir of catechesis? "You have but one master, the Christ" (Mt 23:10).

CHAPTER 11

The Liturgy's Vital Role in Discipleship Ministry with Teenagers

Jim Beckman

There was a blog post a while back that got my attention. It was a story about a grade school religious education class, going into the church to take some time to pray. The teacher took notice of a young boy who was lagging behind, not seeming too excited about this visit. He was new to the class and seemed very sad to her. He had, as she described, "deep, sad eyes." As the class began their prayer, the boy motioned for the teacher to come over to him, which she did. When she was near, he asked her a question. "Is God coming?" It was a palpable moment, and as a teacher myself, such a powerful question from this young boy resonates with me. It turns out this young boy's father had died, which explained the deep, sad eyes. Receiving this question from him was, for the teacher, powerful and moving.

But it was her answer to his question that gave me pause. She explained to this boy how she didn't really have an answer to that question, "No one really does." She continued, "We don't really wait for God to come to us, but rather we bring God to each other, because he is in us." She concluded by explaining how we know God is there: he causes our heart to swell up within us, sort of like "someone pumping it up with air." I guess we can conclude, then, that when our hearts "feel bigger," we can know God is there. The article ended with a quote from Alice Walker, the author of *The Color Purple*: "Have you ever found God in church? I never did. I just found a bunch of folks hoping for him to show. Any God I ever felt in church I brought in with me. And I think all the other folks did too."

They come to church to share God, not find God."[1] Many were inspired by this teacher and this young boy's faith. The reposts and comments on this blog were voluminous, many of them from Catholics.

How would we answer this boy's question? It wasn't clear whether the author is Catholic, but we know our answer as Catholics must be very different. If a young boy asked me, "Is God coming?" my response would be quick: "Oh, he's already here!" To which the boy would most likely reply, "How do you know?" "Well, this is what we believe in our Church, what God has revealed to us about himself. He's present to us in the Blessed Sacrament, which is right over there in that Tabernacle. And every time we come here for Mass, he is present to us in the person of the priest, in the reading of the Scriptures, and in the people as we all gather" (see SC, 7).

These aren't things we have to be cautious or tentative about sharing. These are fundamental truths in which we can be confident! The blog post was powerful, even moving. I was drawn to his deep question and could relate with the whole experience. But that boy needed an answer based in truth, not emotion. He needed something more to hold on to. What about the days his heart doesn't feel like "someone pumping it up with air"? Does that mean God isn't there?

The Critical Dynamics of Discipleship

How do we effectively reach teenagers with the truth about God? After years of active youth ministry, I am convinced that the only way is through what Sherry Weddell calls "intentional discipleship." In my experience with youth ministers and catechists, that term, though, is only vaguely understood. Some think it means using small groups, others that they are utilizing some new resource. For our purposes, I want to be clear what I mean by the term. Discipleship is a relational approach to ministry with teens that converges around three critical dynamics: the relationship we establish with them, the content of the faith we impart to them, and the way this content is applied through mentoring or apprenticeship.

First, relational ministry is a must when it comes to discipleship. We can't disciple someone we don't know intimately. True discipleship inherently involves guiding and directing someone, helping this person navigate personal weaknesses and struggles. I believe this makes it necessary

---

1. Alice Walker, *The Color Purple* (New York: Washington Square Press, 1982).

to do discipleship in a small group context. Large-group style ministry does not allow for the kind of intimate relationships that discipleship demands. Second, discipleship has a content and curriculum. There is content to the faith and through the relational context of discipleship we impart that content to another person. I believe the references in the *General Directory for Catechesis* involving "initiatory catechesis" are speaking to exactly this kind of instruction. Notice how the GDC describes the fundamental characteristics of initiatory catechesis:

> a comprehensive and systematic formation in the faith; . . . more than instruction: it is an apprenticeship of the entire Christian life; . . . a basic and essential formation, centered on what constitutes the nucleus of Christian experience, the most fundamental certainties of the faith. (GDC, 67)

These fundamental characteristics capture the third critical dynamic of discipleship: mentoring. I believe a lack of mentoring is the greatest poverty in ministry settings today. Mentoring and modeling the application of what is being learned is virtually nonexistent in most places. No matter how good one's catechesis is, the young people we are leading will struggle to put it into practice if we don't show them what it looks like, and even help them in the application long enough that they can get traction and be able to practice it on their own. This applies to *any* aspect of the faith—prayer and hearing God's voice, rooting out sin, growing in the virtue of chastity (growing in any virtue for that matter), celebrating the Mass, extending themselves to the poor and less fortunate, etc.

Discipleship and Catechesis

Relationship, content, mentoring: this is what real discipleship looks like, and is actually what catechesis was always meant to be. There's an interesting comment at the very beginning of *Catechesi Tradendae* that helps make this point:

> Very soon the name of catechesis was given to the whole of the efforts within the Church to make disciples, to help people to believe that Jesus is the Son of God, so that believing they might have life in his name, and to educate and instruct them in this life and thus build up the Body of Christ. The Church has not ceased to devote her energy to this task. (CT, 1)

St. John Paul II makes a sweeping statement here in the very first paragraph, making the terms *discipleship* and *catechesis* virtually synonymous.

But this is not what we are experiencing in most places when it comes to instruction in the faith. Call it religious education, or CCD, or whatever you will, but it is not true catechesis if it is not encompassing "the whole of the efforts within the Church to make disciples."

This is also what youth ministry should look like, encompassing all that is involved with helping teens embrace and mature in their faith in order to become authentic disciples of Jesus and fully engaged members of the Church. The defining document on Catholic youth ministry from the bishops of the United States, *Renewing the Vision*, fully supports this idea. In the document, the bishops identify three driving goals that define the scope of youth ministry:

- Goal 1: To empower young people to live as disciples of Jesus Christ in our world today.

- Goal 2: To draw young people to responsible participation in the life, mission, and work of the Catholic faith community.

- Goal 3: To foster the total personal and spiritual growth of each young person.[2]

These are the real aims of youth ministry. These objectives may seem daunting perhaps, but it is our charge nonetheless. Our first resistance might be, "There's no way to spend that much time with every teen." That is why we can't do youth ministry alone. We need lots of other adults and young adults who work together as a team. Every adult realistically can only reach 6–8 teens. So do the math—how many adults will you need?

If youth ministry is about making authentic disciples out of young people, then the whole approach to youth ministry needs to shift to embrace systems and structures that foster intentional discipleship.[3] There are too many programs and events that are giving young people content but not really taking that next step of mentoring them in the faith. This is not limited to youth ministry. The poverty can be seen in all areas of parish life. How do we make disciples? What does it even mean to be a disciple? What does it look like for someone in today's world?

---

2. National Conference of Catholic Bishops, *Renewing the Vision: A Framework for Catholic Youth Ministry* (Washington, DC: USCC, 1997), 9, 11, 15.

3. For a more detailed treatment of a discipleship approach to youth ministry, see the author's recent work, *Discipleship Focused Youth Ministry: A Getting Started Guide for Parishes*, written by Jim Beckman and Eric Gallagher, a publication of DiscipleshipYM.com.

Unfortunately, there are no pat answers or quick solutions to these questions. There isn't a program or a resource we can just go buy that will do it for us. We can be encouraged by the fact that many have made this shift and are seeing incredible fruit from their efforts. Dioceses all over the country are talking about discipleship. And many are wrestling with the most effective ways to implement it. The work takes effort and time— all change does. There will even need to be trial and error as we adapt to the circumstances and unique environment within our parishes. But we have to push any "silver bullet" mindset to the side and be willing to get back to the basics of discipleship. As a catechist, there are tangible things you can do. Let's take a look.

Empower Parents to Disciple Their Own Children

Intentional discipleship is not something we can fully accomplish without a unique collaboration with parents. We have all heard the Church's teaching on this: parents are the "primary educators" of their children.[4] But do we really believe this to be true and indeed *act* like we believe it? I've talked with many who work for the Church who treat this statement like an empty platitude—it's a nice "theory," but in reality WE are much better at teaching young people the faith. We have degrees in theology after all!

The bottom line is parents exercise the most significant influence on the lives of their children, hands down. When Church documents teach that parents are the "primary and principal educators of their own children" they mean it, not simply because it sounds nice, but because it is true. As catechists we must acknowledge this reality and believe it with every fiber of our being. Study after study has conclusively shown that parents have the greatest impact on their own children, particularly in terms of faith formation. Christian Smith, in his landmark study *Soul Searching*, goes so far as to say that if you want to know what a kid's faith life is going to be like, just look at his parents.[5] High percentages of young people simply mimic their parents' faith as they come into their adult years.

---

4. See especially Vatican II, *Declaration on Christian Education*, par. 3.

5. Christian Smith with Melinda Lundquist Denton, *Soul Searching: The Religious and Spiritual Lives of American Teenagers* ((New York: Oxford University Press, 2005), 261.

The Church calls parents the primary educators because she knows that parents have a number of trump cards that no catechist is ever going to have. Parents are *called* to the role they are in, and because of their call, they bear a huge weight of responsibility. Because they have been called to parenthood, they are *uniquely anointed* for it. This means that God is constantly making up for what is lacking in them and is actively involved in what they do through the work of grace. In addition to calling and anointing, parents also have *proximity* and *access*. They live in the same home, at least part of the time, and they have a unique access to their children because of their parental relationship—trust, comfort level, etc. These are powerful assets that EVERY parent has. No matter how close a catechist may get to a young person, they are never going to have these to the extent that a parent has them. And because of that fact, when it comes to teaching and discipling, even an awkward, seemingly ineffective parent is going to be better than any youth minister or catechist could ever hope to be.

If that is the case, then one of the most important roles youth ministers and catechetical leaders can play is to empower parents to be more effective in this role. One of the first things we need to help parents know is that discipleship is spelled *T I M E*. If they intend to lead their own children closer to Christ, first and foremost they must spend time with them. Yes, setting aside time is uniquely challenging in today's culture. With a little creativity and sacrifice, time is frequently found for things we prioritize. Spending time with children needs to be one of those priorities. Please don't buy into the fallacy that it's about quality, not quantity. I have found it to be just the opposite, both in my work over the years with teenagers, and now with my own children. Young people don't really trust someone who won't waste time with them. That may sound counterintuitive, but it's really true. I can't assume that a young person will want to listen to what I have to share with them; I know I have to earn that. When we are willing to spend time with another person, with no real agenda, no task to accomplish, nothing productive to get done, it shows that the person is important to us. When I've invested myself in this way, it has earned me the right to be heard.

That principle as a youth minister has translated well for me as a parent. I know I can't be a friend to my own children in the same way I have been with young people to whom I have ministered. But I can have a relationship with them that clearly demonstrates their importance to me and my love for them. In fact, I'm hoping I have a stronger relationship with my own kids than with any teen I have ever served. This requires a realignment of my priorities. I have to be creative and *make* time for them in my life. Discipleship requires lots of time, lots of conversations, and the firm foundation of a relational context for it to be effective. Parents already have an edge over any other adult. By virtue of their unique relationship, they exercise significant influence over their children's life decisions. Imagine the power of that edge being combined with a parent's gift of time and presence.

Second, if teens are going to mimic our faith practice, then we parents need to practice our faith in a way that is worthy of that emulation! The best way parents can begin to disciple their own children is by modeling a lived faith. We can already see the results of poor faith—or worse, no faith—being mimicked. Contemporary society is inundated with young adults who have completely detached from faith altogether. By and large, they're just doing what was modeled for them by their own parents, so we shouldn't be surprised.

Giving witness to a life of faith requires that we live our faith "out loud," even being more externally expressive than we might sometimes be comfortable with. It shouldn't be forced or awkward. In fact, the more natural our faith is in daily life, the more instinctively it will come up in conversations with our kids. We can share how faith is important to us, how God has been present to us, or how in some way he has blessed us. The point is, in order to have an influence on our children's faith, they actually have to *see* us practicing it. I have met many parents who say their faith is something very private to them; they don't like talking about it with others, even within their own family. All I can say to that is, we have to get over it. We are losing a staggering percentage of young people from the Church these days. Many are leaving in their teenage years, and even more in their young adult years. Most who leave talk about the shallow, empty experience they had of the Church and of faith. They experienced adults, especially their parents, as hypocritical, judgmental, and wishy-washy in their own beliefs. We can and should do much better than this for our children.

Living faith "out loud" means pushing through rolled eyes and sighs of exasperation when we suggest saying a prayer or reading the Scriptures together. It means being vulnerable with our children and sharing what we believe God is saying to us in our own prayer, which inherently means that WE are praying regularly. It means sharing about spiritual experiences we have had and even connecting those to our children's lives whenever possible. It means constantly opening ourselves to the subtle promptings of the Holy Spirit to share on this level with our own children.

I can't tell you how many times I have discipled my own children through casual conversations that just come up because I (1) have made time for them in my day-to-day life, and (2) have been willing to share what is going on in my own faith journey. Discipleship is not complicated, but it does require diligence and consistency. By living our faith out *in front of our children,* we let them see and hear what we believe, how we express our love for God and the charity in our hearts for others, and how we see God working in our lives. Everything we share will influence our children. These are the foundation stones for children becoming authentic disciples themselves.

Finally, we need to help parents pray. If their intention is to make disciples of their children, then they have to start regularly praying *for* them and *with* them. Parents need to pray *for* their kids every day and even let them know that they are doing it. Instead of saying that we're going to pray for them later, we should stop what we are doing and pray for them *immediately and out loud* so they can hear what we are saying. This kind of modeling of prayer is an amazing way to teach our kids how to pray. As my kids get older, I realize more and more what little control I actually have over their lives. This realization has driven me to pray more for them. I find myself on my knees a lot, sometimes in their rooms in the middle of the night while they're sleeping. As parents we have to recognize the spiritual battle going on for the souls of our children and must engage in this battle through prayer and spiritual warfare.

And we shouldn't limit prayer with our children to those times when they need something. We ought to take time to pray with them when *they* are praying. In this way, we can help them navigate prayer time, fruitfully read Scripture, and even ask them what they are hearing as the Lord speaks to their hearts. This may be unfamiliar terrain for parents. That only makes a stronger case for our own need to grow as disciples ourselves. These types of experiences in prayer are regular fare for a disciple. If we are pursuing our own faith and steadily growing, it will translate over time into deeper and deeper faith for our children. Entering into the sacramental life *with* our children is also crucial. With my own children, we read the Sunday Gospel reading in preparation for Mass, I take them to the Sacrament of Reconciliation periodically, and we do these things together. These experiences are even more powerful for them because they are also seeing *me* praying, going to Mass, going to confession, etc.

John Paul II once put it this way: "Only by praying together with their children can a father and mother, exercising their royal priesthood, penetrate the innermost depths of their children's hearts and leave an impression that the future events in their lives will not be able to efface" (FC, 60). When we pray *with* our children, they begin to see that *we* believe, that we have faith, and that we can approach our loving God in the context of a relationship. They witness things in us during these times that are deep and intimate, and these experiences leave a lasting impression on them. That impression will sustain them through many struggles and trials in their own lives, long after they have moved beyond our parenting.

In today's cultural situation, discipling our own children is an urgent challenge for parents. Whether we are in an intact family or a single parent, every parent is called to love and form their children, and ultimately help them become true disciples of Christ. This is a tangible response to John Paul II's exhortation, "The family finds in the plan of God the Creator and Redeemer not only its identity, what it is, but also its mission. . . . Each family finds within itself a summons that cannot be ignored, and that specifies both its dignity and its responsibility: family, become what you are!" (FC, 17). And "family," what you are, or rather should be, is a disciple-making machine!

As youth ministers, we can share these ideas with the parents of the young people in our programs. We can encourage them in their particular gifts for leading their own children to God. This would be a beautiful vision for the parish—pastors, youth ministers, parish catechists, and others collaborating with parents to make disciples of young people. The key for those of us working in ministry is to prayerfully consider how we can more effectively engage in that effort.

Emphasize the Liturgy's Vital Role in Discipleship

Finally we will turn back to the emphasis of this book, the liturgical life. What role does the liturgy play in all this, and how can we harness the power and momentum of the sacramental life of the Church to foster this kind of discipleship in young people? When it comes to discipleship, there is no better setting for it than the font of the sacramental life of the Church. As this book has already made clear, God is generously giving himself in the encounter of the liturgy. A fruitful life of discipleship becomes possible to an extraordinary degree when rooted in that encounter.

When combined with grace and the mysterious life of God found in the sacramental life of the Church, discipleship efforts will shift into a whole new gear. The real work of transformation is actually not possible for us to do in another person's life. That work is up to God. When we foster the capacity for young disciples to access the grace that is already available to them, it's like having a highly coveted back-stage pass; they get drawn into the liturgy as active participants and not just spectators.

Let's conclude by exploring some challenges that will likely emerge when trying to lead young people to a deeper experience of the sacramental life.

Help Them See the Primacy of Grace

In the same way that we need to embrace the fact that parents are far better than we are at leading their own children to discipleship, we need to also be deeply convinced that a teen receiving grace through a sacrament is far better than anything else we could do for them. There is a fundamental humility that we must have before God and the work that he is doing in a young person's life. Ultimately our job is to lead them to him, not to ourselves. The most significant access points that they have to him can be found in the sacraments—namely in the Sacraments of Eucharist and Reconciliation. They may not understand what they are receiving, and may even seem completely unaffected by the experience. We shouldn't judge the efficacy of the sacraments based on what we can observe. Much more is going on than what is visible to the human eye.

I have had countless experiences with young people over the years where repeated exposure to the sacraments on retreats, youth nights, mission trips, pilgrimages, etc. has gradually softened their hearts and opened them more and more to a deeper experience of our faith. We never had a retreat or trip where we didn't make space for the sacraments despite complaints from the teens at times. I will never forget one young person saying to me on a World Youth Day pilgrimage, "Why do we have to have Mass every single day? There are so many other things we could be doing on this trip. When you factor in the travel to and from a church, plus Mass itself, we are wasting so much time!" He obviously had thought through his argument. He even took time to informally survey the rest of the group and informed me that more than 85% agreed with him. This all led to a "family meeting" that evening where I informed the group that the schedule was not negotiable, particularly in reference to daily Mass. I shared with them briefly my love for the Eucharist, but more importantly God's love for meeting us in the liturgy. I knew that they may not get that, so I had to rely on my relationship with them. I basically asked them if they could trust me and trust the schedule that we had spent an entire year putting together. Changing the schedule really wasn't an option because all of our transportation and daily activities had already been built around daily Mass.

By the way, that young man today is a youth minister himself. I don't think these daily Masses hurt him one bit.

Patiently Work Through Their Sacramental Apathy

Many young people don't want to go to Mass, they believe "Mass is boring," and they constantly complain about anything Church-related. How do we help teens grow in their capacity for sacramental desire? I think one of the greatest challenges we face is that teens are never going to fully "get" what we are presenting to them because we can't fully "get it" either. There is a certain mystery to the faith, and it is something our human capacities will never be able to fully take in. How do we draw young people to such a mystery?

First, we need to pray for this conversion to happen. Ultimately, God is the One who brings about desire for him in a person. It's like the old adage "You can lead a horse to water, but you can't make it drink." We have no control over another person's desire, but God can move people and can stir up a desire for holiness within them. We need to pray for that, and then pray some more.

I remember well my experience with one young man. When I first met him, he was constantly speaking about how "made-up" the Catholic faith seemed to him. He would frequently make sarcastic comments to me about the man-made nature of the Church and all the "rules and regulations" the Church tried to force down people's throats. I would find myself cringing when I was with him, jarred by how callous he was towards God and faith in general. I prayed for that young man for months. I remember one night sitting behind him at a parish mission—he only came because his mom forced him to. I started praying for him more intently that night, literally sitting right behind him. My heart was moved for him and I was drawn to the desire that Jesus had for him. My experience of the prayer was so intense; I had myself convinced that he must be having a conversion experience right there. When the mission ended that night, he turned around to me and said, "More crap! How do you listen to this stuff? Who made all this up anyway?" I was floored—so *not* what I was expecting. But I kept praying for him, and for his heart to open.

Months later it did. One Sunday at Mass I came back to my pew after Communion. I was kneeling in prayer when someone grabbed my shoulder. Surprised, I looked up and saw it was him. He was crying and was saying he needed to talk, right then! I went out into the church foyer with him. He started by saying amidst his tears, "Remember that night at the parish mission last year—when I said, 'Who made all this stuff up anyway?' Well now I know! It's Him (God)—he made it all up, and it's perfect. He thought of everything! I get it, I get it now!"

I'm deeply moved now just remembering the moment. It was one of the more powerful ones in all my years of youth ministry. That young man became one of the most significant leaders in our youth ministry, and a little over a year later entered the seminary. He eventually discerned he wasn't called to the priesthood and left seminary to become a teacher. He longs to help young people have a conversion similar to his own. We won't always see the fruit like this, but we have to pray like we know God has the ability to transform hearts. I believe that God gives us just enough evidence of the fruit to keep us going, but never so much that we start thinking it's us who actually bring about the conversion.

As I mentioned earlier, *repeated exposure to the sacraments can eventually lead to a softened heart.* We need to encourage and get kids to Mass and confession as often as we can. We obviously don't want to force them, but at younger ages this consistency is important. Push through the complaining.

In addition to helping them be frequently present to the sacraments, we can expose them to *our* experiences as well. We can share our own experiences of the sacraments and what they mean to us. We can share stories about how we have experienced God, and how we have experienced grace at work in our own lives. Do this often, but naturally, organically. We want it to come up in normal conversations, not just when we are trying to get them to go to Mass and are in the midst of conflict. It's hard to argue with personal experience, so we should keep what we share in the form of testimony. And we should always make what we say a proposition rather than a mandate. Young people don't have to believe what we are saying, so it's important to respect their freedom throughout the conversation.

Help Them towards Sacramental Relevance

As catechists and youth ministers we are constantly struggling to be "relevant" in a teen's world. How do we help make the sacramental life of the Church relevant for them? The temptation here can be to try and adapt the sacraments in a way that will make them more relevant. We think of it as accommodation, which in modern culture is a common and often successful strategy—particularly for Millennials and Gen Z teens. The problem with this is that the sacraments are already an "accommodation" in themselves—God accommodating himself to us, through the tangible signs that are the "matter" of the sacrament, bread, wine, water, etc. If we change sacramental words or signs for the sake of relevancy, we run the risk of taking the focus off what God is doing. The accommodation has to be the other way around when it comes to the sacraments. Our goal has to be to help teens accommodate themselves to the liturgy. He is bringing himself down to our level, and our whole disposition should be to receive as much of what he is giving us as possible.

Years ago I was running a Confirmation program for a parish. The preparation had come to an end, and it was the big night of the ceremony with the archbishop. It was my first year, and I was inheriting a program and lots of traditions that had been done for years before me: like letters to God from all the teens, written on different colored paper and then taped together into a large colorful quilt-like piece that was draped over the altar during the Rite of Confirmation; like each small group producing items that symbolized their group to bring up during the offertory—footballs, basketballs, musical instruments, etc. These ended up being brought forward and placed all around the now very colorful altar; and special intercessory prayers were read by a different member of each small group.

These were all creative ways to try and make the experience more relevant. But I will never forget the reprimand I got that night in the sacristy from the archbishop. His words stung, but the message was clear to me: "Don't mess with the rite, Jim. The rite is beautiful in itself, and you don't want to do anything to take away from that beauty!" It reminded me of words I had heard in my undergraduate studies—"Teach from the rite, to the rite." I was taught that the focus of good sacramental catechesis was the rite itself. We should use the rite to help young people understand what they are about to experience, but in a limited way that doesn't steal away any "plot points" for them. The reception of the sacrament was still meant to be a mystery, so it was important to protect that moment of encounter. It's sort of like how we can tell another person about a great movie without giving away the thunder. We can share in a way that gets them excited about going to see it for themselves. Sacramental preparation should be similar. Somewhere between college and that first youth ministry job, I had forgotten this key principle. Not only had I taken attention away from the rite itself, I hadn't gotten the teens excited about the rite at all. They were much more focused on their offertory items and special intercessory prayers. I'm not sure they even knew what the truly important moments within the rite were. The relevancy temptation is something we need to avoid at all costs. We can't make God more relevant, we can only help foster receptivity.

Embrace the Attention Span Issues with Young People

Liturgical living requires an ability to focus ourselves. How does modern technology create unique challenges for growth in holiness and what we can do about it? Collectively, our attention spans are shrinking, not just for teens but for adults too. Some studies show our ability to remain focused has decreased by more than half, from twelve minutes to five minutes since just ten years ago.[6] One study states that the average teen attention span is only eight seconds.[7] Unfortunately that's less than the average attention span of a goldfish, which is only nine seconds—a sad commentary on American culture! Regardless of the exact number, it is clear we have a problem. And this problem is even more prevalent with teens and young adults. If engagement with the sacramental life of the Church literally requires an investment of our attention, then what are we to do?

The first step to healing any problem is admitting that we have a problem. Many people today embrace—without reservation—the advances of communications technology and all the apparent advantages of multitasking. Perhaps it's time to begin asking if all of our devices lead to healthy humans and relationships. Most of us can plainly see the disruption they cause when trying to pray or engage in Mass.

How do we ask these difficult questions with young people? They will resist any attacks on technology and most invitations to unplug from their devices. We can point them instead to the right information. Discussions can be started about the effects, even dangers, of uncurbed technology use. We can propose alternatives or challenge them to see how attached they really are—such as encouraging periodic phone or social media fasts. One of my fellow professors issues the challenge of a Lenten media fast every year, and it is often taken up by more than two-thirds of the students. These kinds of experiences will help young people see for themselves an unhealthy attachment and foster a desire for change.

---

6. Nicole Plumridge, "Is the Internet Destroying Our Attention Span?" *Psychminds* (blog), August 1, 2013, http://psychminds.com/is-the-internet-destroying-our-attentions-span/.

7. Lizette Borelli, "Human Attention Span Shortens to 8 Seconds due to Digital Technology: 3 Ways to Stay Focused," *Vitality* (blog), *Medical Daily*, May 14, 2015, http://www.medicaldaily.com/human-attention-span-shortens-8-seconds-due-digital-technology-3-ways-stay-focused-333474.

Second, we need to foster a capacity in young people for contemplation. A number of years ago I was on a World Youth Day Pilgrimage—a different one. A young teen approached me on our first day during one of the travel breaks to ask a question. "Could you teach me how to pray?" I looked at him, somewhat surprised by the question. I thought he was going to ask if he could go look in a shop, or go to the bathroom. He explained that he had heard I wrote a book on prayer; he had always wanted to be able to pray, but just never seemed to be able to do it. If I wrote a book about it, maybe I could help him. I asked him a few questions to figure out what his experience of prayer was like—but clearly he had no experience. I tried to explain to him that prayer was not something I could just teach him, I would have to show him. And that would take time, probably every day during the trip, time when everyone else would be shopping or site-seeing. "Do you really want to use your time for that?" I asked him. "Yeah, sure," he said, "that sounds kind of cool." I was actually trying to talk him out of it because that is not exactly how I imagined spending all of my time.

Everyday for two weeks I spent some time with him. I started by talking with him about silence and contemplation, explaining that those were critical dynamics for prayer. We would do these "stretches for silence" just to see how long he could stay quiet. The first day he didn't quite make it to thirty seconds (longer at least than the eight-second teen average). I was hoping to get him to eight to ten minutes of silence, and then start showing him some ways to pray. But he never made it. We spent the entire two weeks stretching, and never made it to ten minutes—until the flight home. We sat together for a while on the long flight home. I got him started with the same routine we had been doing every day. But this time my watch passed five minutes, ten minutes, fifteen minutes. I started thinking that maybe he fell asleep, but he was making other movements that showed he was awake. Finally, after eighteen minutes, he opened his eyes. He had the same discouraged look on his face as any other day as he asked, "How long was that?" I looked at him realizing that he really had no clue how long that had just been. He was thinking it had been a short time, just like all the other days. "Eighteen minutes," I said. At first he didn't believe me; I had to show him my phone to prove it.

The best part was unpacking what had gone on inside him during those eighteen minutes. He got lost in memories of all the places we had been on the trip, and ironically all the places we had met each day to spend time trying to be quiet. Those daily stretches for silence were typically followed by conversations, some that lasted for long periods of time especially later in the trip. He had some great memories of those conversations and the many things we talked about. During those minutes of silence, he started realizing how grateful he was that he took that time every day to slow down and just be quiet. I was amazed. What had seemed like a frustrated effort the whole trip had suddenly blossomed into this deepened capacity for solitude. Several months later he was sharing with me how he was having prayer times that were lasting longer than an hour.

Over the years I have had the privilege of taking groups of teens into stretches for silence, to the symphony, to the opera, out late at night to star gaze, on silent retreats, etc.—all in an effort to get them to tap into something deeper inside them. I am always amazed at the incredible capacity they have for silence and contemplation once we help them get there. In fact, most of them prefer it to their normal state of being. Once they taste it, they keep desiring to go back to it. This is what I mean by fostering a capacity for contemplation. It's a gift that will last them a lifetime. And even more, when we can connect that desire within, and direct it to the sacramental life of the Church, we root them in something that will last far beyond this life.

I want to encourage you. I truly believe that the coming years are going to be a pivotal time for the Catholic Church. Be an innovator! Don't settle for the same old, same old. Be willing to take risks and even make mistakes as you embrace the challenges we face. We have explored many things in this chapter:

- true discipleship needs to encompass real relationship, the content of the faith, and a mentoring approach;
- catechesis *is* discipleship, so it needs to embody these characteristics;
- our greatest asset is the parents of the young people we minister to—we need to hinge on their role and HELP them to be more effective;
- and finally, we must help young people and their families meet God in the liturgy, the life-giving font of the Church.

I pray that in the future—fifty, one hundred or even more years from now—people will look back on this time in history and see the people who helped make the change. May you be one of those who helped move the Church into a time of greater fruitfulness!

CHAPTER 12

Liturgical Catechesis and the RCIA Process

William J. Keimig

A simile can be helpful in approaching a Christian mystery. It can make use of a more understandable life experience to draw us into a less familiar reality. So with that entrée, let me offer a simile having to do with a dead armadillo.

My wife, Heather, loves me very much. I know this for various reasons. One is that she lovingly birthed and parents with me our six children, living faithfully all the—dare I say—"ordinary" things that go with being a wife and mother. But I also know that she loves me because I received in the mail a dead armadillo. You see, my wife recently went down to Florida for her mother's birthday, taking along our eldest daughter Rose. And in Florida, as you may know, they have armadillos, which do not hang around in our more northerly home state of Maryland.

We're a nature-oriented family; we do lots of outdoor stuff. One of the things that you find if you get out in nature is dead stuff. Dead stuff would normally be an occasion to do the opposite of the Good Samaritan's reaction—you know, kind of walk around safely and keep on going. But sometimes, if you do elsewise, it can be very interesting. And so one of the things we're in the habit of doing on our nature walks is taking more interesting moribund finds and skeletonizing them. This is accomplished by a process that unfortunately I do not have time to delve into, but we've skeletonized things as big as a beaver, which can weigh fifty or sixty pounds. You can get some really cool skeletons, which are great for our family science studies (we homeschool, and animal skeletons would be rather expensive to purchase).

Anyway, my wife called me from Florida: "Honey, on the way to church, I spotted an armadillo road kill. Do you want it?" Well, you know anybody's obvious answer, right? "Yeah!" She was offering to grab it on the way back from Mass. She knows my criteria: it can't be too crushed and messed up to have an intact skeleton, and not all eaten up and old. So she went ahead, got it, and mailed it to me up in Maryland. Now I have an armadillo skeleton! Very cool!

I know some of you reading this are actually a bit puzzled so far. You're perhaps wondering if this chapter is in the right book. It may never have occurred to you that someone could show the intensity of her love for her hubby by putting a dead armadillo in the mail. But so it is. Now, the simile part.

If you've been involved in the Rite of Christian Initiation of Adults (RCIA) for any length of time, you know that many people outside of the Church's fold view what we do inside the Catholic world as weird. To some it is a shake-your-head sort of weird, right? It can seem especially weird in regard to what we do in the liturgy. People outside of a "high church" tradition (or sometimes even within a "high church" tradition, like Anglicans or Lutherans who have largely lost the theology of sacramental efficacy) hear what Catholics think about worship and what we daily do about it (like going to church on a weekday, or adoration at some odd hour of the night). Such people often react like perhaps you reacted to my armadillo story. "That's just really weird!" As far as the liturgy goes, and how important Catholics think it is, such folks might say: "Okay, not only is what you do weird, but I could never imagine THAT being an overwhelming way in which God wishes to love me, or me to love him." And we Catholics aren't just saying that liturgy is sort of tolerable if you end up becoming Catholic. No, we say that liturgy is *the* place and experience that makes us feel MOST loved by God, and *the* thing that accomplishes God loving us most perfectly. A non-Catholic might never imagine that this could be so, just like you might find it slightly challenging to imagine that I would feel intensely loved because my wife mailed me a dead armadillo. It's in that category of weirdness for many people trying to figure out Catholics.

What Moves People to See a New Vision?

So that leads to the first question: What's the point of what we're doing here in this chapter? Two things: one is to *understand* the vital purpose of the liturgical experience in the RCIA process, and two is to encourage you in your own love and need for the liturgy so that you can *mentor* others into that same love and need.

In my experience, the only effective way to do liturgical catechesis in an RCIA context is as a *personal witness*. My own awareness of the power of this witness comes not firstly from my years of RCIA ministry, but instead from my years of being a dad. As we've raised our six munchkins, all born and baptized in the same parish community where I've had the privilege of being the director of religious education, Sunday and daily Mass have been constants—in the sense of regular attendance and regular indigence. Grace is always there, but the good Lord experiences a fairly reliable poverty of my attention and attunement. I cannot at this stage of my parenting life offer him much in the way of profound meditative focus at Holy Mass. Yet I can bring to him the constancy of my love by offering the sacrifice of that very desire to be more able to focus, so that my children will be closer to their best Father often. This simple but determined witness that my wife and I give year after year, and the challenging aspects of "pew-parenting" visible to all in such contexts, has elicited many testimonies from others of how it has encouraged their own fidelity to the liturgy. Perhaps others' similar thoughts go unspoken to us. This witness silently says to others, "This family seems to think the Mass is *really* important— even with the rocks and rolls of those kids, they seem to need something that being here gives them."

Liturgy must be need-based. In your own faith life the liturgy must be an uncompromising and unequivocal *need* of your soul, so that you could say, "I *need* the liturgy! I *need* what it offers on a daily basis. I can't imagine life without it." That's what I mean by *understanding* the liturgy, that you've gotten to the place where it is a genuine need for you. Then you become an authentic witness of it to others.

Why Does Liturgy Matter So Much?

So that leads to the next question: What *is* it about liturgy that makes it so enormously important? I like the one-sentence description by the great Benedictine liturgical theologian Cyprian Vagaggini: "The liturgy is connaturally the center and soul of the whole striving toward perfection in the way in which Mother Church officially proposes it to her children."[1] Now, I am nowhere near the theological level of Father Vagaggini, but I'm going to dare to edit him for the sake of simplicity. If we could make his sentence even more succinct, we could say: *the liturgy is the center and soul of the striving toward perfection.* Now, in an RCIA setting that sentence might be off-putting because of the word *perfection.* In our culture, people don't perceive a need to strive for perfection. Not because everybody is mediocre, but because most people don't perceive perfection as a real-world *need.* Yet, they *could* perhaps articulate it as a *desire.* "Yeah, I'd like to be perfect and all that." But they either think it's a pie-in-the-sky thought—an unattainable thing—or they don't actually perceive why their life really has to be directed quite that fundamentally towards being fully perfect. It's okay to just be "good enough." Some might even consider it prideful to seriously consider such a high target. So, to suggest to RCIA participants that perfection is the goal for the liturgy—this is what the liturgy is offering to you—won't cut much mustard. Unless you first define perfection the way the Church defines it.

The secular world might define perfection in rather mechanical terms—an absence of error or ideas like that. But that's not how the Church understands it. Mother Church means it in terms of a call to *intimacy*; a relational term, not a mechanical or utilitarian term. It's the call to say this: "To be perfect or to strive for perfection means you've decided that you want to experience a love that never ends; a Love beyond all telling *wants you* more than you can imagine being wanted; a surpassingly generous and gentle Lover wants to give you the gift of total intimacy forever." Now, phrased that way, could you imagine that people would perceive that as a *need*? Do you want to be loved beyond all telling? Do you want to experience the love that never ends? Do you want to have intimacy beyond your most daring imaginings? And do you want to be able to

---

1. Cyprian Vagaggini, OSB, *Theological Dimensions of the Liturgy*, trans. Leonard J. Doyle (Collegeville, MN: Liturgical Press, 1976), 900.

give it back, just as fully? Could you more easily say that people in an RCIA setting might get interested in that; that they might perceive this offer as a deeply desirable thing for themselves? Is that something worth striving for? Yes, even on a human level, much less a Divine one, any rational person would want to seek something that attractive. The old cliché is that everyone wants to be loved. So taking that and running with it, you're going to teach that we Catholics have something that is the center and soul of the possibility in your life of attaining perfect, wonderful intimacy forever, and to enable you to live in it *beyond* what you're able to strive for as a mere human. The *Catechism* declares that God wishes to make us "capable of responding to him, and of knowing him and of loving him far beyond [our] own natural capacity" (CCC, 52). Would you want that? *That's* what's being offered in the liturgy. That's what it *is*. Living in the liturgy is seeking love like that, and the granting of enablement to actually attain it. It is the offer of awesome intimacy *and* the engine to get to it!

How Does This Vision Get Unfolded in the RCIA Process?

In RCIA, that initial call of the Gospel message that you deliver early in the process doesn't get defined right away. Catechesis is incremental and gradual. You work towards it. You work towards defining that wonderful call in the Old Testament—starting out in the broadest terms with God's loving presence in creation and among humankind, and eventually ending with the fullness and explicit beauty and drama of Christ's love. Outside the Church, you cannot reliably say that everybody wants to be loved *by Christ*. You *can* reliably say that everybody wants to be loved. You start where people are. After awhile, once they understand who Christ is, then bring in the fact that this faith is wholly founded on our universal innate desire for genuine intimacy.

Many times in leading RCIA I've been stunned by the incremental work of the Holy Spirit in souls—taking newly-arrived inquirers from a vaguely sensed need for "something," or a dimly understood aimlessness, to a place many months or even a few years later of unfettered yearning for the balm of receiving Christ in the Holy Eucharist. People living in unending circles of pain, immaturity, or purposeless ignorance come to the point of intensely wanting a simple circle of embodied Bread, trusting that in so receiving they might be able to live differently and be loved without condition.

Father Johannes Hofinger, SJ, famously said: "Here is the last and most decisive reason why teaching through worship is superior to all other forms of Christian teaching. *The liturgy gives what it teaches.*"[2] Catechesis is always *about* Christ. Loving our brethren, and pastorally serving their needs, is always *about* witnessing to Christ. But these both have that annoying preposition in there—that word "about." Catechesis and pastoral care are both "about" the love of Christ, wonderful and necessary as they are. Yet, only the liturgy *gives* you Christ, gives him to you unfiltered: sanctifying grace. In the Eucharist superlatively—as Blood and Flesh, Soul and Divinity—he is touching, healing, and elevating your body, your soul, your humanity—an intimate union.

This is not only so in the Mass. It is evident when a grown man comes out of a first Confession, crying almost uncontrollably, and takes me by the shoulders and says to me, "I did what you said, I held nothing back, I gave it all to God! I feel so free, so free!" He's encountered and received Christ, unfiltered. This encounter is also evident in the celebratory explosion of an elderly woman from a Baptismal immersion, arms flung upward in joy, a living asperges to everyone near the font. And it is evident at the Rite of Acceptance in the quiet, intensely personal weeping of catechumens receiving just a foretaste of those powerful graces as sponsors gently make the sign of our Lord's Cross over eyes and ears, hearts and hands, head and feet. These are indications of an RCIA process that is serving the work of the Holy Spirit in making known "the love of Christ that surpasses knowledge, so that you may be filled with all the fullness of God" (Eph 3:19).

Where Do We Get Off Track?

Yet many people and parishes in the United States attached the acronym "RCIA" to things that aren't RCIA as the Church has described it in the ritual book. Inquirers are sometimes subjected either to *"convert" classes* or *navel-gazing* rather than the fullness of what the Church longs to give.

---

2. Johannes Hofinger, SJ, and Francis Buckley, SJ, *The Good News and Its Proclamation*, 2nd ed. (Notre Dame, IN: University of Notre Dame Press, 1968), 34; italics in original.

"Convert class RCIA" can be described as a process that primarily lives within the catechetical aspect. It's all about the teaching, and there's little focus on the liturgical rites of the process—the rites are just sort of hoops you jump through, poorly explained and sometimes ignored altogether. There are many parishes where the rites, especially the minor ones, like the scrutinies, presentation rites, and preparation rites, simply aren't done. This didactic sort of "RCIA" is actually more of a "convert" class, and the witness given to participants is of relating to the liturgy in a perfunctory way. A catechist who thinks that people attain sufficiently lasting conversions through only teaching lacks the Catholic vision that liturgy is the glue of conversion. Put in a rather earthy way, the liturgy "sticks" you to God. No lesser human aspect of the RCIA process can make up for a failure to form liturgically oriented neophytes. The liturgy is to be seen as the *summit* of what all souls really desire and the *source* of the strength to *experience* a love that bests all others—not merely learned about as an ideal explained in teachings.

In a navel-gazing "RCIA," the pastoral care can become something that's more about having good fellowship, the warm fuzzy kind, with small groups that do a lot of talking, a lot of unguided discussion, but it's mostly subjectivized—how do *you* feel about this or that? This kind of fellowship doesn't effectively foster conversion and change in participants' lives because it isn't founded on divine revelation that is unpacked and reflected on in a context which encourages deepening trust in Church teaching. It's more founded on opinions ("So what did you think?"), and it rarely moves beyond that. Experience and opinion *are* relevant, but only if truth is informing them. In a healthy, balanced RCIA process, pastoral care and fellowship become more than navel-gazing or more than group dialog because they point souls to the liturgical experience, where it is *fact* and *certainty* that God awaits, to love us and to heal us far beyond our poor power to offer human intimacy and solace—*the* elevating experience of being truly loved by our intimate Savior, who can be found here *par excellence*, and whose sacramental graces lead us to sublime depths of fellowship with the Father (see 1 John 1:1–4).

How Does Liturgy Impact RCIA Catechesis?

Put another way, the liturgy matures catechesis and pastoral care. A mature RCIA process is a liturgical, catechetical, and pastoral process that is *led* by the liturgy. For example, RCIA catechetical work is not monolithic; it changes in each of the four periods of the process: precatechumenate, catechumenate, purification and enlightenment, and mystagogy. These four periods each have a different mission for the catechesis, tied to what is happening liturgically. The liturgy guides *why* it changes. In the precatechumenate, however long it ends up being, you're delivering the basic Gospel message, the kerygma, and answering questions like gangbusters, to bring down the barriers to participants making a choice. Why do you seek to bring down the barriers? Because you're eventually going to be offering them the opportunity to go through the Rite of Acceptance or the Rite of Welcoming, and they need to have the ability, as these rites tell us, to say an honest and informed yes to the momentous questions asked in the liturgy.

In the catechumenate period, catechesis is more like laying flesh on bones. The kerygma is like a skeleton and the catechumenate fills it out: the moral teachings of the Church, the sacramental life much more deeply explained, etc. This period prepares participants for what they're going to affirm and assent to at the Rite of Election or Call to Continuing Conversion. The catechumenate period has a clear mission to make sure that the essential things of the deposit of faith are delivered to participants such that they can honestly say, "I am freely willing and ready to come into the Church."

The period of purification and enlightenment, normally the six weeks of Lent, has the critical mission of proximal sacramental preparation and spiritual formation rather than new instruction on aspects of the deposit of faith. In Lent we shouldn't have any essential doctrine left to cover because that should have happened before the Rite of Election—again, catechesis is driven here by a liturgical reason. So what you're doing in Lent is not catching up—you're preparing participants for the sacramental sharing ahead with more spiritually oriented teachings. Some people liken it to an extended retreat.

And then mystagogy, on the other side of initiation, helps those new Catholics by reflecting on the sacraments that they've just received and encourages them to develop consistent and active participation in God's sacramental mysteries. This period helps them deepen their sacramental life—the fact of liturgical participation now achieved once again drives the character of the catechesis. What we've come to call this liturgy-driven catechesis is "teaching to and from the rites." You teach to the rite that is coming up and then afterwards you teach from it. You're aiming to make participants expectant for and presumptive of what occurs in their souls through the graces of these liturgical steps towards full communion.[3]

How Does Liturgy Influence How Doctrine Is Taught in the RCIA Process?

At this point, I'd like to visit the ancient Church formula, *lex orandi, lex credendi*. In a more formal Latin translation, *lex* would be "law," *orandi* would be "of praying," and *credendi* would be "of believing." So, the law of prayer shapes the law of belief. Put more colloquially: "we pray what we believe." RCIA follows this hierarchy. Catechesis (our belief) becomes what it should be because of the liturgy (our prayer) that it lives within. "In the liturgy, all Christian prayer finds its source and goal" (CCC, 1073). In this sense, our Protestant brothers and sisters can't teach in a liturgical-catechetical manner because they usually don't understand the liturgy as so profoundly relevant to catechesis and the goals of conversion. But you do, right? When we say that the Eucharistic liturgy is the source and summit of our life, it isn't just a Vatican II cliché. It's a reality. And only if an RCIA catechist is deeply imbued with that reality does the catechesis become unswervingly devoted to forming liturgical people.

Let's explore an example. Take any common doctrine taught in RCIA. Try coming up with, in a single succinct sentence, how that doctrine connects to the sacred liturgy. Take purgatory. If this doctrine is not taught in a liturgical-catechetical way, participants could learn that purgatory is sort of interesting and clearly true (because of course you teach it as a certitude, not an opinion), but not obviously relevant to their daily

---

3. It's beyond the scope of this chapter to discuss in detail the role of lectionary-based catechesis in the RCIA process, but if your parish uses this form of determining weekly teaching topics in all four periods of the RCIA cycle, then I would suggest reading a piece I wrote a few years ago titled: "On Not Using Lectionary-Based Catechesis as the Primary Method to Determine the Order of Teachings." It first appeared as an article in the *Sower* catechetical journal, and is also published as appendix 6 in the *RCIA Catechist's Manual* available from Liturgy Training Publications. Some dioceses have it posted online as well.

lives. It remains an intellectual piece of information. Participants could be thinking, "Gee, you know maybe I'll end up there someday, or maybe I'll hope to avoid it someday, or maybe my relatives are there." It's an interesting idea. Beyond that they don't think much about it.

Now let's connect purgatory to the liturgy. What does purgatory have to do with the liturgy? RCIA participants are being invited to be part of the worshipping Church which has a daily embattled mission—a reality spreading across the Church fighting on earth, the Church suffering, and the Church triumphant. What else? We pray for purgatory's population—our future heavenly companions, right! We sacrifice for them, have Masses offered, merit indulgences for them, and make use of sacramental grace to live lives worthy of something better than purgatory's cleansing pains. Purgatory might otherwise be an esoteric Catholic curiosity, but the liturgy makes it a daily lived reality. If you connect that for them, you're doing liturgical catechesis, because you're taking truth and making it lived, not just learned. Do you see this? You can do that with each doctrine in the Deposit of Faith, bringing each one *alive*, because making these connections *empowers us do something of great importance with truth*, making us see a *need*.

A Pastoral, Catechetical Vision for the RCIA—Led by the Liturgy

On its *own terms* the liturgy teaches us to *need*. Liturgy is *history made present*. That's what the liturgical year is, the Church's living memory, annually walking through Christ's life and celebrating saints from days gone by who await us in eternity. Liturgy is *mission made present*. Reading liturgical prayer, you become present to its rich concise expression of our fidelity to the Father through his Son's every word and action. Liturgy is *community made present*. This is most obvious in those around us at Mass, but it is also uniquely so through the Liturgy of the Hours, that constantly present global reality of communal prayer, sanctifying time and surrounding each disciple with the love of unseen intercession. Liturgy is *love made present*. This can be seen in each place that our Sacred Scriptures are read to the Father's children gathered, making God's love audible. Liturgy is *God made present*. Every sacramental grace given is Jesus touching, the Spirit infusing, the Father running to solace a child wanting to be nearer.

In the Catholic tradition, liturgy also becomes a pastoral model. Liturgy *models utterance*, how we are to speak of good things to others. Love longs to share itself, and so the Trinity speaks to souls as the blessed readings and beautiful prayers unfold to bring comfort and challenge. Liturgy *models dialogue* with God and other souls. Love longs to speak to the beloved, and so the liturgy is a discourse to form in us a lifelong practice of earnest candor with God in prayer, from the catechumenal encounter to the neophyte experience and beyond in communion with our brethren. Liturgy *models sacrifice* in our Savior's re-presented self-donation. Love longs not to count the cost, and so the liturgy always places the Paschal mystery at the center to show us the way to love without measure. Lastly, liturgy *models surrender* in the docility of a Son to a Father, the great theme of the Mass. Love longs to trust absolutely, and the liturgy invites us to docility, to seek sacramental grace as our means to imitate the Son.

And there are things that catechesis in the RCIA process does *for* the liturgy: "Catechesis is intrinsically linked with the whole of liturgical and sacramental activity" (CT 23). Catechesis *introduces* worship, helping new-comers become attuned to the basic concept of sacred space in which God is unquestioningly present—an increasingly unfamiliar concept today. Catechesis not only introduces worship, it *incarnates* worship by explaining signs, gestures, and beauty. Would you ever start off the first session of RCIA by saying, "Okay, let's get started here . . . in the name of the Father, and the Son, and the Holy Spirit." No, you would *explain* the gesture *before* you offer the opportunity to do it. Catechesis *informs* worship, offering a compelling vision into the mysteries of God—teaching and grounding participants in the nearly unbelievable divine realities and astounding human possibilities made present by liturgical actions. Catechesis *inculturates* worship, bestowing upon each human culture the blessed explanation of what orthodoxy means: that the true Church brings with her a great gift—the certain knowledge, divinely revealed and divinely guarded, of how to praise God *rightly*, to worship him as he desires to be worshipped. Finally, catechesis *invites* worship, ever pointing to the Great Story of "the love that never ends" (CCC, 25), speaking of truths in a joyful way capable of making hearts burn to celebrate: thanks be to God that *this* is all true, that *this* God is real! The liturgy is that celebration.

Praying through this Catholic vision helps you get to a point where you exude love for the liturgy—where it flows out of you. Seek to bring it to every corner of the RCIA room, understood by catechists, understood by small group facilitators. Then participants can't easily miss it.

How Does the Liturgy Anchor the RCIA Process?

For participants in RCIA (and for the faithful serious about seeking sanctity), liturgies are acts of *movement*. What's that mean? Liturgy could just be hoops to jump through. Many might say, "Next week, the rite gets done, right?" Instead, rightly done and explained, RCIA liturgies should be an active movement forward. For example, what happens to an unbaptized adult going through the Rite of Acceptance? It's a movement, a decision made. On the other side of that simple liturgy, this soul is in an authentically different relationship with God and the Church. He or she inherits the Church's motherly attentions with graces and blessings and minor exorcisms in a way that was not the case before that. If such a person dies before getting baptized, what happens? Look up the wonderful answer in the RCIA ritual book or canon law (RCIA, 47).

Catechesis teaches for conversion when it points to and is impregnated with liturgical power. Not just an emaciated Catholic instruction that weakly hopes that all this revelation is interesting and somehow relevant in a poorly defined way: "This is what the Church teaches; thank you for coming; see you next week for the next set of tenets." This is *not* aiming for change. It's not tackling the harder challenges of Catholic doctrine which can only be taught with evangelical boldness and confidence because we can also boldly and confidently point participants to a liturgy that *enables* real human change. Only *liturgical* catechesis is imbued with trusting expectancy that a Father awaits with deeply needed gifts to make saints of sinners. Sainthood is *impossible* without God's sacramental gifting combined with a soul's hope anchored there alone.

How Can a Parish's RCIA Process
Take Steps Forward in this Vision?

At this point, some succinct lists may help take us toward still-deeper practical applications to parish life.

A first question: *What are the benefits to RCIA catechesis that is authentically liturgical?*

- It fosters more genuine and deep conversions to God and his calling on individual lives.
- It allows for more-frequent and more-full appropriation of grace.
- It fosters docility to the ancient ways of the Church.
- It helps people to grasp the immense potential of participation in the liturgical life of the Church.
- It assists in vocational awareness due to the regular focus on saints who have lived their vocations fully.
- It gives participants opportunities to experience their priest's liturgical ministry more often and in more personal settings.
- Because the liturgical year forms the context of parish life, it helps participants become that much more integrated into parish life.
- It helps sponsors, godparents, and team members to be more liturgically aware and in tune with the cycles of the Church's life.

A second question: *What are some simple ideas for incorporating liturgical or paraliturgical aspects in the work of passing on the Catholic faith?*

- Provide guided meditation on the prayers of the RCIA major and minor rites.
- Provide guided meditation on one of the Eucharistic Prayers or other major prayers of the Mass (e.g., the Penitential Act, the Gloria, the Sanctus, the prayers of the Communion Rite, etc.).
- Provide guided meditation on the Divine Praises or other litanies.
- Explain and offer Masses for various intentions.
- Explain and pray the Liturgy of the Hours.
- Explain and pray the Stations of the Cross.
- Explain and pray the Angelus or Regina Caeli.
- Sing common Mass settings.

A third question: *What are some of the dangers when a parish lacks a liturgically centered vision of the RCIA process?*

- RCIA, as proposed by the Church, is viewed as unnecessarily effort-intensive, or it becomes "canned."

- Doctrine is explained without reference to Jesus; his simple call to receive him is lost in the details.
- Not expecting serious progress in souls, because the liturgy's enabling graces are neglected.
- Liturgical rites become solely celebrations of community rather than transforming encounters with Christ.
- Trust given to catechists and leaders never translates into trusting in Jesus, who awaits participants with sanctifying grace.

A fourth question that leads to lots of additional questions: *What are some questions to discuss in a parish setting to improve RCIA?*

- How do we prepare RCIA participants and the parish for the major liturgical rites?
- How do we reflect on these rites after they take place?
- How often and how well do we make available the various minor rites (Celebrations of the Word, Blessings, Minor Exorcisms, Anointings, Presentations, etc.)?
- If we dismiss the catechumens from Sunday Mass, how often do we do so? If not, how can we change things to offer this opportunity?
- What takes place at Breaking Open the Word (Reflection on the Word)? Is it just another teaching session, or perhaps just a sharing of opinions?
- What happens during Lent? Is Lent a time for "interior reflection" or unaltered catechetical instruction?
- Do we celebrate all of the scrutinies, presentation rites, and the Holy Saturday preparation rites?
- What is our Easter Vigil like? How many parishioners attend? Do the elect and the candidates feel welcomed and at home by their experience of the parish at the Vigil?
- Are sponsors and godparents deeply involved before and after the Easter Vigil in giving good witness to their charges of the importance of living a liturgical life? What sort of formation do they receive?

These are the kind of queries that you noodle on in the summertime, when things are normally a bit quieter, even if your parish has a year-round RCIA process. Looking at the lists given here, I would suggest coming up with two things, maybe three at most, to improve in your parish's next RCIA cycle. Focus on just a couple of new things to do really well. Next year, tackle a couple more. For example, perhaps you'll look at the shape of the neophyte year. The difficulties of this year can be very great. Consider how these quotes from the RCIA rites book might lead your parish to come up with ways to foster specific liturgical formation for your neophytes:

> After the immediate mystagogy or post-baptismal catechesis during the Easter season, the program for the neophytes should extend until the anniversary of Christian initiation, with at least monthly assemblies of the neophytes for their deeper Christian formation and incorporation into the full life of the community. (RCIA, National Statutes for the Catechumenate 24)

> This is a time for the community and the neophytes together to grow in deepening their grasp of the Paschal Mystery and in making it part of their lives through . . . meditating on the Gospel, sharing in the Eucharist, participating in the works of charity. To strengthen the neophytes as they begin to walk in newness of life, the community of the faithful, their godparents, and their pastors should give them thoughtful and friendly help. (RCIA 244)

> On the anniversary of their Baptism the neophytes should be brought together in order to give thanks to God, to share with one another their spiritual experiences, and to renew their commitment. (RCIA 250)

After All Is Said and Done, Do We Need the Liturgy?

A final practical suggestion: consider how your parish's neophytes turn out. It can be diagnostic of how you're doing with liturgical catechesis. This is an "outcomes" approach. Some questions to help here: Do your neophytes *really* feel they have a need for the Mass? Do they have a mentality that says, "I need God each day"? Do they understand how the liturgy feeds that? Are they in a mentality where they're willing to fight their sins *daily*? This is what the liturgy provides: the enablement, the grace, to do. Do your neophytes really have a desire for Jesus that is restless and hungry for more, or has your RCIA process somehow passed on a "graduation" mentality instead? When nobody shows up for mystagogy, it reveals an absence of hunger. How did that happen? Normally a big part of the answer is a lack of liturgical catechesis that imbues truths with *daily* relevance, *urgency,* and *trust* in a Father who runs to embrace the hopeful prodigal child at the edge of collapse. Liturgical graces are his saving embrace.

As we close, may we pray that our hearts are evermore open to recognizing our ancient and timeless liturgy as both a grand unfolding of history and a simple act of love. It is a reaching out of God's intimacy, prepared for all eternity. The RCIA liturgies begin the great work of inviting and enabling Mother Church's newest children to grasp that reach of love. Only the power of sacramental grace gives souls a path of hope through the desert of this life, the demons' hatred, and the temptation to despair in our weakness. O Lord, even "our desire to thank you is itself your gift."[4]

---

4. Preface of Weekdays in Ordinary Time IV.

CHAPTER 13

The Liturgy: Our Lifelong Means of Evangelization

I had the privilege of working in two parishes a number of years ago, where RCIA was carried out with much visible fruit.[1] In both cases, not only was the learning of a high quality, the personal accompaniment was as well. Both parishes had a well-formed team of catechists and sponsors who were very good at personal mentoring. The various rites were celebrated in ways that provoked wonder by the radiant expressiveness of their dignity and beauty. At the end of the nine months of formation for Christian initiation, the Easter Vigil liturgy birthed neophytes who were ready, in many cases, for missionary discipleship. With their faith life thriving after such an intensive period of apprenticeship, many of them would ask the next week, "How does this continue?" By "this," they meant the discipleship process. They were flourishing.

If approached as a school of discipleship, *every form* of liturgical catechesis today can be a source of immense fruitfulness in the new evangelization. Effective liturgical catechesis creates a harmonization between kerygmatic learning and the transformative sacramental experience of the Paschal Mystery. Both are integral to living life in intimate communion with Christ.

Liturgical catechesis can be the best of discipleship processes because its aim is to help others become attuned to the One who is Teacher, encountering him uniquely in the liturgy. As we learn to become more present to him in our sacramental experience, we become more and more receptive and docile to his accompaniment and apprenticing presence. We—all of us—can then be consciously apprenticed by the

---

1. I take credit for neither of these success stories. In both parishes, I had no direct responsibility for RCIA, but worked with talented colleagues.

Master Teacher who will form us himself through the proclamation of the Word and through a life charged with sacramental grace.

To sum up what has been proposed in this book, we could identify these three characteristic marks of a liturgical catechesis that is likewise a school of discipleship:

1. *Learning*—The catechist communicates truths about the sacraments which cannot be gained apart from what God has revealed and entrusted to the Church. Those growing in faith through liturgical catechesis learn the way of the Incarnation and how God chooses to give himself to us through a rich language of sacramental signs. It is through this particular way of seeing gained in liturgical catechesis that we come to understand God's transforming presence in the sacraments and are enabled to enter into a true exchange of love, affecting us deeply and supernaturally.

2. *Mentoring*—In order for these truths to lead to a *new way of living*, they must be received person-to-person, accompanied by authentic testimony to the power of the sacraments to transform us in love. Through liturgical catechesis, we learn *how* to radically embrace the way of our Lord as he lives the divine life of self-forgetful love. This way of the true *disciple* is best learned from *real disciples* who can describe it not only from Scripture and Tradition but additionally from their own life experience.

3. *Empowering*—Liturgical catechesis is no mere theoretical teaching, even if done well. Rather, Christians are *equipped* with those abilities and spiritual habits most necessary for entering consciously and with desire into sacramental celebrations. Therefore frequent opportunities are built into liturgical catechesis to learn the art of the sacramental encounter. Only then can we assume personal responsibility for living a vibrant and fruitful sacramental life once formal liturgical catechesis has come to an end.

We catechists must ask ourselves: Do these three actions characterize how we speak of the sacraments, conduct sacramental preparation, and engage neophytes in mystagogical catechesis? If it is needed, adjusting our approach to integrate whichever of these actions is inadequately represented is certainly possible, even if we only take little steps in gradually refining our approaches over time. Three years from now, the effectiveness of our ministry in forming missionary disciples could be greatly enhanced by beginning to make just a few thoughtful modifications today.

The Liturgy: Union with God and Union with One Another

As we learn discipleship in this exceptionally important school, we will also come to realize an essential fruit of sacramental living: our union with one another. Attuning ourselves to God in the liturgy teaches us something very important. As we participate in an encounter that puts us into communion with God, we do not do so as isolated individuals. We find ourselves, in fact, joined to the Son in the Holy Spirit in his praise of the Father—and likewise united with the whole communion of the Church in an action that sanctifies us and brings us close to one another. Pope Benedict XVI calls the communion with God we experience in the sacraments the "root and source of our communion with one another" (SCa, 76). The sacraments, therefore, cause a profound unity—with those members of the Church who we see and those we do not.

This unity begins with the first sacrament of initiation. Baptism joins us to the Mystical Body of Christ, bringing us all into the adoptive love of our Father in heaven. Not only do we enjoy a new relationship with God as his adopted daughters and sons, we have truly become sister and brother to one another.

Liturgical catechesis makes us more fully aware of these new relationships we enjoy with God and with every member of the baptized. One 1990 document, if we apply its general principle to this theme, reminds us of the explicit connection between the knowledge of these new relationships and the realization of them.

> A fully Christian community can exist only when a systematic catechesis of all its members takes place and when an effective and well developed catechesis of adults is regarded as the central task in the catechetical enterprise.[2]

Pope Benedict memorably describes the expansion of relationships that happens for all of us every time a new Christian is made through the waters of Baptism:

---

2. International Council for Catechesis, *Adult Catechesis in the Christian Community* (Washington, DC: United States Catholic Conference, 1990), 25.

Through Baptism, each child is inserted into a gathering of friends who never abandon him in life or in death. . . . This group of friends, this family of God, into which the child is now admitted, will always accompany him, even on days of suffering and in life's dark nights; it will give him consolation, comfort and light.[3]

Each of the four authors in chapters 9–12 focused in some way on the beautifully communal reality of the celebration of the sacraments. The more we are catechized in this school of discipleship, the more we are turned outside of ourselves to grow in authentic friendship with others enjoying this communion—and, of course, with those who are outside of this communion as well. Parish communities that are realizing in their visible relationships what they are on the supernatural level become profoundly attractive places, especially in today's world fraught with diminishing personal connectivity.

In my formative late teenage years, my family belonged to a parish where—through the presence of mentoring priests and catechists—young people were being formed to love the liturgy and encounter God therein. As this happened, more and more teenagers and young adults began to even prioritize daily Mass and focus their energies on living their lives in Christ. Many parents also began to accompany their kids—on Sundays and during the week. One of the enduring memories of my later adolescence is, on a nearly daily basis, talking with others outside the church building after the evening Mass for a good half hour, growing in friendship with amazing people and being formed into a genuine community. *Participating in the Eucharist was, for me, supernaturally transformative of my friendships.* Many of these good people remain among my closest friends today. In the end, this growing Eucharistic community brought new life to many aspects of the parish: Sunday Mass became the high point of the week, prayer groups began to arise, many participated in missionary work around the diocese and at a Franciscan mission in Mexico, and a series of retreats became staples on the parish calendar. Additionally, as people grew in their relationship with God and in their understanding of the essential truths of the faith, many volunteer catechists became available, stepping forward to strengthen catechetical ministries for all age levels.

---

3. Pope Benedict XVI, Jan 8, 2006 cited in *YouCAT: Youth Catechism of the Catholic Church*, foreword by Pope Benedict XVI, trans. Michael J. Miller (San Francisco: Ignatius Press, 2010), 116.

The Liturgy and Our Ongoing Evangelization

By envisioning liturgical catechesis as a school of discipleship, the most important avenue of lifelong evangelization—the liturgy itself—is opened to Christians. Not only is this a sure way to grow in union with God, but through it we are all more likely to truly become missionary disciples.

In the second chapter, we reflected on the teaching of the *General Directory for Catechesis* that the liturgy is a "means" of evangelization (GDC, 46). Because the liturgy makes the Paschal Mystery accessible, we have a nearly limitless potential to move into intimate union with God.

This union changes us, conforming us more and more to the inexhaustible self-giving love of the Blessed Trinity. There is no greater contact with God possible this side of heaven. With such union comes an infinite potential for our ongoing evangelization if we can see and understand. In fact, the Church envisions the sacramental life to be the primary means for our evangelization over all the years of life—moving us more and more deeply into a sustained following of our Lord. She believes such a lifetime of evangelization is possible because of who the liturgy inimitably makes available to us.

This experience of transformative communion with God becomes most fruitful over the years when it is enveloped in effective approaches to liturgical catechesis. Catechetical reflection brings us not only to a considerable understanding of the liturgy, but also a greater desire for God uniquely present in it. Liturgical catechesis, consequently, is best envisioned as a *lifelong process*, taking place in a variety of forms: sometimes in a formal catechetical setting (neophyte catechesis, Bible study, adult faith formation), in small groups, in personal conversations with an experienced mentor, and through personal reading and prayerful study. Liturgical catechesis is a lifelong school of discipleship where we learn the most important ability of the disciple: being in alert communion with the One to whom we seek to conform ourselves. Prioritizing lifelong catechesis in this way helps the parish to flourish, to become a family of missionary disciples.

Through liturgical catechesis, we become more able to see God embodied and made present (by his gracious love for his creation) through sacramental words, signs, and gestures. We are additionally enabled to give ourselves to God through this rich sacramental language. Timothy O'Malley describes this liturgical way of offering ourselves—and being transformed in these acts of self-donation—that can be the fruit of a thriving lifelong liturgical catechesis.

> When liturgical participants sign themselves with the cross, they mark their bodies as a space given over to the Father in love, entering into the primary relationship of obedient love defining of Christian existence. The genuflection of a single person passing before the Tabernacle manifests an offering of the body through ritual action to God, a sacramental enactment of God's very presence dwelling among us. Those who receive the anointing of the sick bestow the entirety of their being, including the pain of illness, to God. . . . Gathering at the Sunday Eucharist, we interrupt the routine of the American weekend, reordering our desires according to the Eucharistic logic of the church. In the act of singing within liturgical worship, our voices, our hearts, are lifted up to God; the violence of human speech, at times dedicated to coercion, reorients itself to the gift of divine praise. The liturgical prayer of the church reforms our speech, our action, placing us once again in that spirit of gratitude that defined the paradisiacal vocation of humanity.[4]

As we encounter and respond to God in his incarnate presence, he becomes more and more incarnate in us. We are then, through our sacramental transformation, able to bear him into the world.

The Blessed Virgin Mary leads us in this school of discipleship and she is, par excellence, the Theotokos (God-bearer). She was uniquely able to see in a sacramental way. How frequently she gazed upon her nursing, utterly dependent infant son, and through his human body with which she was so profoundly familiar, was able to see her Lord, Creator, and Savior. A work of art such as Blessed Fra Angelico's *Madonna of Humility* luminously proclaims the paradox—the sheer mystery—that Mary experienced in the presence of the Word Made Flesh. Lying in her lap, the infant child reaches in need for his mother, who is the source of his human sustenance. At the same time, the mother crosses her hands over her heart in an act of true adoration—as no other mother has ever experienced—for her child, who is God.

The Blessed Mother, our Lord's first disciple, is experienced in seeing the invisible in the visible, the mystery in the sacrament and the Divine Reality to which the signs point. By her fiat, she knows what it is to

---

4. Timothy O'Malley, *Liturgy and the New Evangelization* (Collegeville, MN: Liturgical Press, 2014), 113.

carry Christ within. She also knows how to share the Good News become flesh with others not as a theoretical proposition but as a Life that has become personally embodied in her.

We stand in need of both these abilities—the ability to see and the ability to carry—and she is our sure guide as we encounter God in the liturgy and share in the responsibility for the New Evangelization.

The *Ars Celebrandi*: The Contribution of Liturgists

In this book we have focused on addressing the two challenges of liturgical indifference and decreasing sacramental practice by starting from a renewed liturgical catechesis. There is much that a catechist can do to contribute to a turnaround with these critical issues.

As important as liturgical catechesis is, improving our approaches to sacramental preparation and mystagogy are not the only ways to address this problem. How the sacraments are celebrated also matters greatly. The catechized person must be able to verify in his own sacramental experience what he learns about the sacraments from the catechist.

Perhaps a few brief words would be helpful here concerning the evangelistic potential of how the sacraments are celebrated.

Pope Benedict XVI describes what he calls the *"ars celebrandi,"* the art of proper sacramental celebration. He writes, "the primary way to foster the participation of the People of God in the sacred rite is the proper celebration of the rite itself" (SCa, 38). Later in the same document, he memorably quotes the synod fathers with a great one-line power statement: "The best catechesis on the Eucharist is the Eucharist itself, celebrated well" (SCa, 64). A liturgy well celebrated will draw the assembly into full, conscious, and active participation by virtue of the experience of the celebration itself. The liturgy then becomes an effective means of evangelization for all those who have invested themselves into the prayer of the Mystical Body. Let's briefly describe some of the key ways we can challenge ourselves as liturgists to bear full witness to the liturgy as a transformative place of divine encounter.

First, the presider sets the tone for the whole assembly in how the rite is prayed. More than any other factor, he bears witness to the presence of Christ the Divine Liturgist and our great Physician in how he speaks, moves, prays. A presider who is deeply aware of the presence and action of the Blessed Trinity in a sacramental celebration will carry himself in a way that this truth becomes the inescapable conclusion of those who are seeking to be present to this mystery. It is an extraordinary witness presiders are able to offer to the divine encounter. For instance, many experience deep conversion in the Sacrament of Reconciliation today based almost entirely on how the priest *intently* listens, speaks, and offers absolution. Remembering Jim Beckman's claim that kids frequently mirror the prayerfulness they see in their parents, there may be parallels in the presider-assembly relationship. We must pray for and support our priests and deacons in this immense responsibility they bear.

Music is, of course, immensely influential in how the liturgy evangelizes. Timothy O'Malley writes of the unique dynamic it introduces into the celebration of the liturgy:

> It would be far quicker to read the words of Psalm 51 in the context of our prayer, but to pray with Allegri's *Miserere* within the liturgy is to encounter a musical text that reveals to us what penance sounds like. It invites us to participate in this act of penance not merely through a cognitive assent.[5]

Of course, music need not be Allegri's *Miserere* to evangelize us. There are a rich variety of musical traditions from which we draw today that can elevate us into divine worship. Most importantly, the liturgical musician—as much as the catechist—must be convinced of the truth of the liturgy as a divine encounter. Such a conviction will influence every aspect of how the liturgical musician approaches his or her service to the assembly, motivating a search for music that will make beautifully present to the ear the contours of sanctifying worship.

The overarching question is this: How can liturgical participants sing in such a way that they become more docile to how the Holy Spirit elevates them into contact with God? To this end, liturgical music needs, first of all, to be doctrinally clear and accurate. In this way, it will bear witness to the truth about God and our relationship with him, which is the essential foundation of authentic worship. The language of liturgical music must be the language of direct encounter with the Divine Other who is lovingly offering himself to us. If we are confident that we are in

---

5. Timothy O'Malley, "Beauty and the Liturgy: A Program for the New Evangelization," *The Catechetical Review* 1, no. 4 (Oct. 2015): 6.

the presence of God—just as when we are in the presence of another whom we love—we communicate ourselves in a way that we are directed outside of ourselves and towards the One we encounter. The time to consider ourselves and for musical commentary regarding what the worshipping community is or should be is not in the moment of encounter with God.

In the end, our music is an act of love for God. It is also a vital service to the members of the assembly, who are in great need of assistance in summoning themselves to the exchange of love that is the liturgy.

The atmosphere of the church building itself—in its architecture and its environment, is also important to evangelization. Put simply, what the church looks like ought to bear witness to what takes place within it. The *Catechism* tells us, "In this 'house of God' the truth and the harmony of the signs that make it up should show Christ to be present and active in this place" (CCC, 1181). If the liturgy is the place of maximum divine encounter, the enveloping environment can do much to help members of the assembly to see the brilliant reality of the liturgy and enter into it with anticipation.

The homily is the most explicit form of liturgical catechesis (NDC, 50) and perhaps the most important consistent opportunity to evangelize the faithful and draw them into the mystery. Because it follows the proclamation of the Word, the homily is the apex moment of mystagogical catechesis on a week-to-week basis. Those who have this opportunity to preach should be empowered and supported to make this the highest of priorities. Pope Francis has made liturgical preaching an important focus of his recent calls for renewal. He writes:

> The homily has special importance due to its eucharistic context: it surpasses all forms of catechesis as the supreme moment in the dialogue between God and his people which lead up to sacramental communion. The homily takes up once more the dialog which the Lord has already established with his people. The preacher must know the heart of his community, in order to realize where its desire for God is alive and ardent, as well as where that dialog, once loving, has been thwarted and is now barren. (EG, 137)

For the Holy Father, the homilist serves as a mediator, evangelizing the faithful by bringing them into dialog with God. "The preacher has the wonderful but difficult task of joining loving hearts, the hearts of the Lord and his people" (EG, 143).

Finally, every member of the assembly bears responsibility for the liturgy being experienced by others as an evangelizing act. How we attune ourselves to God, unite ourselves to our prayer, allow ourselves to deeply consider the implications of liturgy to life—each of these aspects of our worship is important confirmation for those surrounding us that the liturgy is a participation in the work of God. Full, conscious, and active participation in the liturgy is not only an act of love for God, but also for our neighbor.

Conclusion

A parish is meant to be an evangelizing community. Well-celebrated sacraments and well-orchestrated liturgical catechesis are both essential in order for Catholics today to become missionary disciples. Catechists and liturgists who see the sacramental encounter with God as the summit and font of the whole life of the parish never tire of pointing those whom they serve to this place of encounter.

Returning now to the contribution of the catechist, what is the potential arising from a revitalization of today's liturgical catechesis, as this book proposes? On the level of each person, this renewal will help the liturgy become a primary means for a transformative encounter with God. Such an encounter can bear great fruit throughout a person's life, giving each of us everything we need to grow into the missionary disciples the world so desperately needs today. Joseph Jungmann, SJ, put it like this: "If in catechesis we should succeed in introducing children to the content of the liturgy, we would open up a well which could supply the adult Christian with 'waters of eternal life' his whole life through."[6]

The outcome of more effective approaches to liturgical catechesis will be children, teenagers, and adults who more deeply desire God and are confident and certain that the sacraments are the most impactful place to meet him. As such a way of seeing spreads, a parish becomes steeped in a culture of transformative liturgical encounter.

---

6. Josef Jungmann, SJ, *Handing on the Faith: A Manual of Catechetics*, trans. A. N. Fuerst (New York: Herder and Herder, 1959), 99. Later in the same book, Jungmann goes on to say, "If we succeed in making the children feel at home at Holy Mass we shall have created a spiritual home for their entire lives as Christians. The Mass will enter their lives at least every Sunday. In it they will discover all the basic truths of Christian doctrine and all the decisive requirements for Christian living. They will find the whole of life ordered towards God and the renunciation of selfishness" (329–30).

My parish church here in Ohio features a beautiful wooden crucifix fixed on the wall behind the altar. Like no other crucifix I have seen, this one speaks to me the language of self-giving love. In my contemplation of this image of our Lord on the Cross, I am struck by the posture of his body, his open hands, the expression on his face. Every feature speaks of his total gift of self, how he holds nothing back. Christ on the Cross is an image of supernatural love, a love that invites and empowers us to likewise give all of ourselves in love. This cosmic exchange of self-sacrificing love is the life of the liturgy. It is the story underlying the work of catechesis. And, for all eternity, it will be the experience of every person who joins in communion with the God who is Love.

BIBLIOGRAPHY

Magisterial Documents

Benedict XVI. *Sacramentum Caritatis (The Sacrament of Charity)*. Postsynodal Apostolic Exhortation. February 22, 2007. Boston: Pauline Books and Media, 2007.

Catechism of the Catholic Church. 2nd ed. Washington, DC: Libreria Editrice Vaticana–United States Catholic Conference, 2000.

Congregation for the Clergy. *General Catechetical Directory*. Washington, DC: United States Catholic Conference, 1971.

———. *General Directory for Catechesis*. Washington, DC: United States Catholic Conference, 1997.

Francis, Pope. *Evangelii Gaudium (The Joy of the Gospel)*. Apostolic Exhortation. November 24, 2013. Boston: Pauline Books and Media, 2013.

Introduction to "Rite of Baptism for Children." In *Catholic Rites Today*. Edited by Allan Bouley, 138–45. Collegeville, MN: Liturgical Press, 1992.

John Paul II. *Catechesi Tradendae (On Catechesis in Our Time)*. Postsynodal Apostolic Exhortation. October 16, 1979. Boston: Pauline Books and Media, 1979.

———. *Christifideles Laici (The Lay Members of Christ's Faithful People)*. Postsynodal Apostolic Exhortation. December 30, 1988. Boston: Pauline Books and Media, 1989.

———. *Evangelium Vitae (The Gospel of Life)*. Encyclical Letter. March 25, 1995. Boston: Pauline Books and Media, 1995.

———. *Redemptoris Missio (The Mission of the Redeemer)*. Encyclical Letter. December 7, 1990. Boston: Pauline Books and Media, 1991.

Paul VI. *Evangelii Nuntiandi (Evangelization in the Modern World)*. Apostolic Exhortation. December 8, 1975. Boston: Pauline Books and Media, 1976.

Pius X. *Tra le Sollecitudini*. Motu Proprio on the Restoration of Church Music. November 22, 1903. In *The Liturgy Documents, Volume Three: Foundational Documents on the Origins and Implementation of "Sacrosanctum Concilium,"* 19–32. Chicago: Liturgy Training Publications, 2013.

Pius XII. *Mediator Dei*. Encyclical Letter. November 20, 1947. http://w2.vatican
.va/content/pius-xii/en/encyclicals/documents/hf_p-xii_enc_20111947
_mediator-dei.html.

The Roman Catechism. Translated by Robert I. Bradley, SJ, and Eugene Kevane.
Boston: St. Paul Editions, 1985.

Second Vatican Council. *Ad Gentes* (*Decree on the Church's Missionary Activity*).
In *The Basic Sixteen Documents: Vatican Council II; Constitutions, Decrees,
Declarations. The Conciliar and Postconciliar Documents*. Edited by Austin
Flannery. Collegeville, MN: Liturgical Press, 1996.

———. *Dei Verbum* (*Dogmatic Constitution on Divine Revelation*). In *The Basic
Sixteen Documents: Vatican Council II; Constitutions, Decrees, Declarations.
The Conciliar and Postconciliar Documents*. Edited by Austin Flannery.
Collegeville, MN: Liturgical Press, 1996.

———. *Gravissimum Educationis*. (*Declaration on Christian Education*). In *The
Basic Sixteen Documents: Vatican Council II; Constitutions, Decrees, Declarations.
The Conciliar and Postconciliar Documents*. Edited by Austin Flannery.
Collegeville, MN: Liturgical Press, 1996.

———. *Lumen Gentium* (*Dogmatic Constitution on the Church*). In *The Basic
Sixteen Documents: Vatican Council II; Constitutions, Decrees, Declarations.
The Conciliar and Postconciliar Documents*. Edited by Austin Flannery.
Collegeville, MN: Liturgical Press, 1996.

———. *Sacrosanctum Concilium* (*Constitution on the Sacred Liturgy*). In *The Basic
Sixteen Documents: Vatican Council II; Constitutions, Decrees, Declarations.
The Conciliar and Postconciliar Documents*. Edited by Austin Flannery.
Collegeville, MN: Liturgical Press, 1996.

Documents of the United States Bishops Conference

National Conference of Catholic Bishops. Committee on the Liturgy. *Rite
of Christian Initiation of Adults: Study Edition*. Chicago: Liturgy Training
Publications, 1988.

———. Committee on the Laity. *Renewing the Vision*. Washington, DC: United
States Catholic Conference, 1997.

United States Conference of Catholic Bishops. Committee on Education and
Committee on Catechesis. *National Directory for Catechesis*. Washington,
DC: USCCB Publishing, 2005.

———. Committee on Education. *Our Hearts Were Burning within Us*.
Washington, DC: USCCB Publishing, 2004.

———. Ad hoc Committee to Oversee the Use of the Catechism. *United States
Catholic Catechism for Adults*. Washington, DC: USCCB Publishing, 2006.

Books

Alberigo, Giuseppi, and Joseph A. Komonchak, eds. *History of Vatican II*. Vols. 1, 2, and 3. Maryknoll, NY: Orbis Books, 1995, 1997, and 2000.

Anselm. *Proslogion*. In *Anselm of Canterbury: The Major Works*, eds. Brian Davies and GR. Evans. Oxford World's Classics. New York: Oxford University Press, 1998.

Arinze, Francis, Cardinal. "Active Participation in the Sacred Liturgy." In *Cardinal Reflections: Active Participation and the Liturgy*, 15–25. Chicago: Hillenbrand Books, 2005.

Barron, Robert. *And Now I See: A Theology of Transformation*. New York: Crossroad, 1998.

Beauduin, Lambert, OSB. *Liturgy, Life of the Church*. 3rd ed. Translated by Virgil Michel, OSB. Farnborough: St. Michael's Abbey Press, 2002.

Beckman, Jim. "Rethinking Youth Ministry." In *Becoming a Parish of Intentional Disciples*, ed. Sherry Weddell. Huntington, IN: Our Sunday Visitor, 2015. 117–37.

Botte, Bernard. *From Silence to Participation: An Insider's View of Liturgical Renewal*. Translated by John Sullivan, OCD. Washington, DC: The Pastoral Press, 1988.

Bouyer, Louis, ed. *Dictionary of Theology*. Translated by Charles Underhill Quinn. Tournai, Belgium: Desclee Co, 1965.

Bugnini, Annibale. *The Reform of the Liturgy: 1948–1975*. Translated by Matthew J. O'Connell. Collegeville, MN: Liturgical Press, 1990.

Carstens, Christopher, and Douglas Martis. *Mystical Body, Mystical Voice: Encountering Christ in the Words of the Mass*. Chicago: Liturgy Training Publications, 2011.

Cavalletti, Sofia. *Living Liturgy: Elementary Reflections*. Chicago: Liturgy Training Publications, 1998.

————. *The Religious Potential of the Child: Experiencing Scripture and Liturgy with Young Children*. 2nd ed. Translated by Patricia M. Coulter and Julie M. Coulter. Chicago: Liturgical Training Publications, 1992.

Cavalletti, Sofia, and Gianna Gobbi. *Teaching Doctrine and Liturgy*. Preface by Cyprian Vagaggini, OSB. Staten Island, NY: Society of St. Paul, 1964.

Danielou, Jean, SJ. *The Bible and the Liturgy*. Notre Dame, IN: University of Notre Dame Press, 1956.

Fink, Peter E., SJ, ed. *New Dictionary of Sacramental Worship*. 2nd ed. Collegeville, MN: Liturgical Press, 1991. S.v. "The Liturgical Movement," by Virgil C. Funk, 695–715.

Forrest, Tom, CSsR. "Why Should Catholics Evangelize?" In *John Paul II and the New Evangelization*, ed. Ralph Martin and Peter Williamson. Ann Arbor, MI: Servant Books, 2006.

Guardini, Romano. *Preparing Yourself For Mass*. Foreword by Henri J. M. Nouwen. Manchester, NH: Sophia Institute Press, 1997.

———. *Sacred Signs*. St. Louis: Pio Decimo Press, 1956.

Haenggi, Antonius. "The Liturgical Education of the Clergy." In *The Commentary on the Constitution and on the Instruction on the Sacred Liturgy*, ed. A. Bugnini, CM, and C. Braga, CM; trans. Vincent P. Mallon, MM, 79–83. New York: Benzinger Brothers, 1965.

Hahn, Scott. *The Lamb's Supper: The Mass as Heaven on Earth*. New York: Doubleday, 1999.

Hofinger, Johannes, SJ. *Evangelization and Catechesis*. New York: Paulist Press, 1976.

———, ed. *The Good News: Yesterday and Today*. Translated and edited by William A. Huesman, SJ. New York: William H. Sadlier, 1962.

———. *You Are My Witnesses: Spirituality for Religion Teachers*. Huntington, IN: Our Sunday Visitor, 1977.

Hofinger, Johannes, SJ, and Francis Buckley, SJ. *The Good News and Its Proclamation*. Notre Dame, IN: University of Notre Dame Press, 1968.

Jackson, Pamela. *An Abundance of Graces: Reflections on "Sacrosanctum Concilium."* Chicago: Hillenbrand Books, 2004.

Johnson, Cuthbert. *Prosper Guéranger (1805–1875): A Liturgical Theologian*. Rome: Pontificio Ateneo S. Anselmo, 1984.

Jungmann, Joseph A., SJ. *Announcing the Word of God*. Translated by Ronald Walls. New York: Herder and Herder, 1967.

———. *Die frohbotschaft und unsere glaubensverkündigung*. Regensburg: Pustet, 1936.

———. "The Good News and Our Proclamation of the Faith." In *The Good News: Yesterday and Today*. Translated and edited by William A. Heusman, SJ, general editor, Johannes Hofinger, SJ, New York: William H. Sadlier, 1962.

———. *Handing on the Faith: A Manual of Catechetics*. Translated by A. N. Fuerst. New York: Herder and Herder, 1959.

———. *Liturgical Renewal in Retrospect and Prospect*. Translated by Clifford Howell, SJ, London: Burns and Oates, 1965.

———. *The Mass of the Roman Rite: Its Origins and Development*. Translated by Francis A. Brunner, CSsR. New York: Benziger Brothers, 1959.

———. *Missarum Sollemnia*. Vienna: Verlag Herder, 1949.

———. *Pastoral Liturgy*. Translated by Challoner Publications (Liturgy) Ltd. New York: Herder and Herder, 1962.

———. "Religious Education in Late Medieval Times." In *Shaping the Christian Message: Essays in Religious Education*, ed. Gerard S. Sloyan, 38–62. New York: Macmillan, 1959.

Kelly, Francis D. *The Mystery We Proclaim: Catechesis for the Third Millennium*. 2nd ed. Huntington, IN: Our Sunday Visitor, 1999.

"The Liturgical Movement: Its General Purpose and Its Influence on Priestly Piety" in *The Liturgical Movement*. Popular Christian Library, ser. 4, no. 3. Collegeville, MN: Liturgical Press, 1930.

Mallon, James. *Divine Renovation: Bringing Your Parish from Maintenance to Mission*. Mystic, CT: Twenty-Third Publications, 2014.

Marie Eugene of the Child Jesus, OCD. *I Want to See God: A Practical Synthesis of Carmelite Spirituality*. Chicago: The Fides Publishers Association, 1953.

———. *Where the Spirit Breathes: Prayer and Action*. Translated by Sr. Mary Thomas Noble, OP. New York: Alba House, 1998.

Marmion, Columba, OSB. *Christ in His Mysteries*. Bethesda, MD: Zaccheus Press, 2008.

Miller, John H., CSC. "Liturgical Studies." In *Theology in Transition: A Bibliographical Evaluation 1954–1964*, ed. Elmer O'Brien, SJ, 174–201. New York: Herder and Herder, 1965.

Mongoven, Anne Marie, OP. *The Prophetic Spirit of Catechesis*. Mahwah, NJ: Paulist Press, 2000.

O'Malley, Timothy. *Liturgy and the New Evangelization*. Collegeville, MN: Liturgical Press, 2014.

Pecklers, Keith F., SJ. "Liturgical Movement I: Catholic." In *New Catholic Encyclopedia*, 2nd ed. Ed. Berard Marthaler. Detroit: Thompson Gale, 2003.

———. *The Unread Vision: The Liturgical Movement in the United States of America: 1926–1955*. Collegeville, MN: Liturgical Press, 1998.

Quitslund, Sonya A. *Beauduin: A Prophet Vindicated*. New York: Newman Press, 1973.

Ratzinger, Joseph Cardinal. *Feast of Faith: Approaches to the Theology of the Liturgy*. San Francisco: Ignatius Press, 1986.

———. *Faith and the Future*. San Francisco: Ignatius Press, 2009.

Reid, Alcuin, OSB. *The Organic Development of the Liturgy*. Farnborough: Saint Michael's Abbey Press, 2004.

Smith, Christian, with Melinda Lundquist Denton. *Soul Searching: The Religious and Spiritual Lives of American Teenagers*. New York: Oxford University Press, 2005.

Vagaggini, Cyprian, OSB. *Theological Dimensions of the Liturgy*. Translated by Leonard J. Doyle and W.A. Jurgens. Collegeville, MN: Liturgical Press, 1976.

Warren, Michael, ed. *Sourcebook for Modern Catechetics*. Vols. 1 and 2. Winona, MN: St. Mary's Press, 1983 and 1997.

Weddell, Sherry. *Forming Intentional Disciples: The Path to Knowing and Following Jesus*. Huntington, IN: Our Sunday Visitor, 2012.

White, Michael, and T. Corcoran. *Rebuilt: Awakening the Faithful, Reaching the Lost, and Making Church Matter*. Notre Dame, IN: Ave Maria Press, 2013.

Willey, Petroc, Pierre de Cointet, and Barbara Morgan. *The Catechism of the Catholic Church and the Craft of Catechesis*. San Francisco: Ignatius Press, 2008.

Yarnold, Edward, SJ. *The Awe Inspiring Rites of Initiation*. Collegeville, MN: Liturgical Press, 1994.

Journal Articles

Burghardt, Walter J., SJ. "Catechetics in the Early Church: Program and Psychology." *The Living Light* 1, no. 3 (Fall 1964): 100–118.

Cuthbertson, Marianne and Caroline Farey. "Liturgical Catechesis." *The Sower* 31, no. 1 (January 2010): 14–16.

Hofinger, Johannes, SJ. "Catechetics and Liturgy." *Worship* 29, no. 2 (January 1955): 89–95.

Jungmann, Joseph A., SJ. "An Adult Christian." *Worship* 27, no.1 (December, 1952), 5–11.

———. "The Pastoral Idea in the History of the Liturgy." *Worship* 30, no. 10 (November 1956), 608–22.

———. "The Sense for the Sacred." *Worship* 30, no. 6 (May 1956): 354–60.

———. "Theology and Kerugmatic Teaching." *Lumen Vitae* 5 (April 1950): 258–63.

———. "What the Sunday Mass Could Mean." *Worship* 37, no. 1 (December, 1962): 21–30.

Kavanagh, Aidan, OSB. "Teaching through the Liturgy." *Notre Dame Journal of Education* 5, no. 1 (Spring 1974): 35–47.

———. "Theological Principles for Sacramental Catechesis." *The Living Light* 23, no. 4 (June 1987): 316–24.

Kloska, Robert. "My Mind Wanders at Mass." *The Catechetical Review* 1, no. 4 (October 2015): 9.

Martin, Ralph. "What is the New Evangelization?" *The Catechetical Review* 1, no. 1 (January 2015): 6–7.

Michel, Virgil OSB. "Back to the Liturgy." *Orate Fratres* 11, no. 1 (November 29, 1936): 9–14.

———. "Timely Tracts: Liturgical Religious Education." *Orate Fratres* 11, no. 6 (April 18, 1937): 267–69.

———. "Timely Tracts: Religious Education." *Orate Fratres* 11, no. 5 (March 21, 1937): 218–20.

O'Malley, Timothy. "The Iconic Liturgy in Pope John Paul II: A Three-Fold Perspective on Liturgical Catechesis." *Assembly* 33, no. 4 (2007): 29–31.

———. "The Kerygmatic Function of Liturgical Prayer: Liturgical Reform, Meaning and Identity Formation in the Work of Josef Jungmann, SJ." *Studia Liturgica* 41, no. 1 (2011): 68–77.

———. "Beauty and the Liturgy: A Program for the New Evangelization." *The Catechetical Review* 1, no. 4 (Oct. 2015): 6–8.

Rosier, Veronica, OP. "The Spirit and Power of the Liturgy: Understanding Liturgical Catechesis." *Australasian Catholic Record* 83, no. 4 (October 2006): 387–405.

Siegel, Elizabeth. "Beyond RCIA: Accompanying the 'Newly Planted.'" *The Catechetical Review* 2, no. 3 (July 2016): 32–34.

Willey, Petroc. "Editor's Notes: Liturgical Catechesis." *The Sower* 32, no. 4 (October 2011): 4.

———. "Liturgy and Catechesis in the *Catechism of the Catholic Church*." *The Sower* 32, no. 4 (October 2011): 18–21.

———. "The Pedagogy of God Part 1." *The Sower* 30, no. 2 (April 2009): 7–9.

———. "The Pedagogy of God Part 2." *The Sower* 30, no. 3 (July 2009): 17–18.

CONTRIBUTORS

Jim Beckman is the executive director of evangelization and catechesis for the Archdiocese of Oklahoma City. Jim has been involved with parish ministry, evangelization, and leadership development for more than thirty years. A graduate from Franciscan University of Steubenville in 1987, Jim has served in various roles of leadership of national, regional, and local ministry ever since. He is a dynamic and passionate speaker and has a great love for the Church, and he has built solid and thriving ministry programs in several parishes over the years.

Sr. Hyacinthe Defos du Rau, OP, is a member of the Dominican Sisters of St. Joseph in Lymington, UK, which she joined in 2000. She has an ecclesiastical bachelor's degree in philosophy, an MA in contemporary history, and an MA in religious education and catechesis. She has been an associate member of the staff of Maryvale Institute, Birmingham, UK, since 2007. She is the author of the Anchor resource for adult faith formation. Since 2007, she has been translating from French the Come Follow Me catechesis for children produced by the Notre Dame de Vie Institute. As well as publishing the English translation of the catechists' books, she trains catechists for this particular pedagogy in schools and parishes in England, Ireland, and the United States. She is currently responsible for adult and catechists formation in the Diocese of Portsmouth, UK.

William J. Keimig is currently the assistant director of the Catechetical Institute at Franciscan University of Steubenville, Ohio. For fifteen years, he served as the director of religious education at St. Mary's of Piscataway Catholic Church in Clinton, Maryland. Along with this work, Mr. Keimig served as a master catechist in the Faith Foundations Catechist Formation Program for the Archdiocese of Washington, DC. Mr. Keimig has served as a speaker in many other settings, including at the annual St. John Bosco Conference in Steubenville, and at major venues in more than thirty dioceses. He served for nine years as the director of the Association for

Catechumenal Ministry (ACM), which assists dioceses in training clergy and laity to do RCIA ministry, and was the managing editor of ACM's series of RCIA texts currently used in thousands of US parishes and in many other countries. He also served for nine years as a volunteer counselor for a local crisis pregnancy center. Mr. Keimig holds a master's degree in theology and Christian ministry with a certification in catechetics from Franciscan University and is completing a doctorate in ministry at Catholic University of America. He also holds a master's degree in public management from the University of Maryland in environmental policy. He and his wife, Heather, have six children running around, Rose, William, Julianna, Theodore, Elizabeth, and Gregory.

Mary Mirrione is the national director of Catechesis of the Good Shepherd (CGS). She began serving in catechesis in 1988 and has worked in the CGS since 1992. She has been a CGS formation leader of catechists since 1997 serving at home and abroad working with those in dioceses, parishes, and in ministry with the poor. She has had a particular call to work with Mother Teresa's Missionaries of Charity throughout the world, especially in Kolkata, India. Mary has served on the board of the National Association, is a founding member of CGS Fund Advisory Board, and is on the international council for CGS. She has a master's degree in pastoral ministry in the Catechesis of the Good Shepherd. She has worked in the Diocese of Phoenix since 2003 as a presenter and formation leader for diocesan catechists and catechetical leaders.

INDEX

Ratzinger, Joseph, 6–7

Reconciliation, Sacrament of, 97, 99, 111, 120–121, 127, 132, 156–157, 159–160, 162–163, 176–177, 188–189, 192, 203, 221

Reformation, 61–62

Rite of Acceptance (or Rite of Welcoming), 203, 205, 209

Rite of Election (or Call to Continuing Conversion), 205

Roguet, A. M., 10

sacramental desire, 52, 69, 90–91, 93, 107, 141–142, 145, 156–163, 170, 190–191, 200, 212–213, 215, 218

sacramental preparation, 72–73, 131–132, 156–157, 159–163, 193, 205, 215, 220

sacramental signs and symbols, 54, 64–65, 72, 111–117, 123, 133, 138, 153, 165–166, 172, 174–178, 192, 208, 215, 218–219

salvation history, 46, 57–66, 133, 166

Second Vatican Council, 2, 11, 33, 39, 43, 48–54, 70, 76, 109, 206

silence, 78, 80, 147–150, 153, 161, 177, 195–196

Sin, Original, 5, 46

Smith, Christian, 84, 184

tasks of catechesis, 20

teaching and learning, 28

Thérèse of Lisieux, St., 9

Trent, Council of; Catechism of, 66

Vagaggini, Cyprian, 11, 93, 95, 109–111, 115 n.11, 124, 135–136, 165, 201

vocation of the catechist, 23–26

Weddell, Sherry, 29, 75, 77, 83, 135, 181

Willey, Petroc, 112–113

wonder before God, 24, 134, 142,162, 169, 174, 177, 214

Word of God, 23–24, 26–29, 32, 53–54, 56, 71, 77, 81, 97, 111, 127, 132–133, 141, 146–149, 153, 159, 161, 163, 167, 170–171, 178, 181, 187, 204, 207

World War I, 37, 43–44

World War II, 37–39

Zsupan-Jerome, Daniella, 123